Enhancing the Doctoral Experience

To all doctoral supervisors and their students, in the hope that their journey is as satisfying as the destination, even as the landscape changes around them.

Enhancing the Doctoral Experience

A Guide for Supervisors and their International Students

STEVE HUTCHINSON,
HELEN LAWRENCE and
DAVE FILIPOVIĆ-CARTER

GOWER

Published by
Gower Publishing Limited
Wey Court East
Union Road
Farnham
Surrey, GU9 7PT
England

Gower Publishing Company
110 Cherry Street
Suite 3-1
Burlington, VT 05401-3818
USA

www.gowerpublishing.com

British Library Cataloguing in Publication Data
A catalogue record for this book is available from the British Library.

Library of Congress Cataloging-in-Publication Data
The Library of Congress Cataloging-in-Publication Data has been applied for.

ISBN 9781409451754 (pbk)
ISBN 9781409451761 (ebk – ePDF)
ISBN 9781472401694 (ebk – ePUB)

MIX
Paper from responsible sources
FSC® C013985
FSC www.fsc.org

Printed in the United Kingdom by Henry Ling Limited,
at the Dorset Press, Dorchester, DT1 1HD

Contents

List of Figures and Tables

Figures

Tables

Preface

Some years ago when I worked for a large university in the north of England an international research student came to see me in a state of some distress. She had an engineering background and had been a participant on one or two of the courses that we ran for researchers. I invited her in to my office and she told me about how her supervisor had recently started to become very critical of her work. She also said that her supervisor had for the first few months of her candidature been very happy with the technical work she had done and she now couldn't understand why their relationship had changed.

I dug a little deeper; it soon transpired that the reason for the fracture in the relationship was criticism by the supervisor of the student's review of appropriate literature. I asked the student if she had that specific document with her. When she took it from her bag I quickly understood what the specific issue might be. The document had, at most, four or five pages.

I inwardly winced and, without even opening the document, I asked her how many references the review contained. 'Twelve,' she replied, and her tonality expressed a complete conviction that that number was plenty.

'And where', I continued, 'did you find these references?'

'Oh,' she said with a continued tone of confidence, 'on Google.'

Since the incident occurred at a time before Google Scholar, I patiently explained why this factor might be the source of the problem and then I quickly marched her to the library and set her up with an appropriately expert literary specialist from her field. She returned later that day in a state of heightened distress. It turned out that her hard work was simply repeating exactly something that a team elsewhere had done ten years before and her (technically excellent) output for the year was not original, or even particularly innovative.

I remember clearly her mixture of confusion, outrage and bewilderment as she asked: 'But why didn't my supervisor tell me all this when I started out?'

This story is not intended to suggest that all international students are naive or fail to understand the expectations placed upon them, but it does raise a number of interesting points about mutual expectations, research quality, shared standards and the supervisory relationship more generally.

This incident, and dozens of others like it, led to the creation of this book.

Acknowledgements

Steve Hutchinson: To Geoff Parker. Thank you.

Helen Lawrence: To Sali Tagliamonte, whose passion for discovery and belief in her students is still an inspiration. Thank you.

Dave Filipović-Carter: I had one that did and one that didn't – but learned much from both. Thank you to M. and D. for tolerating me.

Thank you to the supervisors, students and post-doctoral researchers who contributed their thoughts, experiences and ideas to this book. Without your shared insights this book would have been impossible – or at least fairly boring.

Review of *Enhancing the Doctoral Experience*

This is a practical yet scholarly treatment in support of a vital but underrated academic relationship – that of doctoral supervisor and student. Although focussed on the needs of international students, its sage advice and helpful suggestions are more generally applicable. I wish I had been able to access such material when starting off as a new academic; I anticipate transformational effects when put into practice.

Tom McLeish, Pro-Vice Chancellor (Research), Durham University, UK

Notes for the Reader

First, a confession: none of the three of us are doctoral supervisors. But we all have research backgrounds and PhDs (in zoology, linguistics and law) and, combined, have spent many years in universities in teaching or academic-related positions. All three of us run our own businesses, each of us in our own way helping to facilitate the development of academics and researchers. In this time as freelancers we have each met thousands – if not tens of thousands – of research students, and a majority of those we've met do not come from the UK. Often people who come on courses have specific problems and issues they are hoping to resolve, and it struck us that a vast proportion of these issues are linked to relationships that could be more functional. This book uses the insight and advice we've compiled and given over the years.

In the course of researching and writing this book we've delved into a considerable amount of educational and social science research. Since none of us have an educational research background we've often found the frameworks and terminologies faintly bewildering. I have on my desk at present an article that deals with the pedagogies of transculturation; it's a good academic article, its methodology is sound and conclusions valid. I can, however, find nothing in it that would be of practical value to an electrical engineer (for example) with a Chinese (for another example) doctoral student.

So, despite wishing to produce a book that is academically rigorous, we have at all times been guided by two driving forces. We've attempted firstly to produce a synergy of theoretical frameworks and research findings and to ask the question, 'How could a scholar in any discipline make use of this?', and secondly, we've aimed for the book to be pragmatic and useful for research supervisors (and, by proxy, their research students). After all, we've never met a supervisor who wants to be a bad supervisor, and we constantly meet lots who want to be better. However, as they are faced with myriad other challenges and demands on their time, most of them want to do this quickly and with minimal effort.

With this in mind, the new primary material in this book comes from a number of types of sources: from conversations we've had with supervisors and researchers in dozens of institutions; from scores of questionnaires that were sent to supervisors, post-doctoral researchers and research students, and from a variety of less academically usual sources (such as asking a roomful of international research students to write a piece of advice on a sticky note for a new doctoral student from their own country). Our intention is not to expound a watertight methodology, but to find interesting stories and say something useful.

We hope that this synthesis of scholarly theory and pragmatic sampling has produced a book that provides a framework for students and supervisors to have conversations about their expectations; to discuss what supervision is; to articulate clearly what both parties need in order for a successful relationship to occur, and to build a mutually beneficial endeavour.

These conversations and frameworks are, of course, useful discussion points for students and supervisors who share a cultural and linguistic background, but essentially we hope it will be useful for a number of groups:

- supervisors who are currently supervising, or considering supervising, research students who have previously studied entirely outside the UK;
- prospective and current research students from outside the UK who are considering studying for a doctorate in the UK or through a UK institution;
- supervisors new to the UK who have previously only worked outside the UK;
- supervisors supervising international students in UK universities outside the UK (so-called 'franchise' institutions).

We are fully aware that there are a number of different forms of the UK doctorate, from the traditional PhD to EdD, MD, EngD and practice-based doctorates. While there are of course some differences between these forms, the end product of supervision (to support and guide a student on a journey towards intellectual independence) is very similar. In addition, the majority of the contributions to this book were from people engaged in studying for or supervising PhDs – a situation that reflects the norm within the UK. As such we will, for convenience's sake, refer to the 'doctorate' to encapsulate all forms, while recognizing that this often refers to the PhD. If it seems that the specific circumstances of a non-traditional doctorate differ substantively from what is described here, it falls to the supervisor and student to engage in a discussion about the actual nature of their engagement.

The stories and anecdotes that form some of this book's content were told to us in confidence, so we have protected contributors' anonymity throughout. To help the reader identify whether specific concerns or issues are discipline-specific or culturally specific we've provided a discipline or nationality label for quotes wherever possible. While we have tried to avoid homogenizing terminologies and stereotypes (such as 'Western' or 'Asian'), sometimes we've had to stray close to them in order to protect the anonymity of the contributors. One type of anonymity we've had to include is that frequently research students have been reluctant to discuss specifics concerning the identity of their supervisors. So while the student information is given as fully as possible, the academic label is given merely as 'research supervisor'. We are completely aware that a student from one nationality working in a UK institution with a supervisor of a third nationality is increasingly common, but we decided to simplify matters by using boxes herein labelled 'Supervisory Enquiries' (to ascertain a supervisor's attitudes and beliefs), 'Supervisory Ideas' (to provide tasks, actions and thoughts to help the supervisory process) and 'Discussion Points' (to facilitate conversations).

Since some of the quotations herein are taken, with permission, from conversations (as opposed to academically 'proper' interviews), there has been some editorial adaptation in places. Some of the quotations come from written responses, and here we've again adapted and corrected editorially where there have been linguistic issues.

For clarity, throughout this book we use 'Thesis' with an upper-case initial for the formal document submitted, while 'thesis' with a lower-case initial refers to the argument built therein.

This book is a joint venture, and the concepts and philosophies presented herein are shared or collective. As such, we've shamelessly alternated between the use of 'I' and 'we'. So, to help the reader, the use of 'I' is often found in the personal anecdotes and observations, while 'we' binds the more abstract material.

Finally, we believe that enhancing the effectiveness of the doctoral student and the professionalization of research supervision by providing both with an awareness of, and a toolkit to approach, student diversity can only be of benefit to all concerned. We hope that our efforts provide a source of inspiration and stimulation and a resource that both supervisors and students can use to help build more productive and fruitful relationships.

Steve Hutchinson, Helen Lawrence and Dave Filipović-Carter

Chapter 1

Introducing the UK Doctorate in a Global Context

> *'When I think of globalism I always think of that internet factoid. You know, the one that says India has more top A-grade students than we have students in total.'*
>
> *Research supervisor – Mechanical Engineering*

Over the past decade, in universities and research institutes in many countries, each of us has met hundreds of research supervisors and thousands of research students of varying nationalities. Before we embark on our stories and content let's first consider the context for this publication.

Rise of the Postgraduate

The idea of students moving from one country or culture to study in another is not a new one. The universities of medieval Europe or ancient Islam were 'far more transnational communities of scholars than the modern national universities founded in the twentieth century' (Kim 2009).

Recently however, scholarly migration has increased in scale. Significant proportions of research students in the UK[1] are from outside the UK. Also the absolute number of doctoral candidates in the UK is growing. Depending on which figures are used, this may show a doubling, tripling or quadrupling in less than 15 years. The absolute number of PhDs enrolled is often confusing, as many institutions have in the past registered candidates for an MPhil qualification and then upgraded or transferred a candidate's status to full doctoral registration after a year or more. However, Table 1.1 shows the Higher Education Statistics Agency (HESA) data for numbers of doctorates *obtained* in the UK in 2011/12.

1 Powell and Green (2007) present a figure of 45 per cent, compared to 20 per cent in Australia and 14 per cent in the USA.

Table 1.1 Number of doctorates obtained in the UK in 2011/12

	Full-time	Part-time	Total
UK-domiciled students	8,235	2,770	11,005
EU-domiciled students	2,360	480	2,840
Non-EU-domiciled students	6,055	535	6,590

Source: Data from Higher Education Statistics Agency (2011/12): https://www.hesa.ac.uk/stats (accessed 19 June 2014).

This means that the total number of doctorates obtained in the UK in the most recent data set is just over 20,000, with EU and non-EU candidates obtaining over 45 per cent of them.

The growth in the number of doctoral students is part of a far larger increase in postgraduates generally. This is far more than a strategic student reaction to the recently sluggish hiring economy, showing clear trends regardless of how the economy waxes and wanes. A sensible estimate (taken from Stefan Collini's 2012 book *What are Universities For?*) says that 'in the last three decades the number of postgraduates has gone from about 60,000 to over 530,000'. And while from year to year there is some fluctuation in the absolute numbers of postgraduates (2011/12 saw a small decrease compared to the previous year), there is no denying that the trend is generally an upward one. The HESA 2011/12 data indicate that non-UK-domiciled students accounted for over a third all of postgraduate students in the UK.[2]

An interesting facet of the HESA data is the recent sharp decline in postgraduate numbers from India, which is almost certainly linked to the change of policy at national level towards post-study grace periods applied to visas. One of the post-doctoral researchers we interviewed told us:

> *'One of the key reasons for studying here [the UK] was that I wanted to stay and seek work as an academic here. I was very lucky to get a visa that allowed this. This is now not the case. Some of my friends from home are looking now to study in Canada and Scandinavia*

2 See https://www.hesa.ac.uk/stats (accessed 19 June 2014).

> *as the situation is better. If you want to study here, look into this carefully.'*
>
> *Post-doctoral researcher, India*

The Draw of the UK Doctorate

An increase in doctoral students is, it could be argued, inevitably linked to the growth of MA and especially MSc numbers, but there are many other reasons for this growth in the UK as a destination for international postgraduates.

The UK doctorate is still a massive draw for international students, for a host of reasons on top of the natural recruitment that can come from a linked masters degree. Firstly, the UK doctorate itself is still widely and highly regarded internationally, and so are UK institutions (the 'Oxbridge Effect') and their research facilities.

Add to this the relatively brief period of expected candidacy, which is shorter and therefore cheaper than in the USA and much of Europe, the globally recognized academic standards and the potential employability of UK-educated students. As one international student we spoke to said:

> *'I want to be a lecturer in my country. It is easiest with a PhD from [the UK].'*
>
> *Research student – Sciences, Middle East*

On top of these cost, intellectual and career benefits, and of prime importance for many international students, is the intellectual freedom study in the UK brings. Within reason, candidates are largely free to study whatever subjects are interesting and academically valid. This is not the case elsewhere in the world. Travelling to the UK can allow a student to critically examine a facet of their own nation or culture which they would not be allowed to do from within that country.

Moreover, the UK doctoral system is hugely influential in terms of the quality of the support, training and development opportunities (see Hinchcliffe et al. 2007) and all-round activity that sits between the purely intellectual and the purely pastoral. These aspects of the doctorate hold increasing value in the minds of students who are demanding more for the substantial fees they are paying:

> *'It's expensive. It's a big risk for me. I want to make sure I get the most from my time here. [Such as?] Such as training, networking and opportunities to develop and learn. I'm not going to just sit in my lab.'*
> *Research Student – Biological Sciences, Eastern Europe*

Finally, of course, there is the self-perpetuation of the academic system. In essence this is the role-model attractant of academic tutors at bachelors and masters level ('This lecturer is a "good" academic. I want to study with them'). We will deal with this specific element of the recruitment draw later in the book.

Overall, the UK is an outstanding place to study for a doctorate. It is easy to forget this in the day-to-day grind of academic and bureaucratic pressures, *National Student Survey* league tables and student appeals – but one of the refreshing things about hearing the stories of students was the positivity from so many of them. For instance:

> *'This is a great country. There are so many opportunities here. My friends who are at US and Canadian universities, moan to me [about their experiences] and tell me how lucky I am. It is great here …. I'd tell anyone to come and study here. And I will be qualified, hopefully, in three years. You have so many opportunities to learn. I did not expect so much.'*
> *Research student – Medical Sciences, Saudi Arabia*

Combine this set of favourable conditions with the underlying internationalization and globalization agendas and the exponential growth of our knowledge and research-based economy, and these conditions can only serve to make UK (and UK-franchised) doctorates and related postgraduate qualifications more attractive to the international market.

In 2004 the Department for Education and Skills (DfES) published a policy paper entitled *Putting the World into World-class Education*.[3] This influential document outlined three key strategic goals:

1. the establishment of global contexts of all forms of education;

2. the creation of international partnerships;

3 DfES, *Putting the World into World-class Education: An International Strategy for Education, Skills and Children's Services* (2004): http://escalate.ac.uk/downloads/4837.pdf (accessed 18 June 2014).

3. the identification of links to be made between universities and trade and industry.

In some ways this policy manifesto was pushing at an open door since for some time the universities and colleges of the UK had been aiming at exactly these goals – partly through a desire to widen the experiences of their students and faculty, but also because of cold, hard financial realities. Links between the educational sector and the private sector can lead to financial gain for the institutions as well as placements for students and very real benefits to international partners in terms of top-calibre graduate and postgraduate recruits and cutting-edge intellectual property. There are also benefits for researchers themselves in terms of growing a rich and diverse network to facilitate potential collaborations for future projects. The internationalization agenda, at myriad levels, has led to an overall increase in students from global markets, and this has naturally extended to postgraduate and doctoral recruitment.

So the simple upshot is that the number of international doctoral students in the UK is growing. Therefore, in a time when economic concerns are pressing, universities have a growing cash crop – a group of students who are charged higher fees by institutions than the home equivalent. Our experience has taught us that the hand that takes the money is not always the same one concerned about quality. At undergraduate level the sector has started to respond to the challenges of an international curriculum – and has heeded the warnings from both policy makers and educational researchers such as Rees and Porter (1998), who say: 'Those providers … who do not take account of the special needs of international students, and who do not fulfil their sales promises are likely to be just as much at risk as exporters in any other market.' Yet a fundamental tension here concerns the value, in global terms, of the spread of an educational philosophy which is essentially 'Western' – over-simplistically, one that requires a Socratic challenge to the teacher – held up to be the gold standard and sold to international students, many of whom come from a background where this educational expectation is not the norm.

This book is not about the socio-economic reasons for the growth of the doctoral industry across the board, and is not about the rights or wrongs of taking greater numbers of international students or the intricacies of our universities' fiscal juggling; rather, it concerns one important facet of what doctoral programmes must do to mitigate the risks of our practice not meeting the expectations of our students. *This book is about facilitating and ensuring the effective supervision of international doctoral students studying within the UK system.* And by 'effective', we refer to both the student *and* supervisory experience.

The increase in the number of culturally and ethnically diverse students has led to a number of distinct challenges, not just for the supervisors and the students themselves, but also for their departments and faculties. The primary challenge for all concerned, but especially institutions and faculties, is not the fact that there is a difference between home and international students, but the sheer ridiculousness of two suggestions:

1. that all UK home students are a homogeneous group;
2. that international students are a distinct, homogenous group.

Of course, there are differences that can be expressed collectively. But as Geake and Maingard (1999) observe, there are more individual differences within cultures than there are between cultures. Sometimes the very terms 'home' and 'international' can be a source of exclusion and discomfort, and 'grouping people together in such ways may be useful to differentiate fee status but it is indefensible when it is carried over into everyday parlance and policy documents, whether these be at local, national or institutional level' (Trahar 2011). Although there is much documentation of the difficulties caused to international students by cultural frictions (see Cortazzi and Jin 1997), treating international students as a homogenous group is almost certainly counter-productive. Indeed, as Barker (1997) points out, they may have little more in common than the fact they are labelled 'international students'. As we mentioned in the Notes to the Reader at the beginning of this book, we've focused on the area of international students, and in doing so we've taken the stance that all students are individuals and need to be treated as such – particularly research students, for whom the key engagement with the academy, via the supervisor, is an individual one. We've also flagged areas where differences in language or culture may present specific challenges or exacerbate existing ones.

International Challenge – Local Response

Many institutions serve their international students very well; the research for this book shows an array of good practices from across the sector. But many students report failings from their institutions, some resulting from a mismatch between expectation and reality and some resulting from genuinely poor service to a student who is paying a substantial amount of money.

To meet the challenge of the increase in students from outside the UK, the UK Council for International Student Affairs[4] (UKCISA, formerly known as UKCOSA) recommended that colleges should 'ensure that there are appropriate opportunities for staff development for all those in contact with international students', and often these are manifold when concerned with undergraduate or taught student teaching. However at doctoral level this support for supervisors is not as common. One supervisor we spoke to told us:

> *'I need help with them [his two Chinese research students]. Communication is difficult – not just the language barrier, but at all levels. They're both fantastic students, but it's so hard to supervise them properly. I wasn't prepared for this, at all.'*
>
> *Research supervisor – Engineering*

This common lack of effective support for research supervisors is partly because a doctorate is unlike any other form of qualification. There are no set recipes, no ways to standardize the experience, no 'right' ways to do things and no real ways to compare the experiences of students in a cohort or year group, since these classifications do not exist for the individualistic doctorate.

Research and data from the past decade confirm again and again the long-accepted belief across the sector that the key predictor of a student's satisfaction with the research degree experience is the quality of the relationship they had with their doctoral supervisor. But again, there is no 'right' way to build this relationship. John Hockey (1995) noted accurately that 'there is no set format for effective research supervision'. This means that supervisors often have little to base their supervisory tactics on other than the experience they themselves had as a doctoral student. In addition, the relationship between student and supervisor has traditionally been a private and closed affair – the so-called 'secret garden' model 'in which student and supervisor engaged together as consenting adults, behind closed doors, away from the public, and with little accountability to others' (Park 2008).

The supervisory process has long been known to be a complex one, and pivotal in determining whether a research student is successful (Delamont et al. 1997). However, research supervision is, in itself, traditionally a lightly

4 The UK Council for International Student Affairs (formerly known as UKCOSA) is the UK's national advisory body serving the interests of international students and those who work with them. The UKCISA website (www.ukcisa.org.uk) is a hugely useful starting point for help, support and consideration of the issues faced by both international students and academic faculty in the UK.

researched area (Brockbank and McGill 1998). Moreover, the notion of supervision as a discipline in itself which requires formal training, reflective practice and accreditation is a relatively recent one (see Clegg 1997), and is still only sporadically embraced by the academic community beyond educational developers. Therefore, even between experienced academics there is often little or no consensus about what constitutes 'good supervision', and no agreed frameworks, or what Clegg refers to as 'no discursively secure anchorage for a language of expertise which would be acceptable'. *The challenge of supervising an individual who does not share one's own cultural and educational norms is simply another new layer on top of the myriad complexities of 'traditional' doctoral supervision.*

However, recently the role of the supervisor has been subject to scrutiny (as has the doctorate itself) in an attempt to assure consistency of standards. This standardization has in part arisen alongside the nebulous concept of 'student satisfaction', so the two things are often linked causally – whereas this may not be at all true. However, within the literature there *are* firmer correlations, such as the quality of research supervision being the 'strongest predictor of doctoral completion on schedule' (Leonard et al. 2006). With this in mind, the Quality Assurance Agency (QAA) Code of Practice for higher education research degrees[5] includes devices that aim to regulate research supervision and accentuates the basic role of the supervisor in maintaining quality and consistency across doctoral programmes. It also encourages the use of supervisory teams to provide a framework in which newer supervisors can gain experience alongside those with a successful track record of supervision. While there have been changes in practice brought about by the QAA's expectations of an institution complying with the Code of Practice in terms of supervisory practices, there is still, absolutely appropriately, a huge amount of flexibility in the system to allow for disciplinary differences or individual style.

Sitting alongside the policy drivers and the research data are the findings of the annual Postgraduate Research Experience Survey (PRES),[6] a national survey conducted by the Higher Education Academy. A kernel of an idea for this book came a few years back when we saw the PRES data which showed that one fifth of respondents to the survey felt the supervision they had received did not meet their expectations.

5 Chapter B11, 'Research Degrees', *UK Quality Code for Higher Education*: www.qaa.ac.uk/publications/informationandguidance/pages/quality-code-B11.aspx (accessed 18 June 2014).

6 'Student Experience Surveys': www.heacademy.ac.uk/student-experience-surveys (accessed 18 June 2014).

The conversations and data collection in this book were conducted to find out why there was a mismatch in expectations and, further, what students and their supervisors could do about it, especially when a growing number of research students were coming to the UK with expectations (whether cultural, intellectual, academic, linguistic or pastoral) that might be inherently different to those students (and supervisors) who have been an undergraduate or taught masters students in the UK. At the beginning of the last decade, in a paper written for the Learning and Teaching Support Network, Beattie et al. (2001) found that the major differences in expectations and assumptions about the research supervisory process were not between staff and students per se, but between the different types of students – international and part-time being two of the most noticeable examples.

Furthermore, information from the Office of the Independent Adjudicator[7] (OIA) suggests that pro rata, the quantity of appeals and complaints involving international research students vastly outnumbered those from UK students. Furthermore, postgraduates and international students from outside the European Union are proportionately more likely to make a complaint than undergraduates and home students.

So, in short, the key challenges are as follows:

- an increase in the number of international doctoral students (perhaps related to pressure on supervisors to supervise more students, or at least continue to provide quality supervision within a timetable that is increasingly pressured by other scholarly and non-scholarly demands);

- a potential difference in expectations (and hence potential dissatisfaction) between the parties (often exacerbated by the large fees attached to international study);

- an institutional response that is hamstrung by the individualistic nature of the doctorate and doctoral supervision.

The first step, then, is to consider what the existing resources are for doctoral students and supervisors at an individual level.

7 *OIA Annual Report 2012*: www.oiahe.org.uk/media/88650/oia-annual-report-2012.pdf (accessed 18 June 2014).

International Challenge – Individual Resources

Starting at the student end of the equation, there are many general and excellent books about navigating postgraduate life, such as *The Essential Guide to Postgraduate Study* (Wilkinson 2005) and *The Postgraduate's Companion* (Hall and Longman 2008). This type of book is often aimed exclusively at postgraduate international students – such as *Postgraduate Study in the UK: The International Student's Guide* (Foskett and Foskett 2006). At a general postgraduate level these can be supplemented by a number of books about life as an international student in the UK, such as *The International Student's Survival Guide* (Davey 2008) and *Getting Ahead as an International Student* (Burnapp 2009).

There are many helpful books that already aim to help doctoral students succeed, some of the most popular being *The Postgraduate Research Handbook* (Wisker 2001), *How to Get a PhD* (Phillips and Pugh 2010) and *Succeeding with Your Doctorate* (Wellington et al. 2005). They all contain great advice for students, and it's certainly worth a supervisor owning at least one of them simply to know exactly what their students might be being told about what good doctoral practice might be.

Some of these individual resources are more specialized, either by discipline – such as *Working for a Doctorate: A Guide for Humanities and Social Sciences* (Graves and Varma 1997) – or by student type – such as *How I Got My Postgraduate Degree Part Time* (Greenfield 2000). Again, these contain great insights and helpful thoughts and are recommended reading for niche students and supervisors alike.

While some of the resources listed above deal briefly with the unwritten cultural differences inherent in being an international student, such as Jagdish Gundara's chapter 'Intercultural Issues and Doctoral Studies' in Graves and Varma's *Working for a Doctorate* (1997) and Rugg and Petre's work *The Unwritten Rules of PhD Research* (2004), much of the rest of the genre is written from an Anglocentric perspective. This is entirely right and proper since these works accurately reflect the reality of doctoral study. However, there is often little focus on the – perhaps culturally different – *expectations* of the candidate, and this it seems is where much of the supervisory challenge lies.

For supervisors there are a number of useful sources on the pedagogies about doctoral supervision: *A Handbook for Doctoral Supervisors* (Taylor and Beasley 2005), *The Good Supervisor* (Wisker 2004), *The Routledge Doctoral Supervisor's Companion* (Walker and Thompson 2010), *Understanding Supervision and the PhD*

(Peelo 2011), *Effective Postgraduate Supervision* (Eley and Jennings 2005) and *How to Be an Effective Supervisor* (Eley and Murray 2009), to name a few.

We wholeheartedly urge all research supervisors to engage with the theory and discourse of good practice concerning doctoral supervision as they would with the pedagogical theory and research related to other forms of their teaching and lecturing. These texts can, in addition, have beneficial side-effects:

> *'I borrowed a book on supervision from my professor. It was very interesting to read her perspective. It changed the way I approached her. It is a good idea for others [to read a supervisory book].'*
>
> *Research student, Sri Lanka*

Many books for supervisors deal lightly with the issue of international students or take the sensible position that students, wherever their origin, are individuals and any relationship needs to be constructed on that basis. While we fully agree all that students are individuals, international students *can* provide a particular set of challenges for the supervisor.

Particularly useful in this regard are the chapters 'Internationalisation of Higher Education: Challenges for the Doctoral Supervisor' by Anna Robinson-Pant and 'International Students and Doctoral Studies in Transnational Spaces' by Fazal Abbas Rizvi in Walker and Thompson (2009) and *Supervising Postgraduates from a Non-English Speaking Backgrounds* by Ryan and Zuber-Skerritt (1999).

Generally speaking, books on research supervision start with an exploration of the doctorate itself. Yet the doctorate is not a fixed entity, and the notion of what constitutes the doctorate process changes in reaction to educational policy, but also as a response to wider societal needs and intellectual drivers. It is with a re-visitation of the UK doctorate from the perspective of an international student and their supervisor that our contribution truly begins.

Chapter 2

Doctoral Descriptors within the UK Framework

The rich man thinks of next year, the poor man of the present moment.

Japanese proverb

It's now some years since each of us completed our doctorates. Over the course of preparing this book we've had many a long conversation about what our theses were and whether our doctoral experiences had been enhanced by the supervision we had each received. A pivotal moment in the writing process came when one of us asked out loud, 'What would you tell a new student that a doctorate was, and what makes it special?' Despite the fact that we have each built successful careers partly around helping people to answer this question, it still caused us to hesitate and think. And yet, if supervisors and students don't understand the ends of the doctoral process (as opposed to the direction of the research), then how is any action from either party truly effective?

One of the students surveyed for this book, when asked what would have improved the experience for them, simply said:

> *'More clear guidance about what a PhD entails by supervisors/Department would have been nice.'*
>
> *Research student – Science, Mexico*

So if supervision is to be effective, it would seem sensible to start by engaging with the issue of what the doctorate is. Rather than initially providing a potted history of the qualification, we'd like to pose questions to the reader. The act of supervision requires supervisors to reflect upon and challenge their own perspectives and assumptions; and these questions serve both to stimulate thoughts within the supervisors and to act as potentially helpful discussion points between academics and students.

Enquiries for Supervisors and Helpful Discussion Points about the Nature of the Doctorate

- What actually *is* a doctorate?
- What makes a doctorate special and unique, and the highest level of academic qualification? (How does it differ from a bachelor's or master's-level qualification?)
- If applicable, what is special about the professional doctorate or doctorate by practice you are considering supervising (how does it differ from a 'traditional' PhD?)
- What is the doctorate in the UK? How does it differ from a doctorate in other countries around the world?
- In terms of expectations from the UK higher education policy drivers, how has the UK doctorate changed over the last twenty years?
- What makes a doctorate in, for example, geology or physics the same as one in classics or literature?
- How would you describe the types of success measures and standards required for a doctorate?
- What would you say were the skills, qualities and attributes required from any successful doctoral candidate?

These questions sound very simple, and it could be said that to an experienced academic they are almost patronizing. Yet we've lost count of the times over the years where enquiries like these – made to experienced supervisors – have been met with an incomplete answer or 'I've not really thought about it like that.'

If this seems incredible, then test our assertion by casually asking a colleague or two what they think. You'll find that usually there is something in the answer about a 'high-level', 'substantive' and 'original contribution' and there may well be something about 'independence' – but there will rarely be a clear answer. Moreover, the notion that the doctoral process is bound by a time constraint almost never comes up.

Doctoral researchers are generally worse at answering these types of questions, and the notion that the viva will be based on certain international and institutional requirements is usually an alien one to them. As (fairly typical) feedback on a doctoral effectiveness course we ran for later-stage doctoral students once said:

'It was so useful to discover what makes the doctorate a doctorate. This was news to me.'

Research student – Arts and Humanities, USA

Changing times and increasing academic diversity have led the sector as a whole to address the question, 'What is a PhD?' (see, for example, Park 2007; Reeves 2007). To some extent the absolute answer to this question, while vital to understand, is less important than a shared and agreed understanding and definition from both the supervisory team and the student.

In order for a qualification to be academically viable for the candidate, it is therefore worth both parties examining how the doctoral entity fits within their specific higher education institution, within the UK system, within European educational frameworks, and also how the entire agenda fits within the notion of transglobalism. Moreover, despite the highly individual nature of the doctorate, it is perhaps wise to seek some consistency between localized members of staff as to their understanding and declarations regarding what the doctorate *is*, let alone what it is *for*.

The Nature of the UK Doctorate – What is It?

If we wonder often, the gift of knowledge will come.

Arapaho proverb

There has been considerable evolution in the doctorate as a qualification since its conception in the medieval period (as a qualification primarily concerned with teaching) through the eighteenth- and nineteenth-century innovations of Wilhelm von Humboldt through to the modern qualification we now recognize.

Traditionally, even the modernized 'Humboldtian' doctorate was the preserve of the very best students; there was little in the way of quality assurance and no scrutiny of the supervisory relationship. Candidates were not limited to producing a Thesis within a set period. As such, the doctorate was something undertaken by 'very few people, mostly of high attainment and motivation' (Joyner 2003). Since the 1990s, however, there has been a marked trend globally and in the UK towards increasing numbers of candidates registering for a doctorate (see Halse and Mowbray 2011, among others). This may be in part due to the massive growth of undergraduate education and a lack of capacity for postgraduate research in developing nations (see Zhao 2003b).

This has led funders, governments and financially capable families to send students to the UK (and the USA, Canada and Australia as well as other European countries). Finally, as McCulloch and Thomas (2012) explain (and as discussed in Chapter 1), this phenomenon is partly to do with a simple increase in the number of undergraduate and master's degree qualifications obtained, leading to both an increase in the recruitment pool for doctoral-level study and enhanced status for the doctorate in terms of the employability advantages it offers over more commonplace qualifications.

Primarily, then, the doctorate is a high-level qualification. This is not its key value, but it's the sensible place to start addressing it. It is a time-bound qualification and is subject to constitutional regulations both within an institution and at national and international levels – and in that way it is not a special undertaking. To this end, as a student and supervisory team, it is worth considering the point that there are subdivisions within the doctoral qualification (Prof Docs, PhD by Practice, PhD by Publication, MDs, DEng). Each of these qualifications has its own idiosyncrasies (and these need to be discussed and clarified at the beginning of the process), but they are still doctorates and are bound by the same classifiers and descriptors.

Secondly, the doctorate is about the production of a substantive and original piece of research and accompanying literature. This is the most recognizable aspect of the qualification, and the area most researchers focus their attention upon. However, more is required than a substantive and original contribution. In order to obtain the academic hallmark of the doctorate, a candidate must prove their work to be of publishable quality; among other things, the viva provides an opportunity for independent academics to scrutinize the work and judge it worthy, thus aping the peer-review process.

Moreover, the qualification is about the parallel creation of both a Thesis and a scholar: the publishable, original and substantive contribution and the nurtured, crafted and trained potential academic. In many senses it is the second aspect that ultimately defines the doctorate and answers the question of what is the wider purpose of the doctorate.

The Purpose of the UK Doctorate – What is it *For*?

Instruction in youth is like engraving in stone.
Libyan proverb

The purpose of the doctorate is to produce a recognizably independent scholar, and in that regard it could also be considered to be an acknowledgement of (world-class) expertise. The candidate achieves this status by producing independent scholarship, as discussed in the previous section, but also through a process of apprenticeship (with the supervisor serving as metaphorical master to the doctoral apprentice, who learns by osmosis and from example) and informal and formal training – both 'at the bench' and in more formal courses and classes. Often the notion of training an independent scholar is more problematic for the supervisor than supporting the Thesis, as it is a task that requires a huge amount of interpersonal skill and subtlety.

Finally, the purpose of the doctorate might be considered to be an admission key to the academic club and also a licence to independently add to the stock of knowledge of the discipline. These purposes each require an additional skill set above and beyond those needed for the doctorate as previously outlined.

When I think of my doctorate I think less of the Thesis and more of the skills, competencies and capabilities the process built within me and that my supervisor encouraged. Of all of these attributes, the one I prize most (and the one the best academics have in abundance) is *the desire to want to find out something new*. The other doctoral skills and competencies stem from this one.

Throughout the rest of this book, we've aimed to help supervisors to enhance their students' experiences, but we wanted to do this while maintaining a focal point. In order to allow for the wide variability inherent within the doctoral experience, while ensuring there was sufficient structure to make the endeavour manageable, we've built our discourse around the core recognized framework of what the doctorate is in the UK.

The Standardized Doctoral Framework – the 'Dublin Descriptors'

In part inspired by actions of European universities – not governments – in the *Magna Charta Universitatum* (1988),[1] in 1999 the ministers of education of 29 European countries made a declaration in Bologna, Italy. The Bologna Declaration aimed to establish a European Higher Education Area (proposed in the Sorbonne Declaration of 1998) in which students and graduates could move freely between countries, using prior qualifications in one country as acceptable entry requirements for further study in another.

1 See www.magna-charta.org/library/userfiles/file/mc_english.pdf (accessed 18 June 2014).

The agreed principles of this system were twofold:

1. Member countries should adopt common terminologies and standards so that qualifications are easily recognizable and comparable.

2. The system should comprise two main 'cycles' – undergraduate and graduate; the first cycle would be a degree of a minimum of three years which would be recognizable across the EU labour market, and the second cycle would be a master's or doctoral degree.

Building from this, in September 2003 the Berlin Communiqué[2] established the basis of an overarching framework for qualifications for the whole of the European Higher Education Area, including the differentiation of master's and doctoral levels.[3] This framework was intended to enhance the compatibility of workload, level, learning outcomes and student competences as well as endeavouring to shorten the length of higher education qualifications in some participating countries. The framework was to be established upon the so-called 'Dublin Descriptors' of the Joint Quality Initiative (JQI).

The Dublin Descriptors (first proposed in 2002 for bachelor's and master's degrees and based on the descriptors of the UK, Irish and Danish educational systems) were clarified at several JQI meetings in Dublin in 2004 – during which the doctoral descriptors relating to a third Bologna cycle were added.

These Dublin Descriptors set out the differences between bachelor's, master's and doctoral degrees in a number of key areas, labelled 'Knowledge and Understanding', 'Applying Knowledge and Understanding', 'Making Judgements' and 'Communication' and 'Learning Skills'. The doctoral descriptors for the last of these areas are incongruently less about learning and more about promoting the advancement of knowledge.

Since these initial moves a number of documents and processes within the UK have aimed to clarify and make explicit the skills and competencies a doctoral candidate should possess. In 2001 the *Joint Skills Statement* (JSS) unified the skills doctoral research students funded by the Research Councils would be expected

2 *'Realising the European Higher Education Area': Communiqué of the Conference of Ministers responsible for Higher Education in Berlin on 19 September 2003*: www.ehea.info/uploads/declarations/berlin_communique1.pdf (accessed 18 June 2014).

3 These were explicitly named as separate cycles – second and third respectively – in the Bergen Communiqué in 2005. See ibid.

to develop during their candidature. The JSS was replaced more recently by the *Researcher Development Framework*,[4] which seeks to provide a method of plotting the developmental stages of a range of research and academic skills.

The reason for this brief detour into European education policy is that the Dublin Descriptors offer a helpful framework by which a supervisor and student can choose to operate. There are arguments as to whether or not the nature of academic enquiry and development should be led by rules, especially those from Europe. However, this objection misses the point that these frameworks emanated first from universities themselves and do offer a platform of some certainty from which an academic voyage of discovery can be launched. And, pragmatically, it is a candidate's achievements within the Dublin Descriptor areas that will decide whether they (and hence the supervisory team) have been successful.

The Dublin Descriptors that signify completion of the third (that is, doctoral) cycle stipulate that students must have:

1. demonstrated a systematic understanding of a field of study and mastery of the skills and methods of research associated with that field;
2. demonstrated the ability to conceive, design, implement and adapt a substantial process of research with scholarly integrity;
3. made a contribution through original research that extends the frontier of knowledge by developing a substantial body of work, some of which merits national or international refereed publication;
4. proven themselves capable of critical analysis, evaluation and synthesis of new and complex ideas;
5. shown they can communicate with their peers, the larger scholarly community and with society in general about their areas of expertise;
6. demonstrated that they are able to promote technological, social or cultural advancement in a knowledge-based society within academic and professional contexts.

4 See www.vitae.ac.uk/researchers-professional-development/about-the-vitae-researcher-development-framework (accessed 18 June 2014).

Over the following chapters (especially Chapters 7–12, which deal with each Dublin Descriptor in turn) we will show how the supervisor and international student can work together to achieve successful supervision leading to the timely completion of a doctorate that is fit for purpose.

In order for this to happen effectively, we believe that the first step is not to focus on research technique or analytical methodology, but instead for both parties to clarify and articulate their understanding of what the process will involve, and also to appreciate each other's motivations and priorities.

Chapter 3
Doctoral Motivations

Aim for the highest cloud, so that if you miss it,
you will hit a lofty mountain.
Maori proverb

In order for the doctoral process to be as effective as it can be, and for it to have the maximum amount of benefit for everyone concerned, it is certainly worth all parties considering their motivations for engaging in the process. On a daily basis we meet doctoral researchers with a huge range of expectations and fundamental perspectives. These expectations can be purely intellectual (a desire to study and enquire deeply) or more practical (a desire to hold the title 'Doctor' or secure a specific career objective). Combined with this, a student may have a preconceived intellectual idea of the purpose and value of the research findings. Of course, these motivations can and do change throughout the doctoral process, but it is worth considering what they are at the start of the process.

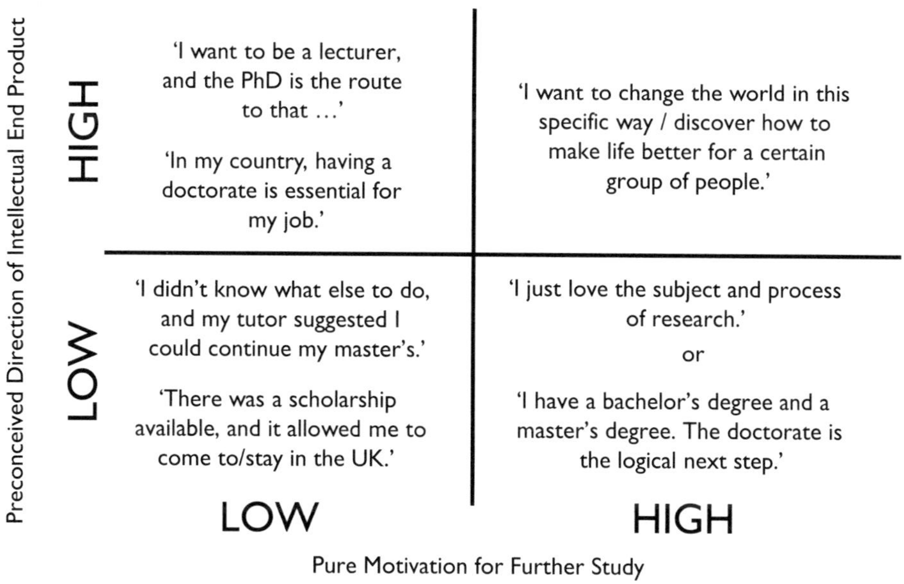

Figure 3.1 Candidates' motivation

It may be helpful here for supervisors to question their assumptions about why a candidate may pursue doctoral study by revisiting their own past motivations for wanting to pursue a doctorate (or other high-level postgraduate qualification). The very simple diagram in Figure 3.1 may offer some food for thought in this regard.

Each individual motivation of each individual student poses certain questions for supervisors, and requires different types of behaviours in response. And a person's motivation can be unclear unless it is explicitly considered and then discussed where appropriate. We accept that motivations are complex, can change over time, and are multi-faceted. This becomes even more important with a relationship that spans different cultures and where motivations may be evidenced in very different ways. Furthermore, we know that 'What motivates you?' or 'What are your motivations?' are not the easiest questions to answer.

Supervisory Enquiries about Motivation

- When you began your doctoral candidature (if applicable, otherwise an equivalent qualification), what was your motivation for doing so?
- Why were you passionate about the *subject*?
- Why did you desire the qualification itself? What did obtaining a *doctorate* offer you?
- Why did you choose the specific institution you were engaged by? Was it even a conscious choice?
- Did your motivation change over the course of your registration?
- How did your motivations affect the type, quality and value of the Thesis you ultimately produced?
- How did your motivations affect the activities you engaged in that sat alongside the production of a Thesis (for example, conference attendance, teaching or writing academic papers)?

Both parties to the relationship, and especially the supervisor (since they may make assumptions based on their own doctoral drivers) need to question their essential motivations, and hence the underlying purpose behind their actions. When building a collaboration with colleagues who have a high degree of technical specialism it can be easy to forget that they are human beings who may have very powerful core motivations.

Having considered these questions, the natural next line of enquiry for a supervisor would be to think empathically about what these challenges posed to their own supervisor.

Supervisory Enquiries about Motivation Challenges

- What challenges did your specific motivations pose to your own supervisor at the time?
- To what extent did your supervisor tailor their style to respond to your motivations?

As can be seen in the above sets of questions, in addition to a student's motivations for discovery and desire for a doctoral qualification, there are also two other factors at play: the student's motivation to study at a particular institution, and the supervisor's motivations for undertaking supervision. In order to explore specific doctoral drivers further, let's first consider the last of these four motivations and address a question the supervisor should be extremely clear about regardless of what students they undertake to support. That question is, simply: *Why do you want to supervise?*

Motivation for Undertaking Supervision

Do not forget what it is to be a sailor because of being a captain yourself.

Tanzanian proverb

The supervisor's own motivation for undertaking supervision is the one element the supervisor can be absolutely clear about before the doctorate process begins. Of course, again, this motivation can change as the research opens up exciting new areas or heads into publishable backwaters – but at the start, where all is possible, we think it is essential for the supervisor to consider their own core motivation for embarking again on the doctoral journey:

> *'Each time I consider taking on a new student I halt the [recruitment] process and ask, 'Why am I doing this?' I don't mean that in a cynical way – the process of questioning my own attitude is very useful. My desire to supervise has changed since I started here; I still love doing it – but now for different reasons.'*
>
> *Research supervisor – Business School*

Supervisory Enquiries about the Supervisor's Desire to Supervise

- What is your motivation for undertaking supervision? (Is the answer 'departmental obligation' fair to anyone?)

More specifically, you may wish to consider:

- What is your motivation for undertaking this supervision, with this student on this topic, and at this time and point in your career?
- What would you consider to be 'a successful doctorate'?
- How structured or unstructured do you prefer to be in your approach to work?

Source: Adapted from Marshall (1999).

There is no need here for us to list supervisory motives. This has been done before, and in any case, it detracts from our core purpose of asking the supervisor to consider their own motivations *and* to build a designed alliance by discussing them with their students. But at a most basic level the discrepancy between the core purpose behind doctoral supervision and the core motivation for doctoral study is the key cause of student concern:

> *'My supervisor seems only interested in publications. I hope a Thesis will come too.'*
>
> *Research student – Biomedical Sciences, Mexico*

Of course, in this example there is an overlap in student and supervisory need since a successful Thesis can and probably should contain material that has already been published in scholarly journals. Lack of alignment in expectations between student and supervisor (denoted in the quote above by the word 'hope') is a real problem within supervisory relationships.

Before any candidate or research area of topic is chosen, it is also worth the supervisor considering some more areas of their own attitudes and beliefs about issues such as style, role and workload.

Supervisory Enquiries about Natural Supervision Style

- Is your natural style dominant – your role being to proactively help shape the direction of the Thesis – or is it based on a belief that it is entirely the student's responsibility to shape the direction, topic and tone of the Thesis?
- If, like many, your style is a mixture of these two, in what circumstances would you prefer to be directive, when would you prefer to reach consensus by open discussion, and when would you immediately hand responsibility to the student?
- How will the support you provide be supplemented by other sources of support?
- For the hypothetical 'normal' student, how much contact time is necessary?
- How much time do you actually have available to supervise? What sort of quality time do you have – to talk, to read and to actually think?

The final question above is contentious – simply because supervisors are consistently under time pressure. Anecdotally, many academics are expected to take on more students than they feel they can sensibly and properly supervise. This pressure can, of course, have a detrimental effect on any student:

> *'The supervisor is not present so much. This can be frustrating.'*
>
> *Research student, Malaysia*

Moreover, the simple *feeling* of being a drain on a supervisor can also cause problems. Peelo (2011) asserts that 'students who travel halfway around the world are often highly committed to what they believe the educational experience will bring them' and 'people who pay large amounts of money do not like to feel that they are a nuisance'. The student 'feeling like a nuisance' is a sign that the relationship is probably not being openly discussed – since they may not actually be a nuisance at all!

In all of our dealings with researchers over the years, time (frequency of meetings and duration of quality supervision) crops up as a problem again and again. And many supervisors also consider that sufficient time is essential when it comes to effective supervision, especially of international students:

> *'You just have to factor more time in to deal with the differences [in supervising international students].'*
>
> *Research supervisor – Engineering*

Indeed, for some, time is *the* most important factor:

> *'My colleagues say that I take over my students' lives. I'm there for my students constantly. We meet every week and they come to my house for dinner at the weekend. I'd rather have fewer students but supervise them properly. Mine finish within three years.'*
>
> *Research supervisor – Psychology*

A few years back I facilitated a supervision training session for post-doctoral researchers who had no supervisory experience whatsoever. As an icebreaker I asked half the group to draw an ideal supervisor from a supervisor's perspective, the other half were asked to draw the ideal supervisor from their own perspective when they'd been a research student. What was fascinating was that the supervisors' drawings of supervisors depicted journeys, with the supervisor as a disembodied but omniscient guide, reaching down from the clouds to help the student over the doctoral terrain. The supervisors drawn from the student's perspective were human beings with large watches (denoting plenty of time), encouraging smiles and big ears for listening – in short, the supervisors valued skill and expertise; students wanted the supervisor to be a human being with plenty of time for them.

Supervisory Enquiries about Workload

- How much time do you currently have to supervise? Is this sufficient? Will this change over the course of the candidature?
- In your experience, broadly, when will candidates need more of your time? Does this fit with your actual schedule? (Of course this is hard to

predict accurately, but there is a need for honesty here from all parties concerned.)

- In your experience, in what areas will different types of students need more of your time?
- How often do you believe it is reasonable for supervisors and their students to meet (for an in-depth one-to-one academic discussion as opposed to a quick technical chat or group discussion)?
- What preparation should each party have engaged in before any supervisory meeting? Do you have time in your schedule to prepare adequately for supervision?

You may wish to revisit these questions for each member of the proposed supervisory team.

Assuming that the supervisor is clear in their mind about their reasons for undertaking doctoral supervision, we must now consider the engagement from the other perspective: *What motivates an international student to come to the UK to undertake a doctorate?*

Within this question are three sub-questions, and we will deal with them in turn:

1. Why the particular higher education institution in question?
2. Why a doctorate (as a qualification)?
3. Why this particular doctorate (the specific topic chosen)?

Each of these questions should ideally be considered before the student is recruited and arrives. However, pragmatically this may not be possible. If it is impossible, then we suggest that these issues are raised as soon as is feasible.

Motivation for Choosing the Specific Institution within the UK

It's worth exploring why your student is considering or has chosen to come and study, not just in the UK, but specifically at your institution. In the Chapter 1 we examined why a postgraduate may be inclined to study in the UK, so our focus here is institutional, not systematic. The choice of institution, especially at doctoral level, is heavily influenced by, if not a direct result of, the supervisor's reputation:

> *'[My university's] reputation did not play a significant part; my supervisor's reputation was very, very important for me.'*
>
> *Research student – Medical Sciences, Hungary*

This weighting can have a profound effect upon an international student (especially one who has invested many personal resources) when the relationship and overall experience prove not to live up to expectations. Frequently, due to cost and proximity issues, an international student may not have physically met with the supervisor prior to their arrival in the UK, and their desire to study with that specific academic may be based solely on published research outputs or reputation. If so, one of the first questions that needs to be addressed is *why* this initial contact was made.

Student Supervisor Discussion Point (Pre-recruitment)

- Why did the student approach you in particular?
- What specifically did the potential student consider to be valuable about you as a supervisor?
- If appropriate, what did they like about any of the specific research outputs you have published?
- What specific elements of the methodology or approaches used in your papers would the potential student change or adapt?

Engaging with these types of questions will give an idea of what type of relationship you and your student may have, and also offers considerable insight into the critical ability and insight of the candidate. We fully appreciate that these types of questions can be difficult for some students to answer (and indeed for supervisors to ask), but this does not mean they should be avoided.

Similarly, an outstanding student may have approached the challenge from the reverse angle. This can be from a purely academic perspective – as in this advice from a Taiwanese researcher to another potential student:

> *'Know your professor's works before you come to UK. I read almost all my professor's works before coming here.'*
>
> *Research student, Taiwan*

Excellent students will also approach the challenge from a different angle and consider the supervisory style as well as their academic output:

> *'Do talk to many potential supervisors, because some are very strange with regard to our typical behaviour. So by considering many options you sort of find out who is closer to you.'*
>
> *Research student – information withheld*

It may be hard for a supervisor to do, as it entails a huge risk to the ego, but a pre-recruitment conversation with a potential student about which other supervisors, research groups and institutions they have considered could be very illuminating!

Yet for all this insight there is often some confusion in a student's mind (especially if the candidate is not experienced in the UK educational system) leading to a belief that a good scholar will be a good supervisor. Certainly there are some stellar academics who are great supervisors, but there are plenty who are not. As Humfrey (1999) says: 'It may be satisfactory to work with a brilliant academic holding an international reputation in the field, but if that academic also recognizes that the student may need support and friendship outside the narrow academic area, then the student – and the institution – is fortunate indeed.'

Herein lies a question, and one that we will explore in more depth later: *How do you design and establish a working relationship quickly?* However, for now, a few other questions may serve to begin this process.

Student and Supervisor Discussion Points about Expectation

- What does your potential supervisee actually seek from a supervisor?
- What did they need in any previous research (dissertation or masters) research projects?
- Do they know how the UK supervisory system works? Have they talked to their colleagues, friends and tutors in their home institution about what the UK system is and how supervision might work? Given the wide variations in doctoral supervision, has your potential student

sought information on this subject from a number of sources before approaching you?

- What type of support does your potential student need from the institution/department?

A student may not know the answer to these questions. We're not sure that we did at the start of our doctorates, but many of the glitches and minor issues that arose over our first years of research could have been avoided if we'd actually talked about these points before we started. Essentially, the purpose of such conversations is not for the student to recognize the supervisor's technical expertise (on the research topic), but for both parties to consider and articulate what supervision might be.

Earlier in this chapter we mentioned that a student may have very non-academic motives for engaging with doctoral study (such as 'The scholarship was available and I wanted to experience the UK'). It is possible that this could be a very destructive element if raised so early in the relationship, and it is unlikely that any student would be explicit in declaring such a motivation. It is important for the supervisor to treat any motivating factor as a positive aspect and to handle differences with their own motivations with sensitivity.

In addition to factors linked to the prospective supervisor, there are other issues that influence a student's choice of institution, and it is probably wise for both parties (and especially the supervisor) to be aware of them – not least because they can have a considerable effect on student motivation at a later point. Sometimes these factors are obvious, but sometimes we in the UK tend to be ignorant of way that the UK is perceived from the outside. For example:

> *'Contrary to what you might see on the news in terms of policy, UK people are friendly to foreigners.'*
>
> *Research student – information withheld*

So what factors influence an international student's choice of institution? Mazzarol et al. (1997), cited in Lord and Dawson (2002), list the following as influencing factors on international postgraduate study site choice:

1. knowledge and awareness of the host country;

2. personal recommendation;

3. cost considerations (cost of living and travel);

4. environment (physical and cultural);

5. geographic proximity to home;

6. existing social links (friends and family already in the host country).

In addition to the supervisor or the research topic and progression, each of these factors (or more likely a combination of them) can affect student motivation, and can be a source of friction between supervisor and student, as in this case:

> *'My supervisor didn't really understand that I need to take my holidays in blocks. Most of my colleagues take weekends off and a week or two in the summer. I don't, but if I'm paying £750 for a flight home I want to go for a block of time. This has caused problems for me.'*
>
> *Research student – Bioscience, India*

Furthermore, as Cotterall (2011) points out, sometimes seemingly unreasonable expectations of supervisors may arise from the fact that 'many international students are socially isolated and don't have other people to turn to'. The point here is for the supervisor to consider the whole set of reasons why the candidate has crossed the world to come and work in their group. Most of the time the reason behind choosing an institution is more complex than simply wanting to work with a specific supervisor. Failure to understand this can cause problems, but embracing and utilizing it can result in a very powerful tool enabling the supervisor to enhance the doctoral experience:

> *'A friend of mine from my country had studied [at this institution] before. They told me that the department had a system to support international students by bringing us together and making available to us an experienced "buddy" who knew the system and knew how we were feeling. I'm really glad I listened to my friend. The system helped me very much.'*
>
> *Research student – Engineering, China*

The research environment component of the Research Assessment Exercise and Research Excellence Framework (REF) has led to research departments and institutions paying far more attention to the atmosphere and surroundings they create for their research students. However, supervisors are not always clear what is available and what is provided by the department and institution.

Since support and provision are continually changing, there is a marked need for supervisors to keep their knowledge about the practicalities and support their institution can offer up to date:

> *'I knew theoretically what a doctorate entailed, such as research design, stats, literature review. It was the other aspects like resources and the research "environment" that I was completely clueless about.'*
>
> *Research student – Medical Sciences, India*

There is of course a workload issue inherent in this, and we're not suggesting that supervisors must be responsible for all elements of pastoral information and support. However, it is important for supervisors to know when they need to offer administrative help and where the appropriate sources of support can be found.

One supervisor told us that he'd asked all of a larger research group's existing students to contribute to a shared resource offering practical advice, links to information and support that new students could benefit from. The students had found such value in doing this that they continued to do it year after year and handed on the resource to new recruits almost as an initiation step. The supervisor told us that this saved him a considerable amount of time dealing with specific queries.

Supervisory Idea to Provide Practical Information

Facilitate the creation of an unofficial research student handbook for the group or department that contains real, pragmatic, practical and even anecdotal advice for new researchers.

Such an approach can reduce supervisor workload and can also address the fact that students sometimes feel their supervisor is not the right person to ask for such information:

> *'Don't expect your supervisor to answer questions about the library and practical questions like that. This is not their job.'*
>
> *Research student – Engineering, India*

If the student feels the supervisor is not the right person to ask, but they do not know who is, this can cause a considerable amount of stress and consume time that would be better spent on actual doctoral activity. Essentially, the more quickly the student is settled, the better. As such, it is worth both parties being aware of what support and provision are in place *before the student arrives* in the UK:

> *'As an overseas student, the first problem I came across was to find clean and tidy accommodation in a friendly area. But I was given very little aid in terms of accommodation except some websites.'*
>
> *Research student – Arts and Humanities, China*

A good starting point may be for the supervisor to talk to an international student who is nearing completion of a doctorate about what resources are available and what they have found particularly useful during their time in the department. Although most academic institutions will have an international office, and many also have an international students' association or student union equivalent which may have literature designed to answer questions such as these, the supervisor is often the first person to whom the student turns. As such, supervisors need to be aware of the practical issues that may arise.

Provision Checklist for Students and Supervisors

What is made available for postgraduate/doctoral researchers in the higher education institution (or local collaboration of them), department and faculty in terms of:

- workspace?
- computing?
- library facilities?
- research environment – seminars, student groups, buddying, mentoring and training?
- language support (departmental and institutional)?
- support with accommodation?
- support with funding/finance?
- support with visas/registration?
- networking and social events?

Is there a buddy or mentoring system in the department? If not, could you introduce a new student to another who has been around for a while and knows about shops, letting agencies, common rooms and so on?

This type of supervisory care and attention can go a long way to help build a strong and productive relationship later on. In addition, though, supervisors who are up to speed on non-academic as well as purely intellectual issues may be a considerable recruiting draw for potential students. However, during the course of preparing this book it's become clear that many academics and administrators from UK universities may be very sympathetic, but have little idea of the concerns of international students when it comes to non-intellectual matters regarding life in the UK:

> *'My supervisor – good for academic matters, not so for any others.'*
> *Research student – information withheld*

As a supervisor, it is probably worth being aware of the support that is on offer *outside* your institution, not least because a student's academic performance is almost certainly going to be affected by certain pastoral non-academic matters.

Wider Help and Support for International Students

A good place to start is the British Council, which offers a range of resources for students and researchers including information on visas, travel, courses, funding and living in the UK:

- British Council – www.britishcouncil.org/higher-education

There is also a specific the British Council resource for students in higher education in the UK:

- Education UK – www.educationuk.org

Supervisors should also be aware of the Euraxess resources, which can be accessed via the British Council website. Euraxess is a joint European initiative providing information and support for researchers who wish to work in Europe.

- Euraxess – www.britishcouncil.org/new/euraxess

The Euraxess website offers a fantastic resource entitled 'The Guide for International Researchers Moving to the UK' which deals with all manner of practical details such as UK entry formalities, working in the UK, the UK research context, pastoral information concerning families and welfare and a host of other information about living and working in the UK:

- www.britishcouncil.org/new/Global/Euraxess/EURAXESS-UK-guide-for-researchers-moving-to-uk.pdf

Supervisors could also be familiar with and point their students in the direction of the UK Council for International Student Affairs, the UK's national advisory body serving the interests of international students and those who work with them:

- UKCISA – www.ukcisa.org.uk

A range of similar support services (such as Host UK) are available at national level to help provide support and education for students who need something less formal and want to immerse themselves in British culture away from the university environment. Host UK arranges for international students studying in the UK to spend a day, weekend or Christmas in a British home:

- Host UK – www.hostuk.org

It is also worth being aware of what is available at a national level in terms of support for researchers and supervisors. Vitae is a good place to start for information on policy, training and career development:

- Vitae – www.vitae.ac.uk

Finally, the National Postgraduate Committee (NPC) is a charity set up to help advance postgraduate education in the UK. As a student representative body it provides a range of advice and guidance for postgraduates studying in the UK:

- NPC – www.npc.org.uk

The questions international students have about living in the UK are not surprising, though it is worth the supervisor pausing for a moment and considering what types of factors may be running through a prospective student's mind. The list and questions below draw on those given in Cryer (2010) and the Euraxess guide mentioned above.

International Students' Possible Concerns

Academic

- What are the academic entry requirements for doctoral study in the UK?
- Will my qualifications be recognized in the UK?
- What is the duration of study?
- How often will I be able to return home?

Finance

- What is the cost of living in the UK?
- Are their regional variations in cost?
- How do I set up a bank account/transfer money?
- How much will the 'international' fee for my course be?
- Is it possible to reduce that fee?
- How can I get details of scholarships that are available?
- Can I claim welfare benefits?

Immigration

- Do I need to get a visa (entry clearance) before I travel to the UK?
- What conditions must I meet to be a student in the UK?
- How long will I need to get a visa for?
- Can I bring my family with me to the UK?
- Can I come to the UK to attend an interview for a position?

Working in the UK

- Can I work part-time while I am studying in the UK?
- Can my family work here while I study in the UK?
- Can I stay in the UK to work after I have finished studying?
- Do I have to pay tax if I work while studying in the UK?

General

- How do I find somewhere to live in the UK?
- Does the institution have accommodation for graduate-only students?
- Does the institution have accommodation for families or couples?

- Can I get childcare in the UK?
- Can my children go to school in the UK while I am a student there?
- Can I get free healthcare while I study in the UK?
- Can I use my driving licence from home to drive in the UK?
- Will my language be adequate? What support is available for me to improve it?
- Is help available for me if I have disabilities or special requirements?

A certain responsibility must be carried by the supervisor for ensuring that they are aware of the needs and concerns of their students, and it is to everyone's advantage if the supervisor is aware of the possible issues and has some ideas about where support may be available before problems arise:

> *'I highly appreciated the support from my supervisor and department. They made sure that the admin/paperwork at the finance and registry offices were done ASAP. It saved me at least four to six weeks which I would have otherwise spent waiting to hear back from them. It's amazing to see what a couple of phone calls can do.'*
>
> *Research student – Medical Sciences, India*

Simple steps can be surprisingly effective here. One student we spoke to talked of her extreme surprise and deep gratitude that her supervisor had taken the trouble to attend an international students' event simply to find out more about his student:

> *'Make time to learn something about the student's culture.'*
>
> *Research supervisor – Social Sciences*

Regardless of any particular student they may be considering working alongside, it is certainly a good idea for the supervisor to become familiar with the issues above and others that concern many international students. Moreover, it would seem sensible for supervisors to ask to attend events and talk to a variety of individuals from countries and cultures different to their own. Finally, a good supervisor will share experiences with colleagues and keep a note of cultural confusions and factors specific to international students.

Yet no matter how good the supervisory practices, the main responsibility for addressing these questions must lie with the students themselves. Nongyao Premkamolnetr (1999) (cited in Cryer 2010) says: 'For starters, [international] students had better make themselves familiar with the universities and countries that they are going to spend some time in. Thus they should find out as much information about those countries as possible, in terms of, for example, government, religions, culture, languages, weather and ways of life.'

This sentiment was reflected by a number of responses to questions we've asked about what advice students would give to prospective doctoral candidates from their own country. Here are two fairly typical ones:

> *'Students should learn the culture before learning the subject. Research the place so you can make the most of it.'*
>
> *Research student, Poland*

> *'Remember to take advantage of the academic support services your university has, and [as a student] you must factor in the higher cost of living expenses.'*
>
> *Research student – Arts and Humanities, Nigeria*

Finally, the most important thing here is that the supervisor should understand the magnitude of these types of non-academic concerns:

> *'I give my students my mobile phone number. I tell them that I'm there for them, wherever and whenever. They don't call very often – but if they do, it's never an academic issue.'*
>
> *Research supervisor – Science*

After all, the candidate is an intelligent adult (and a professional researcher), possibly with considerable life experience, and is capable of solving problems for themselves with just a little local knowledge. A supervisor who belittles a problem or has no time for non-academic issues is likely to be heading towards far more serious academic issues. In addition, these types of pastoral factors tend to exacerbate each other. Issues concerning a researcher's family, finances, visas, children and childcare will obviously distract focus from studies. Even if these take only a day or a week away from the full-time programme, this can still mean that the student feels their progress is slow or they are falling behind. Linguistic difficulties, for example, can mean that the perceived need to catch up may be even more overwhelming:

> *'At the start I was very slow to commence my studies. I had many things to do so I could live in this country. My supervisor was asking*

> *me all the time to be in the lab. I didn't know what to do. It is as if I was a only a part-time researcher but had a full-time position. This was a hard time.'*
>
> *Research student – information withheld*

One of the many contentious concepts in academia at present is the notion of the student as a consumer who needs to obtain 'value for money' from their experience, as if an experience is a commodity that can have a true price put upon it. However, international students *do* pay considerably more for their doctoral experience – through increased fees, higher travel costs and not uncommonly lost income from themselves, their partners and families. As such, supervisors have a duty to ensure they understand that there are special circumstances surrounding international study, that candidates *can* find answers to non-academic questions for themselves with a little help, and that the resources are in place, both institutionally and at a departmental level, to ensure that the student can derive the maximum value from the actual academic doctoral experience.

Motivation for study for a Doctoral Qualification

> *A nation's treasure is in its scholars.*
>
> *Chinese proverb*

Having established the motivation for postgraduate study in the UK and at a specific institution, the next key question to consider is why a potential student specifically wishes to obtain a doctorate. Long experience in the field has taught us that there are many candidates who obtain a doctorate but are considered something of a failure by their supervisors because they don't pursue an academic career. A doctorate is certainly a natural precursor to an academic career, and this is usually precisely the supervisor's experience, yet this is not the only way for the candidate to be successful. Supervisors need to establish the basic motivation for the student pursuing a doctorate, then consider firstly how much it matters whether this motivation aligns with their own, and secondly whether this core motivation is likely to cause any supervisory challenges. Furthermore, establishing the motivation for seeking a qualification is likely to be a very powerful tool in helping the student to make decisions about which research lines to pursue, which publishing and writing strategies to adopt and what career decisions would be beneficial:

> *'Try to understand what it is that drives them to do their PhD; I find understanding motivations helps me to understand how to get them through the lows.'*
>
> *Research supervisor – Linguistics*

For any student, there is a huge amount of risk attached to undertaking a major qualification, but for many international students this risk can be amplified for a number of reasons.

Firstly, regardless of the student's source of funding, stakeholders and family back home will expect a student who is away for three or more years to return a success. This should not be taken to imply that international students are all intellectual big fish in small ponds who come to the UK to prove themselves in the academic capital, but it is important to acknowledge the high stakes involved in their success:

> *'All the time, I think I must not fail. This helps me, but I am tired too.'*
>
> *Research student – Biosciences, Vietnam*

In addition, many international students may have near-contractual reasons for obtaining a doctorate, such as their employment at their home university depending upon it. Again, this motivational stimulus can help to provide focus, but it also can be a major intellectual burden.

According to the direction from many universities in the UK, a doctorate is a qualification which a competent and capable student who is properly supported and supervised can complete within three years of full-time study or the part-time equivalent. The problem for many international students here is that this time scale is taken at face value, and they are not aware of the institutional regulations which often offer a three-year research period followed by a fourth year to ensure that the Thesis writing process is complete. They also tend to be unaware at the start that many research supervisors interpret this institutional guidance as meaning the doctorate is simply a four-year qualification. Indeed, most of the science students we meet who are into their fourth year of study are still in the laboratory collecting more data. If the official line is that the doctorate is a three-year piece of work and the candidate's study visa or financial backing reflects this, then they are likely to feel a great deal of stress if the supervisor is not aware of this and doesn't modify expectations to fit the timescale. Moreover, anecdotally, international students who return home in order to write up their Thesis are much less likely to complete it without major complications – and sometimes not at all:

> *'Sometimes, when work is hard, I remind myself that, God willing, I could be Doctor.'*
>
> *Research student – information withheld*

Supervisors therefore need to understand the purpose of the obtaining the *qualification* from their international students' perspective. Intellectually, this question is often clouded, at both undergraduate and master's level, by the financial costs of study. Binsardi and Ekwulugo (2003) note that 'students are not buying degrees; they are buying the benefits that a degree can buy in terms of employment, status, lifestyle'. Moreover, Humfrey (1999) cites Kogan and Kogan (1983), who say: 'we will have to look carefully at all applications. I say this with tears in my eyes; there will definitely be a lowering of standards. We will have to accept some people who have money and not quality.'

While both of these assertions may contain some truth, at doctoral level the picture is more complex. Nevertheless, there are sometimes cross-cultural differences in expectations concerning the purpose of pursuing a doctorate. For instance:

> *'I think most students in China learn for the degree itself, which [is] normally related to better job, better pay etc. But in the UK the purpose of PhD study is mostly about interest and creativity.'*
>
> *Research student – Computer Science, China*

Again, it is worth considering what expectations the student has of the doctoral qualification itself, and to do this some time in advance of establishing whether the student understands how to process a dataset or how to grapple with the technicalities of a valid research method.

A doctorate certainly means different things to different people from different cultures, and it would seem sensible to step back a little and remind ourselves that regardless of culture or origin, the doctorate is still a very special qualification:

> *'It is most important for me to show my colleagues and friends that I can do this, and so could they.'*
>
> *Research student – information withheld*

As a supervisor, surrounded by professorial, academic and post-doctoral associates all the time, it is often easy to ignore the standing the doctorate has outside academia. It may be recognized as a high-level intellectual qualification, but it's often considered to be ill suited to the needs of any sector apart from (and even including) the academic one. In short, it is not necessarily a commonplace qualification nor seen as a valid one. It is worth the supervisor pausing to reflect on how a doctorate may be viewed from another country or culture – especially a country that perhaps does not have a strong, formal scholarly history. This standing and associated expectations of success among a researcher's friends and family can exert an enormous strain on the student. A simple enquiry and acknowledgement of such factors by the supervisor can produce significant results in terms of building the student–supervisor relationship.

On top of a prospective or new candidate's career expectations and cultural differences pertaining to rational for pursuing doctoral study, there is also the question of the student's professional expertise and history to date. It is essential to consider these at an early stage, partly to help build the relationship, but also (as Clegg 1997 points out) because issues of race and culture (and also gender, sexuality and political leaning, among other factors) within the supervisory relationship may be important, as the 'nature of the experience is implicated in the interpretation of data'.

Previous Student History – UK Study

A relatively common previous career history here is that of the student who has already completed a bachelor's or master's degree in the UK, and has perhaps already been tutored or supervised by the same academic they intend to work with at doctoral level. Rather than assume that this student knows the ropes and understands the academic system, it is worth the supervisor making enquiries as to whether the student understands the nature of doctoral-level study and comprehends the key differences between the doctorate and any previous qualifications.

A very useful conversation to have here, either before or soon after recruitment, focuses on the topic 'What is good research?' Following a 'Starting Your PhD' workshop, one student observed:

> *'I asked my supervisor what he considered "good research" to be. This was amazing. So simple and so helpful. My supervisor said he'd found it a really interesting meeting too!'*
>
> *Research student – Bioscience, China*

This conversation (or asking the student to go and think about it in preparation for a future discussion) can cut through a huge number of potential problems, as it refers to the core values and standards of what research is all about.

Student and Supervisor Discussion Points about the Nature of Research

- What is good research?
- What is good doctoral research?
- What contribution does your honours or master's dissertation make to the field?
- Is this the same meaning of 'contribution' that will be required of your doctoral research?
- What do you consider the UK doctorate to be?
- How do you think the UK doctorate is different to your previous research projects?
- What have experienced doctoral students told you about the PhD process?

Previous Student History – International Study

The next category of student is those who have undertaken previous postgraduate study, but not in the UK:

> *'It sounds like such a basic thing to do, but I've started asking potential students why they specifically want to come and study within the UK system. I found this approach to be initially more productive than discussing research technicalities.'*
>
> *Research supervisor – Biosciences*

If a student already has a postgraduate background it may be tempting for the supervisor to believe that the candidate is fully aware of the rigours of research and the demands of higher-level study, but this may not necessarily be the case:

> *'My previous student already had a master's degree from abroad, but we literally had to start from scratch, though. This set things back, and was disappointing for me and really tough for him.'*
>
> *Research supervisor – Computer Science*

While rudimentary enquiries cannot prevent this type of situation (and of course it is sensible to also enquire about the specific details of the master's qualification), they can begin to address some of the fundamental issues concerning the differences between qualifications in the UK and abroad.

Student and Supervisor Discussion Points about Moving to the UK

The questions in the 'Student and Supervisor Discussion Points about the Nature of Research' box above are valid here too, but in addition:

- What was the reason for moving to study in the UK?
- In what way is the UK doctorate different from a doctorate where you've studied previously?
- Which papers were the key influencers on your master's dissertation?
- What methodologies did you choose to employ? Why did you choose them?

Previous Student History – Employment and Professional Career

Over the last few years within the sector we have collectively met international doctoral students who have come to the UK to study having previously pursued careers as judges, business leaders, police chiefs, headteachers, lecturers, military leaders, senior civil servants and even a prime minister, or who are currently engaged in are on sabbatical from these posts. The wise supervisor will consider these circumstances very carefully and think about what this professional experience can add to the research process and what recognition the student needs for it:

> *'Compared to my home country, I feel that professors [here] lack structure. They do not take professional experience into account, which my MA Thesis supervisor in the US did. He also wanted to know about my cultural background.'*
>
> *Research student – Arts and Humanities, Germany*

As previously observed, these students will have a considerably different expectations of a doctoral qualification compared to students at the beginning of their careers who want to gain professional recognition. This 'downgrade' in status from a well-paid and respected member of society to that of (in the words of one researcher we spoke to) 'a lowly student' can have a considerable impact on a researcher's confidence, and we'll explore this specific issue later. This category of student often has a high level of relevant and pragmatic expertise – and this can cause tension if it is not handled carefully by the supervisor:

> *'Spend a lot of time finding a supervisor who will not over-supervise if you are quite comfortable in your abilities.'*
> *Research student, USA (with 25 years of professional experience)*

Regardless of professional experience, though (and depending on the specific discipline), this type of student may not have undertaken a master's degree and it may also be some time since they were last in a 'student' mindset. We will return to this particular category of student in more detail in Chapter 6 when we examine how to build a successful doctoral relationship.

Student and Supervisor Discussion Points about the Student's Previous Career

The questions from the previous discussion boxes above are valid here too, but in addition:

- What will the doctorate offer you professionally?
- How has your career prepared you for doctoral study?
- What specific help and support will you need?
- Whose work or whose doctorate inspired your desire to engage in doctoral study?

Student Motivation for the Subject

> *A thousand-mile journey begins with a single step.*
> *Australian Aboriginal proverb*

In so far as student motivation is concerned, we have examined the motivation for studying at a specific institution and the motivation for obtaining a doctorate. The third essential type of motivation is the reason for choosing *this specific* doctorate – in other words, why is this specific niche area of study exciting and engaging for the student? In many ways this is the simplest motivation to elucidate, and also does most to enhance the supervisor's ability to truly engage with the student. As before, this issue can be raised before recruitment or soon after arrival, and we left it until the last of the three motivational facets to consider since it's perhaps the easiest to address conversationally.

Earlier in this chapter we posed the question of why the reader had chosen their doctoral discipline, and this same question can easily be used to help a student articulate their rationale for wanting to commit to the programme of study. Indeed, in the darker days of the doctorate, when progress is slow and the end is nowhere near, this motivation is sometimes the only factor that can keep a student going.

If a student has produced a research proposal, this aspect of motivation is far easier to raise in conversation. However, if the research direction is already focused prior to the arrival of the student, then it requires attention from the supervisor.

Student and Supervisor Discussion Points about Student Motivation

- Why is this particular area exciting for you?
- What value will academic discovery in this area add?
- What sort of impact do you think discovery in this area could have?

One of the hallmarks of academic research is its neutrality. Arguments should be balanced, findings should be questioned, and a core premise of any Thesis is that what is being presented is merely an idea with sufficient evidence to back it up. Therefore, to be successful, academic researchers must be objective. As human beings, however, we each face the challenge that everything we do is shaped by our previous experience, culture, tradition and history. Students' own personal, professional and political concerns often have an impact on the subject matter being researched, and our experience tells us that students, especially international students, from the social science and humanities disciplines are most likely to fall into this category. This can pose specific challenges for a research supervisor:

> *'I find it particularly hard when [the student's] personal and professional history is very much linked to their study topic and Thesis. It's hard to both encourage them and remind them to be objective.'*
>
> *Research supervisor – Education*

Since one of the key descriptors of doctoral success concerns a student's ability to conceive and design research with scholarly integrity, we will examine this difficult supervisory challenge in greater detail later in the book.

In summary, we are suggesting that it would be extremely prudent for each party to consider their motivations and to discuss these at the earliest possible opportunity. These motivations are fourfold:

1. the supervisor's motives for supervising;
2. the student's motivation for choosing the supervisor, the institution and the UK;
3. the student's motivation for studying for a doctoral-level qualification;
4. both parties' motivations for engaging with the specific area of research.

It's essential to remember that none of the areas explored nor the questions we've posed so far will help the student to conduct a successful piece of research. But exploring these areas will help both parties to establish solid bedrock upon which to build an effective supervisory relationship, which in turn will make it easier to produce a successful piece of research and complete a doctorate that is fit for purpose.

The next step is to consider what expectations each party has of their respective roles as doctoral supervisor and student.

Chapter 4
Doctoral Expectations

Think before acting; and while acting, still think.
Bulgarian proverb

Having explored and established all parties' motivations for undertaking the doctoral or supervisory process, we now turn to exploring what each party will expect from the process itself and from each other. Through a process of understanding, articulation and discussion, we believe that the various elements of the supervisory relationship can build a designed alliance which benefits all parties.

It is here, though, that many of the fundamental problems with supervising an international doctoral student lie, as the parties' expectations of what will happen may be fundamentally different. As Kam (1997) states:

> *The quality of research degree supervision depends as much on the supervisor's ability to meet the needs of a student as on the student's expectation of her or his own responsibilities in relation to those of the supervisor. This mutual understanding of role expectation is crucial to the success of the supervisory process.*

The mismatch in expectations crops up repeatedly for us, both as part of our everyday work and especially as part of the research for this book. This quote is fairly typical:

> *'I don't know what was my expectation [of the PhD]. Certainly not like this.'*
>
> *Research student, Brazil*

There have also been some tentative explorations of the expectations of UK academics working with international students (see, for instance, Fallon and Berman Brown 1999), but the literature on the subject often raises more questions than it addresses. Yet a disparity in expectations does not necessarily mean that the doctoral process is doomed from the start, and a workable situation usually emerges as time progresses:

> *'I think I had a good experience with my supervisor. But it was not at first how I expected it to be.'*
>
> *Post-doctoral researcher – Computer Science, India*

The trouble here is that the 'implicit 'rules of engagement' and boundaries to be negotiated' (Park 2008) are just that – implicit, and many international students lack the cultural decoding mechanisms necessary to establish which particular rules the process is bound by. This situation is exacerbated by the fact that these rules differ between institutions, departments and supervisors. Brown (2008) notes that academic difficulties may arise not just because of linguistic differences, but also because of a failure to understand or communicate at a cultural level – something that may not have been anticipated. But candidates who reported a largely positive doctoral experience were much more proactive about considering expectations and actually raising this topic as part of the supervision process. Austin (2011) suggests that a mapping exercise can be useful in managing mutual expectations. This can facilitate discussions about important competencies and the construction of a useful action plan:

> *'Reading about your role and the supervisor's role and what to expect from the supervisor is so helpful.'*
>
> *Research student, Saudi Arabia*

> *'When I'd been a PhD student for about a week my supervisor and I sat down and she asked me three questions, which I remember even now. They were "What do you want from the next three years?", "How do you work best?" and "What do you want from me?" These questions weren't about my project or the science, and they took me aback a bit. But I would say that this was a most useful place to start. We have a new PhD student just started in our lab and I made sure that I asked him to think about the same questions before he went to see his supervisor!'*
>
> *Post-doctoral researcher, Spain*

At undergraduate level (driven perhaps by financial agendas) there have been attempts, both historically and latterly, to internationalize the curriculum and to cater intellectually for students from different cultural backgrounds (McNamara and Harris 1997). However, regardless of the good intentions of the institution, several studies (see, among others, Ryan and Hellmundt 2003; Powell 2003, especially pp. 159–76) report a mismatch between the expectations of international students and their teachers. Academic staff also report frustration at feeling inadequately trained to deal with the needs of international students and not understanding the source of their difficulties. At a doctoral level, this consideration does not necessarily have to be so difficult since the relationship is (at least in part) conducted on a one-to-one basis:

> *'I reckon it's probably important to spend a little while finding out about my students ... partly about what they know, but also about their backgrounds and expectations ....*
>
> *[Does the cultural background of a student enter into this?] Yes, absolutely – though I just start from the assumption that all of them are different individuals and work from there.'*
>
> *Research supervisor – Management Studies*

There are a number of different expectations to consider here – not least those of the candidates themselves, whose expectations of the doctoral and supervision process and expectations based on their own underlying motivations to study will shape their actions considerably. We will deal with the candidate in Chapter 5, as these expectations cannot really be known until the student has arrived and commenced work. Prior to this, it may be useful for the supervisor to consider the contextual expectations the student has of the doctoral system within the UK. It may be (as, for example, in Evans and Liou 2011; Harman 2003) that the international student is better acquainted with the US doctoral system and so is expecting a different structure of study and research. Even if this is not the case, the institutional expectations and supervisors' expectations of their own role, of the candidate and of how any supervisory team might work may all have a considerable role to play.

As before, let's consider what a research supervisor *could know for certain* in terms of expectations – namely, those of their institution and those of themselves.

Institutional Expectations of Doctoral Supervision

As we've already discussed, the doctoral supervisory process is a highly personal one, so there is often little formal guidance on how to conduct it. Even when formal guidance is issued, it is sometimes only loosely followed:

> *'We have to keep records of meetings. My professor is expected to do this, but he doesn't. He said that I should do it. I'm not complaining; I find it helpful.'*
>
> *Research student, Italy*

It is worth the supervisor being very clear about what the institution expects of the candidate and the supervisor. This is partly common sense to ensure that they are doing their job 'properly', and partly because students are increasingly conscious that any explicit rules of engagement are easily accessible to anyone on the Web, and any dissatisfaction can be amplified if a candidate can see in black and white that the supervisor is not fulfilling their obligations in accordance with institutional policy.

Supervisor Enquiries about Institutional Expectations

At your institution:

- What does the institution expect from a research student?
- What are the regulations concerning the candidacy, the time allocation and the production of a Thesis?
- What specific information is offered in the research student handbook or guidance provided by your department?
- What do your institutional requirements[1] specify about provision of a supervisory team?
- What institutional requirements are laid out with regard to conducting a training needs analysis at the start of the doctoral process?
- What does the institution/department expect in terms of monitoring student progress (for example, probationary periods, transfer/differentiation processes, upgrade or confirmation reports)?
- What does the institution/department expect in terms of monitoring the supervisory relationship (for example, records of meetings/student-led feedback reports)?
- What guidance and/or compliance measures does the institution/department offer to ensure sufficient quality and quantity of supervisory meetings?

1 To ensure QAA Code of Practice compliance, see 'Code of Practice for the Assurance of Academic Quality and Standards in Higher Education – Section 1: Postgraduate Research Programmes (2004)': www.qaa.ac.uk/Publications/InformationAndGuidance/Pages/Code-of-practice-section-1.aspx (accessed 18 June 2014).

Of course, once these aspects have been researched by the supervisor (we use the word 'research' here carefully – these external expectations and drivers are not static), the next sensible step is to have a conversation with the student about these expectations, and when they require some negotiation between the two parties (for instance, in a case where a record of meetings must be kept, but it is up to the individual partnerships to determine how this might happen), to reach a clear agreement on who must do what by when to ensure institutional compliance.

Supervisory Idea about Compliance and Regulations

Could you provide your research student with national, institutional and departmental links to documents relating to good practice and ask them to either simply consider them, or teach them to you to 'ensure that you are up to date'?

Another factor that is essential for supervisors to consider is their own expectations of the role they play as supervisors.

The Supervisor's Expectations of the Supervisory Role

Our first teacher is our own heart.
Cheyenne proverb

I remember vividly an occasion from my childhood when my parents reprimanded me, unjustly in my opinion. 'That's not fair!' I clearly recall saying, and there and then I made a resolution that when I was a parent, I would not behave in such an unjust and draconian manner to my kids. I would be a cool parent and never, ever act in such an 'unfair' way. Last week, with my own children, who are about the age I was then, I acted in exactly the way I promised that I would not. The example we are set by our elders, parents and educators is an extremely powerful one.

We encounter this type of situation with doctoral supervisors. That is not to say that supervisors are parents and researchers are children, even metaphorically, but often a supervisor's default style is affected less by their current student, and more by either how they were supervised when they were a student, or – if their experience was poor – exactly how they *wanted* to have been supervised. In each case the downside is the same. The relationship is governed by the expectations and experiences of one party only. These expectations often drive the relationship, especially if the research student has a strong cultural background of deference towards elders and educators. If the doctoral experience is to be a positive one for any of those involved, the supervisor needs to be able to articulate exactly what their expectations of their own role are and then use this as a discussion point to establish what the candidate may respond best to.

To articulate some differences in default supervisory attitude, we find that a combination of three existing models works very well. The first is that of Gatfield (2005), who proposes a paradigm of supervisory style based on the supervisor's focus on either research structure or student support, or both. The second is the work of Anne Lee in her 2008 article 'How are Doctoral Students Supervised?' In this she outlines some fundamental styles of doctoral supervisor ethos and behaviour, and in many ways this builds on Gatfield's work, but Lee incorporates the element of 'relationship development', which goes beyond the supervisor simply offering support to the student. Using these two approaches as a basic template leads us to two questions (the answers to which are not mutually exclusive) that supervisors must address before they engage with supervision:

1. To what extent do you place a focus on helping the candidate to complete the doctorate successfully?

2. To what extent do you focus on developing a productive working relationship with the doctoral researcher?

The third model we've drawn inspiration from is the Situational Leadership work of Hersey and Blanchard (1977), which concerns how a leader handles a team at different stages of maturity through the lifecycle of a project.

In combination, these models and the answers to these questions give one of six main supervisory styles (see Figure 4.1). This detailing of what we consider to be the six core supervisory roles devotes only minor consideration to how the international student experience can be enhanced. However, if supervisors are aware of the focus they would prefer to place on the supervisory process, then it can only help them to choose the appropriate specific supervisory behaviours which would work best for their students and seem most authentic and valuable to the supervisor.

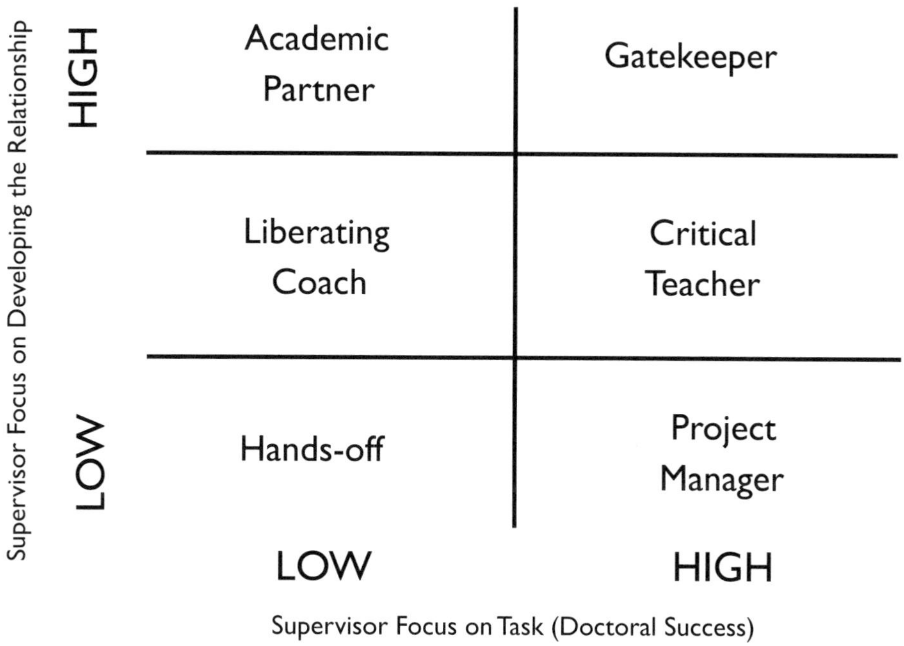

Figure 4.1 Supervisory approaches (1)

There is some overlap between adjoining styles, and this model is obviously a gross simplification. Moreover, we present the styles with no implied judgement or hierarchical order. Each of these styles has advantages and disadvantages and raises specific challenges with regard to the supervision of international students. Most supervisors will adopt a balance of these six styles at different times throughout the candidature, and with different students, but essentially their core beliefs about supervision are driven by one core style. These styles are:

- **project manager** – focus on collecting and analysing data and completing research outputs;
- **critical teacher** – focus on challenge and Socratic enquiry;
- **gatekeeper** – focus on encouraging academic participation and involvement;
- **hands-off** – focus on leaving students to work by themselves;
- **liberating coach** – focus on allowing the candidates to question and develop themselves;

- **academic partner** – focus on building a long-term academic relationship.

If I think about my own two PhD supervisors, I can immediately recognize that they had two very different core styles, and even in the absence of any detailed information about the model and classifications, I can place each of their demonstrated focuses in two separate areas.

> **Supervisory Enquiries about Being a Student**
>
> - How were you supervised? What was the balance your supervisor adopted?
> - How did this change over time?
> - How would you have *liked* to have been supervised? Would this have changed over time?
> - If you had multiple supervisors, how did their styles and role expectations differ?
> - What balance have you adopted with previous research students you have supervised?
> - Has this default balance changed depending on the cultural and educational background of your previous students?

Having considered initial supervisory expectations of the role, we'll provide some detail about each of them to examine the advantages and challenges of the approach in relation to international students.

The Supervisor as Project Manager (High Task, Low Relationship)

> **Core Supervisory Style**
>
> Supervisory emphasis is placed on managing the research project. The supervisor provides the ground rules and structure for the doctoral process as well as advice (or stronger direction) on research methodologies, timescales, ethics, and logistical steps (see Vilkinas 2002). Supervisors adopting this style may issue timetables or schedules and to an extent see the doctorate as a job of work, complete with weekly meetings and timetabled structures. Little focus is placed on explicitly developing the partnership between student and supervisor – though this may sometimes happen anyway.

The generic advantages of this style are obvious, especially if the doctoral student will be working as part of a team which has a shared stake in the outputs of the research work. Many of the supervisors we spoke to adopted this essential style and focus. For instance:

> *'Lay down a schedule which includes review points, and keep it updated. A PhD is a project and needs to be managed as such.'*
>
> *Research supervisor – Business School*

Moreover, a desire for this type of approach is often evident from some of the international researchers we spoke to, especially those in the early stages of their research:

> *'If I am asked to advise a new student, I say to find a supervisor for whom structure and deadlines are not a foreign land.'*
>
> *Research student – Biosciences, Saudi Arabia*

For all of the clarity and consistency this style provides, it is worth considering whether the supervisor as project manager really addresses the fundamental point of whether the candidate will be an independent scholar by the end of the process. This type of supervisory style combined with a lack of challenge or critical ability from the student can easily produce the 'I did it like that because my supervisor said to' answer that so exasperates doctoral examiners.

For any supervisory relationship it is worth challenging any assumptions (cultural or otherwise) about what style of supervision a student may prefer. A clear tension within this style arises with students who have already engaged in postgraduate work in the UK, where more emphasis may have been placed on speculative self-directive learning than on tightly managed structured work. Furthermore, it is not inconceivable that if the supervisor has been very directive and hands-on throughout the research process, then a student (especially one who has paid a considerable sum of money) might expect the supervisor to contribute substantially to the actual written component of Thesis production or be present to help answer questions in the viva. These expectations might seem preposterous, but we've heard them both from students on a number of occasions. In this way, supervisors as project managers may simply be storing up problems for themselves in the long term, as few supervisors wouldn't baulk at that level of contribution.

A further tension can also result from the 'newness time multiplier' that exists around research as a process of apprenticeship and training. This means that when an experienced research supervisor says that a particular task should take a certain amount of time, they mean that it would take *them* that amount of time – not the apprentice. This is a generic condition, and not unique to international students. Phillips and Pugh (2010) offer similar advice to PhD students generally: 'Overall you must realize that it takes a significant amount of time for any new doctoral student to settle in and begin useful research work. Because of these additional difficulties, you must not become impatient if it takes rather longer for you.' If the student is in a situation where they are new to the language, culture, climate, environment, specific style of research technique and a host of other variables, then this difference in expectation about time taken can only be exacerbated:

> *'It is important for supervisor to understand the pace that you are able to work in. For example, it took me three months to really settle in with my environment, and the next six to really look into my work.'*
>
> *Research student, Brunei*

A supervisor who perceives that the student's progress is (for whatever reason) 'slow' may unconsciously take on a strong project manager style to drive things forward. It is, however, worth the supervisor pausing to reflect before acting.

A sensible supervisor, if driven by this core style, will want to facilitate a handover of responsibility to the student as soon as the student is able to handle it (if only to minimize supervisory workload), but no sooner. Core to the handover is the question of how much control the project manager needs and how much they trust their student.

Supervisory Enquiries about the Role of Project Manager

- How much control do you as supervisor need over the direction of the project?
- How can you help the project stay 'on track' when by its very nature the doctorate is a voyage into both independence and discovery?
- To what extent do students need to prove themselves in order for you to trust them?
- How might you gain trust (and establish whether you can trust your student) quickly?

As a starting point, the supervisor as project manager has a great deal to offer the student in terms of making progress quickly. If the student experience is to be enhanced, the supervisor must then begin to engage the student's critical faculties. This may simply mean changing the tone of supervisory meetings from 'I say, you do' to 'We talk and I decide', then to 'We talk and you decide.' This progression is also a manifestation of the blurring of the role expectations boundary to (or the chronological segue into) the style of supervisor as a critical teacher.

The Supervisor as Critical Teacher (High Task, Medium Relationship)

Core Supervisory Style

The supervisor places an emphasis on challenging the student to think. Their role is based on teaching the student via the principles of Socratic enquiry – and as such any finding or thought within the thesis could be questioned – even right until the end of the process of Thesis production.

One of the key doctoral descriptors outlined in Chapter 2 focuses on a successful student's ability to constructively analyse and criticize research findings – whether the candidate's own or within already existing knowledge. As such, the supervisor adopting the style of a critical teacher offers many advantages – not least that at the viva the candidate will be challenged by an experienced academic of high intellectual position, and learning to question and give and receive criticism is part of this process. One supervisor told us that supervisors must:

> *'Let him or her [the student] know that challenging ideas is part of intellectual discourse and is something that is valued.'*
>
> *Research supervisor – Social Science*

Doctoral students often recognize the value of the supervisor's role here, but recognition, acceptance and action are all very different:

> *'I have to learn to act against my Chinese culture. I know why I must do it. But it is hard.'*
>
> *Research student – Engineering, China*

However, the critical teacher style has a number of drawbacks – especially for international students. Firstly there is the issue of the expectations of a student who may be very used to a correct/incorrect style of education:

> *'Change the idea (from Chinese universities) that the supervisors are the "teachers" of your course – self-learning is important.'*
>
> *Research student, China*

Of course, it is one thing to request that our students be critical, and another to expect complete honesty and a no-holds-barred approach to academic debate from day one. This applies to any student, let alone one facing cultural differences resulting from different backgrounds. For example, as Chan (1999) points out: 'the Chinese prefer not to express their true opinions so as not to embarrass or offend others'. This factor is one that, with time and gentle reinforcement, can be resolved – but the supervisor must be prepared to wait for this to happen and encourage it gradually:

> *'The thing I found frustrating was that, in my first year, I kept finding what I thought were answers and my supervisor just asked more questions. It wasn't what I was expecting at all.'*
>
> *Research student – Computer Sciences, Middle East*

Simple strategies like posing the challenges in advance of a meeting so that the student has time to consider their responses can really aid translation and understanding. Such preparation can help both culturally and linguistically in allowing a student to formulate a meaningful response to a challenge:

> *'It's hard when my supervisor calls on me when I am not expecting it. I don't like this as I am not prepared.'*
>
> *Research student – Sciences, Indonesia*

For supervisors acclimatized to the UK system, it is an intrinsic idea that a candidate can also challenge the insights and ideas of the supervisor, though it is worth mentioning that some individual supervisors are more tolerant of challenges than others. Culturally, however, this can be a sticking point for some international researchers – especially those who have not developed in a Socratic educational system:

> *'In my country there is much to remember. Learning is done by remembering. And the teacher is in charge. You must not question. Here it is very different.'*
>
> *Research student – information withheld*

There is a paradox here: in order to become what the supervisor intends, a doctoral candidate must break away from concerns about the supervisor's intentions. And a while great doctoral supervisors are doubtless worth listening to, they will encourage their students to listen when being told not to take everything the supervisor says at face value. As one supervisor smilingly told us:

> *'I tell my students that they must challenge my ideas. They respond "OK." This isn't really what I have in mind.'*
>
> *Research supervisor – Engineering*

The next issue with the critical teacher style is that of student confidence. In an academic world built around intellectual criticism, and with the traditional model of academic discourse being 'You're wrong because ...', it's important to realize how easily constructive criticism can become constructive *criticism*, as opposed to *constructive* criticism.

Supervisory Enquiries about the Role of Critical Teacher

Consider your driving force when you are commenting on your students' work.

- Are you seeking to criticize, to find the flaws in their work or their argument in the traditional manner of academic discourse?
- Or are you looking for opportunities to build, to provide the student with the materials to construct a solid piece of work?

There will be a place for both approaches at different stages of a student's doctoral candidacy.

- Which is right for your international student now?
- In view of this driving force, what will you need to bear in mind?

With students who may be culturally, institutionally and linguistically inexperienced, this focus on challenge and criticism – however well intended – can result in a considerable erosion of student confidence. As one student told us:

> *'Supervisors – give positive feedback! The PhD is full of the shadow of self-doubt.'*
>
> *Research student – Medical Sciences, Hungary*

The 2011 Escalate project, published by the Higher Education Academy (Trahar 2011), provides the example of a doctoral researcher (Paola Signorini) who noticed that the feedback from her supervisor constantly contained the word 'you' ('You are not clear in this section,' or 'Why do you say this?'). Subsequently, the student realized that she was interpreting the commentary as a personal criticism and changed the way she listened to her supervisor's comments:

> *'When they [supervisor] said: 'What did you mean?', I mentally rephrased it as 'What does this section mean?'; 'You did a good job' was paraphrased as 'This was a good piece of writing' or 'good piece of fieldwork'. Once I did this, my self-confidence increased.'*

This type of insight requires a great deal of reflection and linguistic dexterity from the student, so, as a critical teacher, the supervisor must be very careful to ensure feedback focuses on actions, not personalities. We will fully examine the giving and receiving of feedback in Chapter 9.

The supervisor will be offering feedback from an existing intellectual set of perspectives, frameworks and philosophies. In the humanities and social science disciplines, this can cause a number of challenges if the student has different frameworks and core philosophies. Trahar (2011) quotes a different research student (Shawanda Stockfelt), who writes:

> *'What I am calling into question is my capability to accept or reject a westernised epistemology. Let me re-emphasise, I have no problems with most of these philosophies of knowledge, but with the overzealous attempt in academia for one to use these as lenses through which you "see" your research .... Why?'*

Supervisors should consider how attached they are to accepted 'Western' research philosophies and whether a blend of cultural philosophies (often referred in educational literature as 'transculturation') may offer a valuable way of furthering the discipline itself as well as the practices of both student and supervisor.

In the UK, people typically believe that as a nation we are diplomatic but fairly direct. However, seen from the perspective of someone from outside, this is not necessarily the case:

> *'If your supervisor says that he has "one or two minor comments", in my experience this means a significant rewrite.'*
>
> *Research student, Germany*

Supervisors adopting the critical teacher style must therefore be aware that the messages they transmit are not always received in the intended way. The perception (or reality) of a power imbalance between student and supervisor can add to this communication difficulty. As Palfreyman and McBride (2007) say:

> *Supervisors should be aware that the use of indirect suggestions (e.g. 'perhaps you might want to look at X': a politeness strategy that suggests equality) may create the impression that the student has the option not to follow up on the suggestion when, in fact, the existence of the power relationship means that the student does not have an option.*

Such a situation can be exploited by the supervisor to 'steer' the student towards research areas or data collection that are only of interest to the supervisor. Perhaps worse, though, is the idea that a student can become critically dependent on the supervisor's insight, and thus lack independence. This phenomenon is amplified in – but not limited to – a relationship where the student has been educated in a Confucian system.

Finally, the critical teacher approach – in isolation – can result in no small dissatisfaction for a student who has travelled some distance to work with a world expert:

> *'What annoys me about my supervisor is when I ask him a question, and he asks me back what I think .... Why would I need his advice if I already knew?'*
>
> *Research student – Earth Sciences, India*

Supervisors adopting the critical teacher style have a delicate path to tread between over-criticizing, allowing the student to become critically dependent, focusing on action not the person, being too attached to their own personal critical frameworks and unintentionally suppressing the student's creativity.

If the critical teacher approach is to be truly effective, then the supervisor needs to encourage the student to speak and discuss – and the process needs to flow in both directions. The supervisor must provide a platform and opportunities for the student to actually perform in a 'real' academic environment. One supervisor told us that in the past he had taken a fundamental position of affirmation and support with his students until he felt that they were able to handle whatever criticism he offered. He said that he'd had to revise his strategies when a particularly forthright student, following this change of approach, had complained to him that it was 'as if he didn't like her any more'. The problem here again is not the supervisory tactic ('criticism'), but that the underlying motivation ('it's necessary and the student is good enough') is not clear to the student. The relationship or alliance between the two parties has not been deliberately designed.

The Supervisor as Gatekeeper (High Task, High Relationship)

Core Supervisory Style

The supervisor places an emphasis on investing in the relationship, facilitating the project and promoting opportunities for the student to network and disseminate their findings.

We've already stated our belief that a doctorate involves more than acquiring skills and knowledge. It's also about enabling a candidate to work on building a leadership position, either purely intellectually or within their specific career area. This is core to the supervisor as gatekeeper style of supervision. The supervisor invests in the relationship to facilitate the project and the opportunities associated with it that allow the research student to build a network that actually works. This means the supervisor must trust the student enough to encourage and support their participation and involvement in the academic community.

While this approach poses challenges to any student, it is interesting to note that as some of the funding councils in the UK move towards a cohort-based approach to the doctorate, and institutions in collaborations respond with a doctoral training centre model, the doctorate may well become less isolating, more team-focused and externally facing, and the basic supervisory role may well change to reflect this.

Even with a 'traditional' supervision model, the gatekeeper style seems to be universally welcomed by students (providing the opportunity is not too challenging and presented too soon), regardless of their culture or background:

> *'My supervisor is friendly. He is helpful and he includes me and introduces me to people. It is strange when my postgraduate friends complain about their experience. I love it here.'*
>
> *Research student – Arts and Humanities, Pakistan*

Helping to involve students and immerse them in the academic world demonstrates a great deal of trust and faith on the part of the supervisor, so it can be highly motivating.

One of the senior academics and experienced supervisors we spoke to while researching for this book reflected on his own experience as a PhD student in the physical sciences, working under the supervision of a renowned academic. In his first week in the lab, an eminent guest lecturer came to the department and this brand new doctoral student was introduced to the guest by his supervisor with the words, 'I'd like you to meet my colleague.' Being introduced as his supervisor's colleague had two major impacts on the young researcher. First, it resulted in him feeling that, despite his inexperience, he was a member of the academic community in his own right. The second was that his motivation to deserve the title 'colleague' served to keep him focused on his research throughout his candidature.

Encouraging students to attend seminars, introducing them to colleagues, taking them to collaborative meetings or their first academic conference do not need to be dependent on whether they have any research outputs. Obviously, later in the project the student will be seeking opportunities to present, but in the early stages this type of outward-facing supervision leads to a number of advantages for the student:

- objective triangulation and benchmarking about what constitutes quality academic research;

- learning what rules and norms are appropriate in the academic world;
- discovering potential new research areas and techniques in advance of the published literature;
- motivation from the trust an experienced academic, with a carefully nurtured personal reputation, has placed in them;
- inspiration to get involved in such activities in the future (to disseminate their own outputs);
- hearing critical feedback being given and received;
- (for some students) opportunities to improve their academic English;
- motivation resulting from the fact that they feel academically involved and treated as serious professionals in their own right.

The last of these is, unsurprisingly, important for some students:

> *'Sometimes I feel that PhD students are the black sheep of the university, they are not real students, but not real staff either.'*
>
> *Research student – Sciences, Hungary*

We will deal with the whether the label of 'student' is appropriate for doctoral candidates in Chapter 5, but essentially, any supervisory step that allows the doctoral researcher to feel more involved and central to the core academic action can only be a good thing. As the relationship develops, the supervisor adopting the gatekeeper style will probably be advising the student about publishing (and may even see joint publication as a natural student–supervisor activity), making introductions to editors and publishers and perhaps involving the student in future post-doctoral collaboration plans. It is worth noting here that all of these laudable intentions and activities actually result in an independent scholar, and not one who is, at the end of the process, still steered by the supervisory lead. This process, in order to be truly effective, needs to occur through conscious design.

For students who are engaged in a larger project with tight deadlines and research targets, there are sensible reasons why gatekeeping may not be core to how their supervisor sees their role. To an extent, though, this reticence misses the point that the doctorate is not just about producing results, and a gatekeeper supervisor is actually paying a great deal of attention to 'doctoral success'. In addition, such reticence about gatekeeping can lead to resentment in a student who expects to be more than a poorly paid research assistant. Many international students we've spoken to are either unaware of the greater need for doctoral students to learn the cut and thrust of academic debate at conferences, or feel (linguistically or culturally) that they can't ask to attend:

> *'I want to attend the [deleted] conference .... It's local and cheap to attend, but my supervisor told me that I can't afford the time. I'm thinking of taking it as a holiday.'*
>
> *Research student – Social Sciences, South Africa*

Facilitating a student being part of a wider network and involved in the academic community doesn't have to be an expensive process. The wise gatekeeping supervisor will also help the student to understand the appropriate academic etiquette in the UK system – how to make approaches to other academics and what types of requests and behaviours are appropriate or inappropriate. The gatekeeper supervisor will make local introductions and involve the student in local seminars and journal groups. Simply guiding students to recognize that they can make valid academic contributions can be powerful in itself, especially if this is not the case in the students' home educational systems:

> *'Hierarchy is not as important in this country. ... [Students,] do not be afraid to approach professors, as they might be genuinely interested in you.'*
>
> *Research student, Poland*

Anecdotally, it seems that the key impediment to gatekeeping as a supervisory style is not money or time, but ego. Sometimes a supervisor may not think a student is academically or linguistically ready – and a 'poor' performance from the student could reflect badly on the supervisor, group or department. Sometimes, however, it seems there is something less wholesome at work:

> *'Some [academics] seem to treat their PhD students as their own private research assistants. This is more the case if the student doesn't understand the UK system. You come across students who won't share their ideas at seminars for fear their supervisor will perceive it as infidelity.'*
>
> *Research supervisor – Civil Engineering*

Even in the above example there is still a possibility (depending on the interpretation of the words 'fear' and 'perceive') that the student's discomfort is the result of cultural or linguistic misunderstanding – which can be alleviated if the relationship is built on solid design.

The UK doctorate (to return to the Dublin Descriptors described in Chapter 2) involves helping students to discover new areas of research contribution and acquire the skills to communicate and share research In short, we believe that gatekeeping is a good supervisory style to adopt.

However, one major drawback with gatekeeping is that it can put pressure on students and requires a great deal of semi-blind trust from supervisors. A cautious supervisor may wish to be flexible in their strategy and gradually move into the gatekeeping style from that of critical teacher. A similar transition could be made to the critical teacher style from that of project manager, as shown in Figure 4.2.

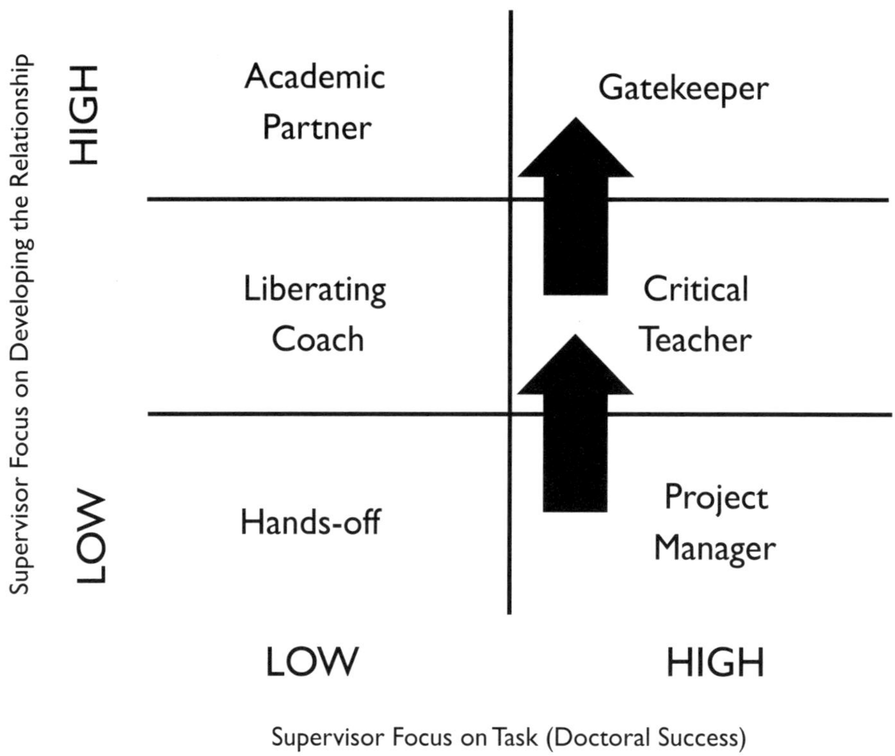

Figure 4.2 Supervisory approaches (2)

For such transitions to be successful requires:

- a high degree of flexibility and emotional intelligence from the supervisor;
- an understanding from the student (or shared dialogue between the two parties) of why the change in strategy is occurring; ideally, this understanding should be reached before the transition occurs.

If these conditions are not met and there is a sudden difference in supervisory behaviour (as pointed out by Gurr 2001), this can result in conflict with an autonomous student, or the feeling of 'benign neglect' or expectation overload in a dependent one. As is ever the case, effective supervision is a very special job – perhaps more akin to an art than a science – and knowing what strategy to adopt when requires huge skill.

So far in this section we have examined supervisory styles which emphasize doctoral task completion. The other three styles place far lower emphasis on this aspect of supervision.

The Hands-off Supervisor (Low Task, Low Relationship)

Core Supervisory Style

Supervisory emphasis is placed on allowing students to do whatever they feel necessary. In some ways this is the classical model of research supervision, as it requires something akin to candidate independence from day one. The onus is placed very much on the students to seek help and support from wherever they need it. There is often little direction from the supervisor in terms of completing the doctorate, or in terms of building a quality relationship with the candidate. For a candidate who is capable and strongly autonomous, there are advantages to this supervisory style. For candidates who lack independence or simply need interactions as part of the learning process, there are sizeable disadvantages.

For many research supervisors, this traditional model was the way that they themselves were supervised. Certainly, many of our friends and colleagues who completed a doctorate in the mid- to late twentieth century experienced this form of supervision. My personal experience of it was a primary supervisor who handed me a doctoral Thesis, told me to read it and said he'd see me in a few months. This role is clearly far harder to realize in the days of supervisory teams and progress monitoring.

However, it is important to consider that there may well be cultural expectations from the student about what should be expected from a supervisor, and what a student views as 'hands-off' supervision may in fact be something else entirely:

> *'It is normal to feel shocked and confused with the different approach to education in the UK, and the level of independence given to the students, unlike education systems in the Middle East. Therefore, students would feel lost and confused if they were not fully guided by their supervisor.'*
>
> *Research student, Middle East*

It is easy to criticize this approach to supervision (and plenty of students do), but some supervisors we spoke to expressed a strong belief that this style of supervision was beneficial to both student and supervisor. For instance:

> *'I make sure we [supervisor and student] have enough contact so things don't drift, but from the start I tell my students that I will leave them alone. They know where to find me. My door is open, but I won't chase them. That's the whole point: they're meant to be independent. Most of mine respond very well to that approach.'*
>
> *Research supervisor – information withheld*

In addition, many supervisors (who may primarily have a high task focus) acknowledge that their students' need for supervision comes in peaks and troughs, and sometimes there is no real need for a supervisory session at all. Again, such fluidity within the relationship only works if expectations have been discussed and the relationship is a designed alliance.

James and Baldwin (1999) observe the power of this phenomenon:

> *Consider this scenario in which a group of students and their supervisors were provided with a structured opportunity to 'talk straight' with each other about their working relationship. One supervisor emerged shaken from his discussion. He had found out that an international student had been expecting far more direction from him than he had realised – and more than he considered appropriate.*

> *He had been working with this student for eighteen months. During this time, it seems, the student had formed a judgement that the supervisor was negligent.*

Students who contributed to this book, from a range of backgrounds, recognized that the onus was on students to manage their supervisors so that they obtained whatever supervision they needed. For instance, two students were asked what advice they would offer a new international student in their department:

> *'Be prepared to track people down for answering questions: Many people pass the responsibility.'*
>
> *Research student, Ireland*

> *'Do not expect things to be handed to you on a platter. Ask for help and guidance. But find out what "proactive" means and be proactive.'*
>
> *Research student, India*

For supervisors of international students, the challenges of adopting a well-meaning hands-off style are manifold:

- to ensure, in advance, that the candidate's level of autonomy matches the supervisor's hands-off style;
- to ensure that the student understands and is truly happy and accepting of this level of attention, steering and support;
- to ensure that the student understands that there are other support and information sources available and the student is fully empowered to access them;
- to ensure that the quantity of contact is sufficient to maintain institutional standards;
- to ensure that the quality of any limited interactions is absolutely first-rate.

However, even if most of these conditions are met, lack of understanding by students about roles and responsibilities can result in dissatisfaction and confusion. This could stem from a feeling that the supervisor 'should' be taking control of the process, or that the supervisor is too busy, or even that the student has insufficient new material to warrant a meeting:

> *'He [supervisor] hasn't ever asked me for a meeting. Must I always do this?'*
>
> *Research student, Spain*

Supervisor Questions Concerning Quality and Quantity of Contact

- How much contact is appropriate at any given stage of the doctorate?
- Generally, how often would you expect to meet with your students? For how long each time?
- Is new data necessary for a meeting to be useful?
- What would you consider to be the ingredients of a high-quality supervision meeting?
- What ground rules do you discuss with your students about how much contact is necessary and whether tangible progress is required in order for a meeting to occur?

Also, the actions of a hands-off supervisor who delegates many of the technical aspects of functional supervision to a post-doctoral researcher, technician or (in some cases) a more experienced research student may well cause value-for-money dissatisfaction:

> *'I did not meet my supervisor often. Either it was a post-doc who supported me day to day, or we had supervision as a group. [What happened there?] Each week someone had to present their findings. We all sat and listened. Our professor would ask a few questions, and then everyone went back to work.'*
>
> *Post-doctoral researcher – Chemistry, Spain*

In addition, there is a linguistic and cultural challenge for the supervisor whereby lack of instructional clarity can lead to the student feeling that the quantity and quality of supervision is 'hands-off' whereas in fact it may not be.

Both parties need to ensure that whatever they say to the other is fully understood:

> *'My supervisor told me to get a feel for what is in the literature. A feel? What's that?'*
>
> *Research student, Greece*

Sometimes, especially if an international student has to return home for a protracted period (for instance, to write the Thesis) or is engaged in long periods of fieldwork, the supervisor may have little choice but to adopt the hands-off style. Extended periods of fieldwork are proportionately frequent with international students in some social science and ecological disciplines, and even with modern communication technologies the quantity and quality of meaningful supervision can suffer:

> *'The biggest challenge in this area is that [the student in question] is doing fieldwork for several weeks and sometimes months at a time. We keep in touch by Skype and phone, but it's hard to have a conversation that is anything more than functional.'*
>
> *Research supervisor – Biology*

It is our contention that supervisors whose students are engaged in long periods of fieldwork need to actually increase, where practical, the quantity of supervision they offer. Student on fieldwork may be isolated from many of their research networks and even from much human contact. In these cases the supervisor may offer a human face and a friendly ear that can make all the difference. Our experience tells us that supervisory relationships that remain strong across geographical divides are those that have been designed by student and supervisor alike – and are ones where both parties are comfortable with asking for what they need from the other.

We've already discussed how supervisors may need to adopt different styles as students become more capable and experienced. A final thought here is to note that a hands-off supervisor may find that switching to another of the six supervisory styles is very difficult, as the student may either have become autonomous and have no need for the supervisor's intrusions or be in crisis and resent the supervisor for allowing this to happen through adopting the hands-off style.

There are two remaining supervisory roles to explore, the first of which is very easy to explain.

The Supervisor as Liberating Coach (Low Task, Medium Relationship)

Core Supervisory Style

The academic liberator is in many ways a task-neutral extension of the Gatekeeper and Critical Teacher approaches – but with increasing autonomy for the student. The supervisor places an emphasis on encouraging the student to critique themselves and become independent at an appropriate pace. The advice given may be non-critical and more reflective than that from more task-focused supervisors.

Supervisors who adopt the style of liberating coach, rather than demanding autonomy from their students, place far greater emphasis on enabling growth or development within their students. In many ways this style is strategically sensible, since if the supervisor has achieved their desired outcome then the candidate should have become a fully rounded independent author and the doctorate is a phased transference of authority in a specific niche area. Many supervisors recognize the value of their role in this transformative process:

> *'I want them to be able to totally do it for themselves. My role is to help them get to that point.'*
>
> *Research supervisor – Music*

> *'As far as I'm concerned, my chief role [as a PhD supervisor] is to train my students to function without me.'*
>
> *Research supervisor – Chemistry*

One of the core functions of the liberating coach style is to help students to develop as reflective practitioners, yet this also requires reflective practice from the supervisor (see Zhao 2003a), and to a certain extent the liberating coach approach requires a greater degree of supervisory reflection than other styles because it is a far more dynamic role:

> *'As a scientist, I know what I'm doing. As a supervisor, I have to constantly think.'*
>
> *Research supervisor – Biological Science*

This dynamism can help both parties to improve their practice, but in order to do so, the relationship must be built carefully, have clear reciprocal benefits and requires empathy and trust (Sullivan and Glanz 2000). The student may assume that a supervisor with research authority is omniscient with regard to supervision strategy, but of course this is not the case – and this fact needs to be acknowledged and discussed.

Enquiries about Personal Supervisory Style

- What are your supervisory strengths and weaknesses?
- If your previous research students were asked to categorize your supervisory style, what would they say?
- In any given supervisory situation, what support can you offer your student?
- In any given supervisory situation, what support do you need from your student?

For supervisors of international students, this dynamic process can require more effort (both upfront and overall), since students' expectations of the supervisory role may differ and the stakes for some students may be considerably higher:

> *'I think very carefully about how I am going to encourage or criticize or motivate or challenge every one of my students. I do this more for my two international students since we don't share so many reference points.'*
>
> *Research supervisor – Psychology*

We chose the label 'coach' deliberately, partly because of the neutrality that word can convey. In some ways the coach is a combination of other roles – but with the added advantage that the student does not become dependent on supervisory assistance. As such, it is a role that will change a great deal over time:

> *'Research evolves, technology evolves, student's needs evolve; we [supervisors] need to evolve.'*
>
> *Research supervisor – Engineering*

Supervisory Enquiries about the Doctoral Journey

- What is the 'journey' you perceive research students will undertake?
- What skills will they need at each stage?
- What is the supervisor's role at each phase of the journey?
- What do you think the student/supervisory relationship should be at the end of the doctoral journey?

Most international students who spoke to us about supervisors who took this highly flexible approach were often very positive about its impact on their experience:

> *'My supervisor's style has changed. It impresses me that she's able to adapt to what I need. I should probably tell her.'*
>
> *Research student – Biosciences, Canada*

Some, however, found the lack of clear structural direction to be a challenge. One researcher who vociferously did not wish to be identifiable at all was vocal in her frustrations:

> *'I want guidance about what direction to take. That's why I wanted to work with him. We sit and talk and discuss, but choices are left to me. I want to be supervised.'*
>
> *Research student – information withheld*

For other students, though, the challenge of working with a supervisor adopting the liberating coach style was almost the opposite. As one student asked me:

> *'She [supervisor] is encouraging me to go in my own direction and find my own paths. Is this OK? Can I do this?'*
>
> *Research student, Philippines*

This attitude was surprisingly common among the international students we spoke to, and was at first somewhat confusing to us, since it seems to misunderstand the whole point of the doctoral process. Actually, what it reveals is not naivety about the doctoral system, but the lack of a clear expectations-led design between a willing student and a supervisor serving as a liberating coach.

As Cryer (2010) says, sometimes all that is needed is permission from the supervisor that independent work, creative thought and argument are acceptable.

If the supervisor wants to adopt the liberating coach style, four key principles seem to be necessary, the first of which is by far the most important:

1. Base every action on conscious design (or actual enquiry) – and discuss and articulate this design regularly (the short-term time costs of doing this are outweighed heavily by long-term student independence).

2. The student will have – or be able to find – answers. The liberating coach's role is to ask the right questions.

3. The supervisor should primarily focus on those parts of the research that provide the student with the most intellectual motivation. Let the student lead (but the supervisor must keep an eye on what needs to happen in order for the Thesis to be fit for purpose.)

4. The supervisor should focus only on the student's intellectual pathway. If it happens to align with the supervisor's research agenda, this is a great advantage – but not essential (see Principle 3 above).

Supervisory Enquiries about the Liberating Coach Style

- What effect might these principles have on your current supervisory style?
- Can you think of any incidences where (especially due to cross-cultural issues) these principles would not be applicable? (Revisit Principle 1 and ask this question again.)
- What effect would holding an 'expectations' conversation with any of your students have?

Over time, and with careful conscious design, many research supervisors find that their initial stance as critical teacher transforms into that of liberating coach, as they can trust the student with an appropriately rigorous critical approach. (In the same way, a supervisor who adopts a heavy project manager style may find that once the project has been 'managed' there is little left for them to do except take a hands-off role.) Similarly, once the student is free, a liberating coach has the choice to switch to a hands-off style.

One of the key advantages of the gatekeeper and liberating coach supervisory styles is that they both provide an opportunity to move to a state of full academic partnership with the student. The advantages of building a long-lasting academic relationship are potentially huge for any supervisor and student or post-doctoral researcher. However, the supervisor of an international researcher has the additional possibility of having a collaborator, friend, colleague and ambassador who will spread their network internationally. To that end, among others, the supervisory style of academic partner, transcending formal supervision, is one which many supervisors invest heavily in from the very beginning:

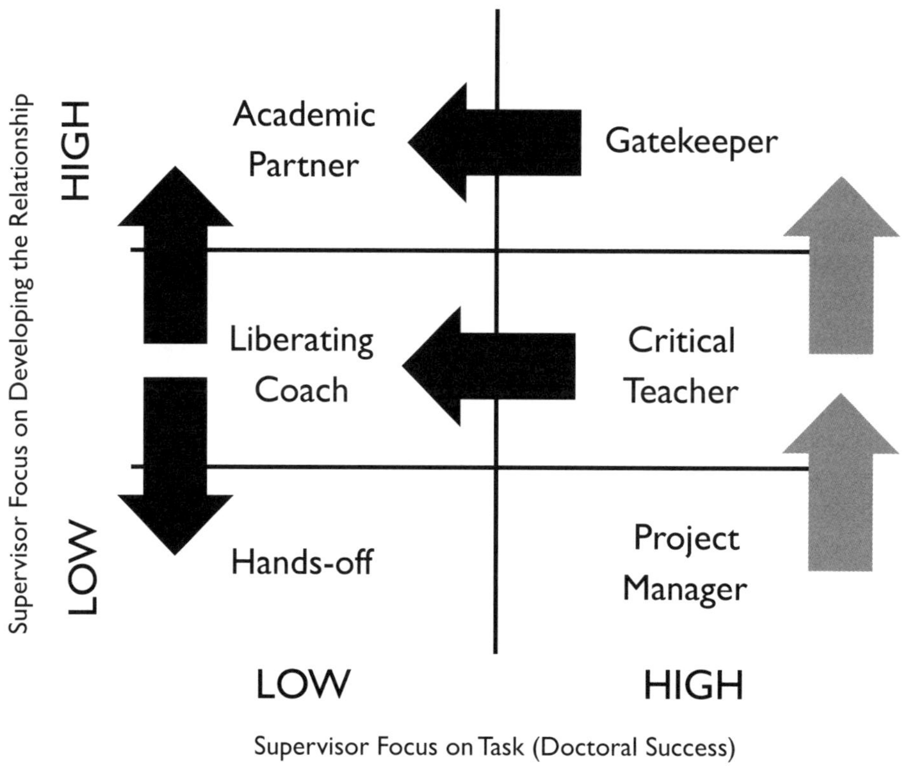

Figure 4.3 Supervisory approaches (3)

> *'I think I learn as much from my students as they do from me. This is particularly true with graduate students. I always say: "Two heads are better than one. You learn from me, but at the same time, I am learning from you." I want my students to know that I respect and acknowledge their efforts and am proud of their achievements. Perhaps the greatest joy in supervision comes from what you get in the end: an incredibly stimulating group of colleagues and friends.'*
>
> *Research supervisor – Arts and Humanities*

The Supervisor as Academic Partner (Low Task, High Relationship)

Core Supervisory Style

In this supervisory role, the supervisor places primary focus on building a relationship with the view to establishing long-term research partnerships. This is not to say that if the supervisor places a focus in this area then the doctoral task is not important. This is a comparative function and usually it means that the supervisor is confident that the student sufficiently autonomous. It is also worth noting that supervisors exhibiting other role preferences will also pay attention to building a productive relationship – but supervisors in this area will focus primarily on relationship-building.

For all the international students we spoke to, a supervisor who paid attention to the relationship and the human being in front of them was a positive aspect of the doctoral process:

> *'As an Indonesian student who is studying abroad for the first time in the UK, I found great value in the human culture here. My supervisor totally supports me, not only in my study, but also in daily life. Even though I am still learning, and everything is new, he always gives me great appreciation. In my culture it is not like this. I think I am lucky to have a UK supervisor.'*
>
> *Research student – Mathematics, Indonesia*

Moreover, both international students and supervisors generally recognized that paying attention to more than the research topic alone was a useful strategy:

> *'Students should know their main supervisor outside their profession.'*
> *Research student, New Zealand*

However, several supervisors told us that relationship-building was a core motivation and purpose when supervising:

> *'Many of the MA students I supervise have potential to do a doctorate. The ones, international or home, I encourage to pursue a PhD are the ones who I can envisage working with in the long term.'*
> *Research supervisor – Arts and Humanities*

It seems that the academic partner style emerges over the course of the doctorate, partly as both parties establish mutual trust, and partly as the research student starts to become an independent 'equal'. However, some supervisors simply focus on partnership from the outset, and see the candidate as a fellow researcher with whom they can explore new areas. This approach clearly has potential payoffs and risks attached to it – but if it is to be effective, it needs to be consciously designed and clear to both parties.

Supervisory Enquiries about the Role of Academic Partner

- Are doctoral researchers more colleagues than students?
- Regardless of the individual, when will you know that you can treat a budding researcher as an intellectually equal colleague? What stage or competency must they attain?
- How would a candidate know that they had reached such a level?

The supervisor as academic partner can also direct strategic focus to the relationship. This can offer a useful long-term payoff if, after the doctorate, the student remains in the academic sector (and, of course, it is nice to have friends around the world anyway), but is there a supervisory payoff if the student graduates and returns home to take up a non-academic position? Lee (2008) quotes a supervisor who says they felt angry after a student left and never looked back after several years of working together. To an extent here, it helps if the research area both student and supervisor are pursuing is aligned and applied. One supervisor we spoke to said that none of his students who have left academia are 'useful in any research sense' to him, but that this was due to the pure nature of his work. He told us of colleagues who had fostered long-term industrial and knowledge exchange partnerships with their ex-doctoral students who had moved outside academia. Other supervisors told us of global collaborations with media, culture and the government and policy sectors that resulted from continued relationships with their former doctoral students. And these benefits are clearly reciprocal. Indeed, as Humfrey (1999) says: 'at the highest level, the benefits [of international education] could be global understanding and harmony – more realistically, they should at least include the facilitation of friendships across international boundaries, more effective development of the global knowledge base and more interesting programmes for students at every level'.

However, in order for this supervisory style to be effectively in enhancing the international student's experience, their expectations have to be aligned with those of the supervisor, and any issues concerning the perceptions or realities of the power dynamic must be addressed. There's also the question of whether relationship-building and partnership are the core purposes of a supervisory relationship. With this in view, many supervisors tend to build the relationships via a combination of other styles initially, and gradually emphasize the value of a collaborative relationship as the doctorate progresses.

As we have mentioned on multiple occasions, it is essential for the supervisory relationship to be built on the principles of a designed alliance. These conversations can take place in advance of the student arriving, but usually emerge over the first few weeks and months. We will therefore return to international students' expectations when we consider cultural factors and building the relationship.

However, there are two other major role expectations any sensible supervisor should consider when supervising an international doctoral researcher: how any supervisory team might function, and how group supervision will be organized.

Expectations of the Supervisory Team

One of the notable developments in doctoral supervisory practice over the last decade or so has been the rise of the supervisory team. Often a primary supervisor is supplemented by a secondary supervisor or adviser. This may be for interdisciplinary reasons within the project or to comply with the QAA Code of Practice for Postgraduate Research Programmes:

> *'My supervisor says that my adviser is just a bureaucratic necessity. I don't know if I should go to see him.'*
>
> *Research student – Social Sciences, Egypt*

However, these regulations were set in place to provide a safety net, to provide students with second opinions and perspectives or an alternative if the primary relationship was incompatible. The worst-case scenario for a student who has risked much to study in a particular area is where a sole supervisor leaves an institution, resulting in a situation like this:

> *'As for my supervisor, that is a horror story, for the man left the university after my first term, without previous notice to me. [Why not?] He said he didn't want me to get "more nervous". Wonderful!'*
>
> *Research student – information withheld*

It is therefore essential for prospective supervisors and their departments to ensure that the supervisory team is in place prior to the student's arrival and that each member of the team knows how their role complements that of the other supervisors:

> *'I felt neglected and, yes, unwelcomed. It's not nice when you cross half the world (literally), leave your family, your friends, a good job, your house, etc., to come here to be told nobody wants to work with you.'*
>
> *Research student – Social Sciences*

International students we spoke to largely valued the role of any supervisory team, and many of them offered direction in this regard to future international students:

> *'Make sure that they [supervisor] have thought about who a good second supervisor would be.'*
>
> *Research student, USA*

Also, many of them recognized the value of different supervisory perspectives and the need for different styles of relationship:

> *'I think I have been lucky with my supervisors, but I had no choice as to who they were. They give different angles and approaches, and the mixture works. I am friendly with one; the other, we are just professional. But I keep both of them informed and involved.*

This works well. Some of my colleagues in a similar situation are not so lucky.'

Research student – Sciences, Eastern Europe

However, the quality assurance, balance and complementarity that supervisory teams bring can also cause problems, in that the student can sometimes be caught between conflicting intellectual perspectives (see Manathunga 2012). This is particularly the case if one supervisor holds a more senior position in the department. In addition, and anecdotally, it seems that cross-cultural gender issues can also cloud supervisory team and student interactions.

One way of resolving many of these issues (as suggested by Okorocha 2010) is that research students and all members of the supervisory team should meet together regularly, if not frequently. This approach can be enhanced if students are encouraged to keep and use documentary records of meetings. Another strategy is for the student (as in the quote above) to ensure that all members of the supervisory team are kept informed of actions and decisions. The 'primary' supervisor has a role to play here in providing guidance to the student that they should keep all team members involved and how to do this most effectively.

Finally, the wider their perspective and experience base, the more confidence an individual has in handling challenging situations. Multiple supervisors can offer a student a variety of different opinions and styles of questioning (though the student must be clear that there is usually only 'difference', not 'correct' and 'incorrect' in supervisory opinion). In addition, one key advantage of the team supervisory system is for supervisors to learn from each other about supervision styles and techniques.

Supervisory Enquiries about the Supervision Team

Prior to an international student's arrival:

- Are all the supervisory team members in place?
- If an appropriate second supervisor or adviser is to be determined as the research develops, is there a clear timeline in place for this process?
- Are all the team members aligned in terms of the purpose and scope of the doctorate?

- Have any relevant issues concerning shared intellectual property from potential collaborative outputs been discussed?
- Has the supervisory team met to discuss how supervision will be conducted?
- Have the supervisors had a conversation about complementary supervisory styles?
- If the direction of the doctorate is to be emergent, have the supervisory team discussed who will take responsibility for which elements of the work?
- Are there any other stakeholders who will contribute funding, support, equipment or experience? Are you clear about what they will expect in return?

When the student arrives:

- Have you ensured that they have an appropriate understanding of the above?

Expectations Regarding Group Supervision

Group supervision (where multiple students are supervised jointly) has become more prevalent in science and engineering disciplines, and particularly in the opening phases of the doctorate (see Samara 2006, for instance). This is also an effective workload protection device for busy supervisors, and makes sense if multiple students in a cohort are using a similar technique or are at similar stages of a process.

There are mixed views as to whether this type of academic enculturation is appropriate and whether any student gains access to an appropriate quality or quantity of supervision by this method. Regardless of the position taken here, there are a number of inherent drawbacks that can significantly affect the experience of an international student. The first is whether or not having day-to-day supervision conducted by (as one research student described them to us) 'a lowly post-doc' represents sufficient return on investment. The second is whether the student is gaining the requisite academic language debating capabilities from this form of supervision:

> *'Mostly supervision is done by the post-docs. My supervisor asks us to meet once a week or fortnight. These meetings are useful – but some students just don't speak.'*
>
> *Research student – Chemistry*

A third major disadvantage is that some supervisors lack the skill to facilitate a group in order to add value for all it members. Some clearly do:

> *'I don't ask my group [supervisory meeting] to present their data. I ask them to bring a problem or issue for discussion. Then the group and I provide advice. This started out as an accident, but it's very useful and it gets all the students to contribute. They also seem to be more communal and supportive.'*
>
> *Research supervisor – Engineering*

Several supervisors told us that they consider group supervisions to be a useful *addition* to their existing one-to-one meetings as they provide a chance for the skills and knowledge of the wider group to be shared, which results in greater team cohesion and opportunities for more experienced students to develop their own academic leadership capabilities.

Supervisory Enquiries about Group Supervision

- Are group supervisions set up to facilitate student engagement or solo reporting?
- Do the more experienced students and post-doctoral researchers have a role in supporting newer colleagues?
- To what extent are your current students and post-doctoral researchers aware of the possibilities of group supervisions, or do they consider them merely a supervisory time-saving device?
- To what extent are all students encouraged to contribute and help or challenge each other?
- Are there any conflicts within the group concerning individual protection of intellectual property, and how do you plan to handle such issues?

In short, effective group supervision *can* considerably enhance international students' experience, provided it's conducted with the right intent and sufficient awareness. If it's seen as a device which allows busy academics to abrogate their responsibilities, then it can be a major source of confusion, dissatisfaction and complaint.

In this chapter we have examined the expectations of the institution (linked to international agendas) and those of the department and supervisory team. All of these factors need to be considered prior to student registration (or at least soon after). However, the real challenge for the supervisor begins when the student arrives and the candidature commences.

Chapter 5
Starting the Relationship and Beginning the Journey

A day of travelling will bring a basketful of learning.
Vietnamese proverb

Up to this point we've considered the institutional and supervisory expectations of the doctoral process and speculated on students' motivations for doctoral study. In this chapter we present an essential model of how the supervisor can ensure that the student can get down to the business of engagement with doctoral scholarship as soon as possible.

The Engagement Conversation

Assuming that preliminary conversations are productive and there seems to be scope for the student to pursue a doctorate, there will come a moment where both parties need to formally engage, contracts will be signed and the student will agree to commence registration on a certain date. We've already mentioned that, prior to this formal step, an interview or face-to-face meeting is recommended and a Skype meeting or videoconference is highly valuable. If at all possible, a telephone conversation (exploring motivations and expectations, as set out in the previous chapters) is the absolute base level of pre-doctoral contact.

In this final pre-registration conversation, supervisors must ensure that they have satisfied themselves and their institution that they have clear answers to a number of questions. These may be purely intellectual.

Supervisor – Intellectual Pre-arrival Enquiries

- Am I certain that this student's intellectual qualifications are clear and comparable to a bachelor's or master's degree from the UK? Do I have sufficient evidence to think that, on the basis of their qualifications and other evidence, this student is academically capable of commencing a doctorate?

- Does this student meet the institution's or department's language requirements for postgraduate research?
- Am I confident that this student is sufficiently diligent to self-study with little academic structure?
- Do they have a grasp of what the UK doctoral system actually demands of the candidates?
- Do they have a grasp of what doctoral research is and what it is not?
- Do they have at least an elementary understanding of the role of the doctoral supervisor?

Or they may be administrative.

Supervisor – Administrative Pre-arrival Enquiries

- Does this individual have all of the residency permits and visas necessary to study in the UK for the period of the candidacy?
- Dependent on the field of study, are there any specific issues or permissions needed to ensure that the student has suitable security clearances?
- Do they have enough money to live, work and study in the UK?
- If the student is proposing fieldwork, is there sufficient funding to account for travel costs to the field site(s)? Are there any other considerations in this area – for example, are other visas required?
- Do they have a grasp of the logistics of the UK system of research/ doctorate?
- Have I ensured that I have met all institutional requirements prior to agreeing to a student commencing their registration?
- Has the student considered the questions and issues, and sought information as laid out in the box headed 'International Students' Possible Concerns' in Chapter 3, page 36?

The issue of funding is a contentious one. Many students commence their doctorate with insufficient funding to last for the full doctoral process. If the candidate believes that a doctorate will take a maximum of three years, then it could be argued that most of them come with insufficient funding to extend beyond this time frame – though running into a fourth year is very common. Many students we spoke to believed that their supervisor had a role in helping them to obtain research funding:

> *'If you're from outside the EU, make sure your supervisor will continually advocate for more funding for you.'*
>
> *Research student, USA*

Many supervisors will of course help their students to do this, but they are certainly not obliged to do so. If a student (especially one who is unfamiliar with normal UK funding application processes and channels) takes time away from doctoral study to seek more funding, this will obviously detract from the time available for scholarship. In addition, any funding gaps can lay heavy on a student's mind, leading to an inability to focus on the core business of research. Because they did not have full funding in place at the time of registration, many international students we've worked with have been essentially part-time, as they have had to hold down a job on top of 'full-time' study. In these cases the student has usually registered for the doctorate based on one year of pre-obtained funding with the expectation that additional funding will be generated during their candidature. It seems that research students often base their assumptions about how much part-time employment they can undertake from their experiences with previous qualifications. A doctorate, especially one with a packed laboratory schedule, leaves little time for paid employment, and students should be aware of this prior to accepting a research position. In addition, there are not always opportunities for paid teaching assistant or demonstrator posts, and again financial caution should be urged before a student registers since these factors frequently cause huge problems of workload management and consequent friction between the candidate and supervisor.

The student will also have a number of concerns and questions, but in our experience the initial conversations are often led by the supervisor, and the student may assume that if the supervisor doesn't ask a question, this demonstrates tacit approval. It is worth the supervisor revisiting the questions detailed in Chapter 3 to ensure that the candidate is clear about their expectations – and to do this prior to agreeing to supervise the student.

Of course, in science and engineering disciplines, many institutions or conglomerates now run a doctoral training centre model. The engagement 'moment' actually happens over the course of several weeks or months as students complete laboratory rotations and have opportunities to engage with a variety of potential doctoral supervisors. Even within this acclimatization period, it is worthwhile for potential supervisors to discuss these issues (rather than just the technicalities of the project) to ensure that all parties are clear about the nature of the relationship upon which they are about to embark.

It's also worth noting that once the student and supervisor have signed the institutional documentation declaring that they wish to register to embark on a doctorate, then they have agreed to be bound by certain conditions. Supervisors should read the fine print and ensure that their students do the same. In our experience, most students (regardless of background) are unaware that they are in no small way contractually bound.

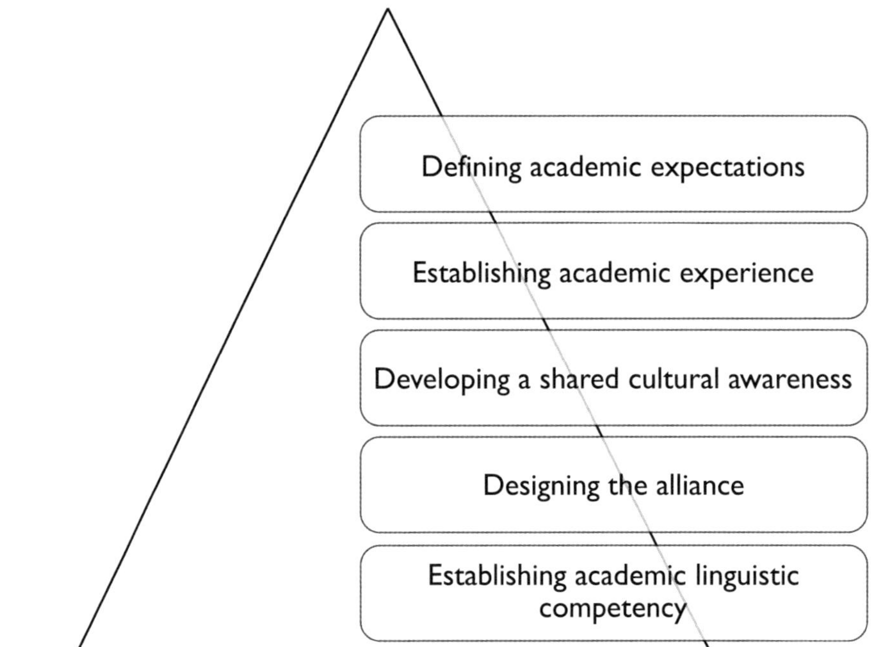

Figure 5.1 Steps in the embarkation process

Once the student has been recruited and has arrived in the UK, we believe that there are a number of steps a supervisor needs to ensure are followed in order to enable the student to set about the business of focused research more quickly. Some of these steps are very simple, and some are more involved. Similarly, some of these steps will need to be revisited throughout the course of the doctorate, and some can be dealt with quickly and then never need to be touched upon again. Figure 5.1 shows the six steps in the embarkation process.

We believe that all of these steps should serve (at least in part) as a precursor to the student and supervisor actually engaging in intellectual debate. This is not a novel concept, and stems from the work of Abraham Maslow, who in the article 'A Theory of Human Motivation' (1943) proposed a similar hierarchy of needs.[1] Self-actualization, at the top of Maslow's hierarchy, includes many of the behaviours required for successful completion of the doctorate, including morality or ethical behaviour, creativity, problem-solving and open-mindedness. However, in order to be able to function at this level, Maslow's theory is that all 'lower' needs must be met. This includes the most basic physical needs (shelter; food; water and so on) as well as a sense of belonging and the confidence that comes from achievement.

Maslow's hierarchy, while not uncontested, makes conceptual sense. Anyone who has tried to focus on an abstract task while cold or hungry will appreciate the importance of meeting the body's basic needs in order to work effectively. Likewise, it's not controversial to suggest that it's difficult to focus on work while concerned about one's own or a family member's well-being – although it's true that some people cope with emotional turmoil by keeping their attention on their work. Maslow's hierarchy builds from the base up, and so does ours. The relevant question at each stage is: *What is the supervisor's role in an international student meeting their own needs (as well as providing institutional quality and mutually beneficial research outputs)?*

As mentioned above, it is not our intention to suggest that the supervisor should become a counsellor or an expert on student accommodation, and independence is a quality that is prized among researchers. However, a degree of pastoral responsibility and emotional intelligence on the part of the supervisor is, we believe, a reasonable expectation.

1 Maslow's seminal article was originally published in *Psychological Review* (1943), 50(4), pp. 370–96. It is reprinted in Maslow (1987).

Step 1: The Bare Essentials – Basic Pastoral and Physiological Needs

The research supervisor may well be the international student's primary point of contact in the UK, and it would not be unprecedented if the student knew no one else at all in the host country. A doctorate is an isolating experience at the best of times, and for an international research student, the experience can be much more so. Younger postgraduates are often a long way from family and friends upon whom they may still be dependent, both practically and emotionally; older ones may well have brought their immediate family with them, resulting in additional and different pressures.

There are many practical things a great supervisor can do to pay attention to the personal and pastoral needs of a doctoral student. As with many relationships, the 'rules of engagement' are set early on, whether these are made explicit or not. If the first meeting involves the supervisor talking about the research project, occasionally asking the new student a question, then this is how the relationship will continue. However, if from the first contact it is acknowledged that practical and personal issues are acceptable topics of conversation, it will be easier to discuss them when non-academic issues become a problem.

International students may need advice and support about many practical issues outside the university environment, so they should be familiar with their university's guidance about:

- accommodation;
- shopping and food;
- healthcare;
- travel and transport;
- childcare;
- employment;
- banking and finance;
- language support;
- inclusive chaplaincy services.

In the pre-arrival contact and in the first week, it is worth making sure that the candidate has secured suitable accommodation, has access to the money required, and that any visa issues are being attended to. In the same way that the supervisor is not a counsellor, the role also doesn't include that of letting agent, banker or immigration adviser. However, it can be invaluable to have an informal conversation about which areas are good to live in, where the banks are, what is reasonable to expect from a landlord and so on:

> *'When I arrived, no one told me anything of practical use. I didn't feel I could ask my professor about the library or [computing] registration. I also didn't know who anyone else in the department was.'*
>
> *Research student – Arts and Humanities*

Even if the supervisor can't explicitly help, it doesn't hurt to ask how things are going and to reassure the student that these issues are significant. It is also worth the supervisor ensuring that a proper postgraduate international student induction process is run at institutional level (or to lobby strongly for one if there isn't) and to have a conversation with their student about the value of what they discovered during the course of it. In our experience, international students often miss the formal induction offered by the university as they are bound by different term times or are busy arranging accommodation. Institutions are becoming more sensitive to this, but it still remains a concern.

It is often the simplest things that make the greatest difference to an international student's ability to focus on the doctorate itself. Seemingly trivial elements that cropped up in conversation with international students that made academic focus difficult included bland food (though one student told me that the spicy food was confusing: 'No one told me that your national dish was curry!'), the cold and the drab, grey clothing on the streets. While researching this book, we lost count of the number of times the weather was mentioned by international students as a challenging aspect of UK doctoral study:

> *'[In Malaysia] … we have many different cultures and types of people. So I found it very easy to come to Britain. [What advice would you give to someone coming to Britain to do a PhD?] I'd say two things – work hard and bring a warm coat.'*
>
> *Research Student – Biosciences, Malaysia*

Of course, supervisors are busy and are often somewhat removed from the core needs and drivers of a new student (regardless of nationality). Okorocha (2010) recommends that institutions provide an experienced international student to mentor new students who arrive in the UK. Whether the formality of such a setup is practical is debateable, but many of the researchers we spoke to found great value in their informal peer support networks:

> *'It was very lucky that I met some other students from my country who told me what to do.'*
>
> *Research student – Engineering*

However, this was not universally the case, and sometimes it actually hindered the process of acclimatization:

> *'My department paired me with another [experienced and international] student from a different country to my own. He said he'd found it easy to adjust to life in this country, and that I should too. This was not my experience at all.'*
>
> *Research student – Physics, China*

Therefore, there is a need to exercise a degree of sensitivity in brokering any formal mentoring process – and here the supervisor can play a key role.

Supervisory Ideas to Aid the Acclimatization Process (1)

- When a student accepts an offer of a place, it is worth finding out whether there are other students (graduate or undergraduate) from the same country in the institution or department, and offering to put them in touch with each other.
- Ask a carefully chosen established international student to help new students to find their feet. If they have research interests in common, so much the better.
- Ask an appropriate and experienced international student to give the new student a tour of the campus or to sit with them and annotate a campus or town map with instructions of where to go and what to do.

There are many advantages to a peer support or buddying system for all parties concerned (see, for instance, Ku et al. 2008). For example, one student spoke to us with great feeling about a peer support scheme his institution had established in which international students were paired with a native English-speaking peers. The international student gained a great deal of benefit (regular and reliable support, improved language skills and increased confidence), while the peer supporter gained an increased skill set and an enhanced curriculum vitae. In spite of the benefits offered and the number of papers and studies that recommend them (for instance, Lord and Dawson 2002), peer support schemes are not commonplace, and few of the students we worked with in preparation for this book knew about or mentioned any.

Supervisory Ideas to Aid the Acclimatization Process (2)

- Make sure that there is a clear focus on practical issues within the first few meetings, and ensure that these issues are not subordinate to purely research-related topics. Invite questions about anything. A simple 'How's it going?' will elicit less of a focus on research and more on practical concerns at this point.
- On arrival, ensure that the student has their own workspace and access to the necessary swipe cards and computer/library registration.
- Be aware that your student may well want to work at different times and days of the week to you, so ensure that they are able to do so.
- Several students we spoke to were somewhat nonplussed by their academic department closing down for vacations and religious holidays that, in some cases, the majority of students did not celebrate.

The bottom line here is that supervisors must ensure that their students are able to meet their basic physiological needs. However, there is an inherent tension in this arrangement, especially with a hands-off supervisor who believes that the candidate should be independent. Peelo (2011) notes astutely that 'some supervisors feel immensely uncomfortable when faced with apparently dependent behaviour' – which represents 'non-academic' behaviour, and that 'a student who presents as unhappy and frustrated can appear to be demanding at a personal level, which is not necessarily the supervisor's area of expertise (where they may feel confident in solving research problems)'. As such, the supervisor's duty is not to solve a student's pastoral problems, but to ensure that the student has the necessary tools, information and support to solve the problems themselves.

Step 2: Establishing Academic Linguistic Competency

Don't speak unless you can improve on silence.
Spanish proverb

For many students and supervisors we spoke to, the linguistic competency of their international students posed the greatest problems:

> *'I know that their language capability is not great, but I don't know what to do. The centre [the university's English language support centre] offers help, but what they need is practice. I can only give them an hour or so a week of supervision at most. I have other [English as a first language] students who get less [supervision].'*
>
> *Research supervisor – Sciences*

> *'I think the hardest part is language. Although my English is good, according to most people, and I have no problem in daily communication, it's still a little bit hard for me to get all the messages. I will miss some points as I do not pick up some words, or even completely lost after I miss some words.'*
>
> *Research student – Sciences, China*

It is important to recognize that many international students speak English as a native language and many are even fluent in four or five languages. However, it's also important to realize that academic English is very different to basic conversational English, and even native speakers, however well practised, can struggle with the intricacies of academic debate. As one student told us:

> *'Regarding language, I'd advise two things. One – don't worry about your accent. This is not so important. But secondly, the level of language required is far more than the [English-language] entry level.'*
>
> *Research student, China*

To ensure that the research student can thrive, it's essential for the research supervisor to acknowledge the student's linguistic ability (personally, I'm in awe of candidates who can participate in an intellectual debate in their second or third language), especially if the student is feeling unsure about every other facet of their intellectual and pastoral life. Supervisors must also ensure from the earliest possible opportunity that every student has the language support they need to function academically. Of course, limited language capability does not just impede a student's ability to express their thoughts and ideas, it can also (as outlined in Kim 2011) affect their ability to engage in other academic tasks, such as presentations and networking, that are part of the academic journey towards independence. Although linguistic difficulties may cause some problems for international students initially, as long as their language capabilities improve (though this is not always the case), research indicates that a mismatch between student and faculty expectations is more likely to be the source of ongoing problems (see Lin 2001, among others).

Some years ago, my department (a university central services skills training provider) was asked by an academic engineering department to provide some academic English training for its large cohort of international research students. We suggested that the department contact the English as a Foreign Language unit, since teaching English language wasn't within our remit. We were told that the unit had recommended us as they didn't deal with the 'higher academic-level' English the department required. We met with academics from the department and asked for more information about the issue, trying to establish whether the area of need was for written English or spoken English at a higher academic level. The supervisors told us that what was really required was basic and simple English-language skills, since many of the students in question lacked routine conversational abilities. This didn't surprise us, as we were also used to having fairly strained conversations – but it did worry us. The department in question had a sensible IELTS[2] (International English Language Testing) requirement and an acceptable doctoral completion rate. So we went to meet with a group of students, and sure enough the conversation was extremely stilted and difficult, and did not, to our minds, match the IELTS requirements.

The IELTS requirement for postgraduate study in that department was around Level Six or Seven. The IELTS descriptors[3] define these two bands as follows:

> **IELTS Level Six:** *Competent user: has generally effective command of the language despite some inaccuracies, inappropriacies and*

2 There are several types of examinations of English for Speakers of Other Languages (ESOL) standards: the TOEFL (Test of English as a Foreign Language), which uses American English and is mainly for university admissions, the IELTS (International English Language Testing System), which uses British/Australasian English and is used for university entrance and migration, and the Cambridge ESOL exams, which use British English and are accepted by some universities and employers.

3 IELTS Overall Band Descriptors can be found at www.ielts.org/institutions/test_format_and_results/ielts_band_scores.aspx, and specifically for spoken English at www.ielts.org/PDF/UOBDs_SpeakingFinal.pdf (accessed 9 June 2014).

misunderstandings. Can use and understand fairly complex language, particularly in familiar situations.

IELTS Level Seven: *Good user: has operational command of the language, though with occasional inaccuracies, inappropriacies and misunderstandings in some situations. Generally handles complex language well and understands detailed reasoning.*

On paper, these levels seemed sensible – and indeed, this 'competent to good' area is still the level required by many academic departments for postgraduate study. However, our conversations with the students suggested that their actual level was far below this – the standards of English on display were limited to modest at best. We began to suspect that either there was something wrong with the testing process, which seemed unlikely due to its internationally recognized scrutiny and quality, or perhaps that the students in question had somehow circumvented the test. This again seemed highly unlikely – despite media reports of IELTS tests being leaked or students paying for stand-ins to sit the exam for them.

So why were the actual capabilities at odds with the scores? In the end, the answer was simple. The students we spoke to were all living together in the university's graduate accommodation; they were all working together in the same workshops and offices; they all ate together and almost exclusively socialized together, and they only saw their supervisors perhaps once per fortnight. They simply weren't speaking any English – and despite their standard of English being adequate, in the intervening months and years of living and working in the UK their English capability had actually fallen dramatically.

Supervisory Enquiries about Language Support

- What language expectations does your institution have? These expectations could be purely objectively measurable such as International English Language Testing (IELTS) scores, or a mixture of objective scoring and subjective description as to expectation.
- What about your academic department?
- Is the IELTS (or TOEFL or ESOL) requirement sufficient for the high-level critical debate demanded at postgraduate research level?
- Where are the institutional sources of support for students who need help with:

a. English as a foreign language (both spoken and written)?
b. academic English (both spoken and written)?

- Is it the supervisor's role to help enculturate the student – not just academically, but linguistically as well?

Language requirements vary immensely from department to department, and it is not unknown for language requirements to be based on an amalgamated score. This means that we have often met students who have a good standard of reading and writing, but whose spoken English is not really adequate, even to hold a basic conversation. We've wondered how such students are able to cope with a dense academic conversation, let alone at a viva defence. At undergraduate or master's level, students are often required to be producing written work very early on, so the reading and writing components of testing are obviously far more necessary. At doctoral level (particularly in the science and engineering disciplines), many students are not required to write a great deal until some time into their candidature. However, regardless of culture and discipline, all students should be participating in high-level academic critical debates with their supervisors from day one. There are a number of works on cross-cultural academic linguistics (for example, Matsuda et al. 2006; Canagarajah 2002), but these are generally purely academic in tone. More pragmatically, supervisors can help to develop academic language capability in a number of ways.

Supervisory Ideas to Assist in Building Academic Linguistic Competency

- Ask your student to share what aspects of academic English they find most challenging. Target these areas as you seek input from your student in a number of ways. Ask them to write a short report on a journal article, or give a brief presentation, or formulate different questions, or interview you. Vary the nature of the linguistic challenges you set, and ensure that you follow up with good feedback on the language, not just the academic knowledge and facts.
- Suggest that a group of postgraduates from your department get together informally to discuss progress. It doesn't matter whether the group members are native English speakers or not, just that they use English as the medium for communication and stop people and ask if they use words or phrases they don't understand.

- Give specific feedback. If there are problems in written work, be clear as to whether the problems lie in the ideas or their expression. If you're not sure, ask your student to talk to you about the ideas before you comment.
- As your student becomes more competent, conduct supervisions in the form of a 'mini-viva'. You could use their master's dissertation or a research proposal, experimental design or prototype chapter as content on which to base the meeting. Explain what you are doing, and ensure the student is able to both academically write and defend what they have written. This has the added advantage of acclimatizing your student to realizing that academic corrections are normal.
- Encourage your student to keep records of supervisory meetings – use these to inform the next meeting and ensure that any misunderstandings are clarified.
- Ask your student to reflect on what level of English is required to write and defend a Thesis. Asking a post-doctoral researcher with the same or a similar native language to share their experiences may be very helpful.

The key elements for the supervisor are twofold: that the student builds to an acceptable level of language competence, and that the student feels they can discuss their work and their doctoral challenges. It is important that supervisory feedback and institutional linguistic compliance measures are not overwhelming to the student, merely adding to the myriad challenges they face:

> *'Never keep a problem to yourself, always seek help and talk about your issues and fears. We are all here to learn, so treat it as a learning curve, not an assessment of your abilities.'*
>
> *Research student, Middle East*

Linguistic ability can make a major difference for students in all manner of unexpected ways. For instance, bureaucracy and administrative information (as is found in codes of practice and student guidelines in every institution) are often very dense and impenetrable. As a result, even a well-intentioned student can end up getting embroiled in them. Institutions may have a duty to use plain English wherever possible, but this duty extends to the supervisor too. Often we find that linguistic capability (and cultural understanding to a point) can lead to a student confusing advice with legally binding policy, such as in cases where a student reports that their Thesis 'must' be 80,000 words long when this figure is merely a departmental guideline.

The core traps linked to language capability are time management and confidence. A student who needs to take longer to linguistically process information may suffer time management issues in relation to expectations and peer achievement. This can lead to lack of confidence, which may then lead to a vicious circle. International students will often sacrifice extracurricular activities in order to keep up with their expected work rate, becoming more isolated as a result and leading to greater difficulties. This problem is not isolated to research or administrative activity. Departmental expectations that research students should be involved in teaching activity can also put an enormous linguistic strain on international researchers.

The supervisor and student both need to bear in mind the holistic nature of higher study, and consider what expectations are realistic and what support is necessary. Finally, perhaps all parties need to consider who really bears the obligation for providing linguistic backing and training for a student – particularly in light of the ever-increasing fees for international students. As Pat Cryer, author of *The Research Student's Guide to Success*, says: 'once an institution has accepted a student, it bears the responsibility to provide the resources necessary to complete the programme of work – which includes language support' (Cryer 2010).

Once the base academic and linguistic competencies have been established, it is important that the student and supervisor design an effective relationship or alliance in order to work productively with each other.

Step 3: Designing the Alliance

Don't think there are no crocodiles
because the water is calm.
Malay proverb

If the doctoral process is to be mutually beneficial, then the supervisor and student need to establish the boundaries, ground rules and joint processes by which the relationship will operate. This concept sounds sensible in theory, but there are of course linguistic, cultural and academic barriers to having such a candid conversation, not to mention the connotations of power imbalance implied by the words 'supervisor' and 'student'. The relationship between a student and a supervisor should be an alliance that is designed by two consenting adults, so it needs a sound communications base.

> *'The supervisor – what is his job exactly?'*
>
> *Research student – information withheld*

Since one element that vexes some international (and UK) students is that there is no clear definition of a supervisor's job, then pragmatically it is perhaps worth acknowledging this lack of clarity and building a mutually clear relationship in collaboration with the student.

The notion of a designed alliance can be captured by the idea that a supervisory relationship might begin with an informal chat about the question: *'So, how are we going to do this?'* Of course, there are problems with this philosophy (not least the potential tension inherent in the informality), but this question, however it is discussed, establishes two vital components of the student–supervisor relationship.

Firstly, this conversational opener establishes the notion that *the research process* (the 'how') is important and is something that needs discussion and input from all parties. Second, it establishes is the notion of *collegiality* ('we'). This simple word encapsulates, for us, the difference between a doctorate and other forms of student endeavour. Yes, the doctoral Thesis is a showcase of individual excellence, but the doctoral process may be far more of a team effort.

In our experience, the designed alliance conversation happens less frequently than it should (in all walks of professional life). For the doctoral relationship, this is sometimes because of the 'rush to the bench' (getting the actual research under way as quickly as possible), or sometimes because the beginning of the candidature is taken up with other matters:

> *'My supervisor and I never talked about supervision or our roles. And we never talked about our working relationship. It would have been useful, I think.'*
>
> *Research student – information withheld*

However, in our experience this stage is often bypassed because the student takes cues about how to behave and what to expect in the early stages from the supervisor. And if the supervisor doesn't mention expectations and the notion of what would make for a mutually successful and beneficial experience, then the student won't either. It is here that the supervisor really has to lead. As Kouzes and Posner observe in *Encouraging the Heart* (2003): 'it's pretty arrogant for someone to assume that just because he's the leader he naturally knows what's right for others without even bothering to inquire or observe'.

Leadership in the supervisor's case, especially at this stage in the relationship, is about providing an example of how the relationship might commence – with honesty, openness and disclosure. We are not alone in recognizing the value of such endeavours; Halai (2011) states that 'building a relationship is the most important part of supervision at the doctoral level and trust is a very important part of this equation'. This is difficult, but a carefully designed alliance may well help to avoid situations such those indicated in the two following instances:

> *'I feel that I cannot ask my supervisor the same question twice.'*
>
> *Research student, Kenya*

> *'Don't talk too much about your weakness in front of [your supervisor] because they will bear it in mind.'*
>
> *Research student, Oman*

We have never met a supervisor who has said that they would object to being asked a research question more than once, nor have we ever met one who says that they would deliberately be looking to exploit a student's weak points, so the fact that that students perceive that these are possibilities is indicative of either a rogue supervisor or a poorly designed alliance.

A good starting point for these conversations is to consider each party's motivations and expectations about the doctoral process (as laid out in Chapters 3 and 4), but the questions typically focus on the 'Why?' Designing the alliance is about concentrating on the 'How?'

Student and Supervisor Discussion Points about Designing the Supervisory Alliance

- How are we going to do this?
- What do we need to know about each other if we are to work together effectively?
- How do we each like to learn?
- What do we each need to perform at our best?
- What did you learn about yourself from your previous major projects?

- What type of professional relationship should we have?
- How do we see each other's role?
- What types of pressures do we each respond best to?
- What types of support do we each need?

Of course, it is possible that neither the student nor the supervisor have thought about these issues before, and it is highly unlikely that a design conversation will take place once at the start, then never again. The value here is, of course, not a relationship that is instantly ready to be productive, but three longer-term benefits:

1. The tone is set for a relationship that is mutually beneficial.

2. It indicates potential problem areas before they are even troublesome – thus nipping issues in the bud.

3. It allows a host of assumptions from both parties (including status, power, culture, responsibility and more) to be openly questioned and safely challenged. Okorocha (2007) suggests that the responsibility for leading on this agenda lies with the research supervisor, and she too suggests that supervisors should examine their implicit assumptions about international students, question their validity and initiate conversations with students about issues (including cross-cultural communication) they don't understand.

In many walks of life an individual's effectiveness is limited by persistence in holding on to the notion that their beliefs are true, that their beliefs are based on real data and that the data they select are the real data. Peter Senge (1994) outlines a helpful tool called the Ladder of Inference, based on the work of (among others) William Isaac and Chris Argyris.

In their model they essentially state: 'our actions are driven by our *beliefs*; our beliefs are formed from *conclusions* that we draw; we draw conclusions from *assumptions* that we make; our assumptions are made about the *meanings* of certain data; the data is not complete and is a small *selection* of the whole picture'.

Designing the alliance is about disclosing beliefs and revealing what assumptions lie behind them. Sometimes both parties in a relationship need to help provide full data for the other, and sometimes meanings need to be clarified. What is important here is that actions are not driven by unchallenged or unconfirmed beliefs. For supervisors, this means challenging their own assumptions about what will work, or questioning their cultural assumptions based on previous students. For students, it is about questioning their own assumptions about what the supervisor will do and what the doctoral process will be like. As one international doctoral student, with beautiful irony, once wrote to me on a feedback form from a research workshop:

> *'[I learned on the course] that my main task was to become independent. My supervisor never told me this.'*
>
> *Research student – information withheld*

As the relationship develops over time it may be necessary to revisit the design process, and in fact it is helpful to do so consciously. Generally speaking, though, a relationship that is built on the principle of a designed alliance will continue in this vein without formal intervention, and the key aim here is for the supervisor and student to foster an atmosphere where each party can perform effectively, not one where attention to personal and pastoral needs and the resultant emotions take precedence over research.

Finally, a good supervisor will gradually build up the student's responsibility for this design process. This could begin by encouraging the student to ask specifically for whatever help and support they need. As the book *Postgraduate Study in the UK: The International Student's Guide* advises international students:

> *Do not be afraid to ask for the things you need or to work in a way that suits you best. This does not mean, of course, that you can demand that your supervisor does exactly what you want, but you should see your working relationship as one that can be 'managed' as much by you as by your supervisor.*
>
> *(Foskett and Foskett 2006)*

Of course, designing an alliance with another individual is difficult to get right even if that individual shares common educational, cultural, stylistic and aspirational reference points. If that individual hails from another country, culture and educational system, then it can pose great challenges. As such, it is important that both student and supervisor start to develop (or build upon existing) awareness of each other's culture.

Step 4: Developing Shared Cultural Awareness

Abroad we judge the dress; at home we judge the man.
Chinese proverb

We live in a multicultural society, and higher education, especially at postgraduate level, is a microcosm of this. Throughout this book we've discussed international students and the UK system, whereas the reality is that often the supervisor will also be from outside the UK. This diversity of culture and expectation can be incredibly complex, so it is important for supervisors and students to pay some attention to differences (cultural, national and institutional) to ascertain where difficulties may occur. As we stated at the start of this book, we have at all times tried to avoid stereotyping; statements about culture are inevitably stereotypical, so they should be taken as guidance only.

When a research student from any background runs into problems or is not producing the quality or quantity of work the supervisor expects, it is probable that this is not a purely intellectual problem. Indeed, as long as the pre-recruitment process was sound, the vast majority of students who commence a doctorate are more than intellectually capable of doing so. The problem often lies elsewhere:

> *'Most of our technical conversations were fine. Most of the language was scientific and universal – so it wasn't a linguistic thing. He was missing the appropriate understanding culturally.'*
> *Research supervisor – Medical Sciences*

Over the last few decades there has been a large increase in interest in the so-called 'socialization' of individuals to the beginning levels of practice in a professional role (see Weidman and Stein 2003; Weidman et al. 2001; Anthony 2002). Since a doctoral student is in the process of learning to *be* a researcher (as well as *do* research), it is worth examining how this socialization process actually occurs. Socialization is taking place as a 'new' individual (in this case a student, or a supervisor who is new to the supervisory system) acquires knowledge, skills and attitudes. Essentially, this phenomenon can be said to have occurred when a new individual accepts the *validity* of the norms, standards, patterns and values within a system. These prevailing norms are the unspoken rules of the institution, faculty, department or group, and their origins are often unclear. Academic socialization (and thus, to an extent, doctoral independence) seems to be based on three key factors:

1. an environment in which the professional norms are clear and with which the participants agree;

2. interactions, both formal and informal, between the faculty and the students that are mutually beneficial;

3. a supportive environment in which the faculty are committed to the students' success.

Supervisory Enquiries about the Rules of Academia

- What does it mean to you 'be' an academic?
- What are the unspoken rules of engagement within your department, school or research group?
- Where did these 'rules' originate? Is there a sensible rationale for them, or is it a case of 'that's just how we do it here'?
- To what extent do you believe that the three conditions listed above are met in your department? What is currently lacking?

Our world is shaped by values, perceptions, expectations and assumptions. Many of these come directly or indirectly from the culture in which we develop and are raised or adopt. Cultural differences are not good or bad – they are what they are. We agree here that differences should be recognized and potentially valued as a source of intellectual improvement for both parties and that 'we can improve our teaching by studying our students' learning – by listening to and learning from our students' (Ramsden 2003). Essentially, the more people know about their own culture and the more they learn about other cultures, the better communication is likely to be. This makes it easier to design an effective alliance and also to avoid stereotyped cultural assumptions. To make the most of the cross-cultural differences within the relationship and to embrace any diversity of approach or belief in a positive way requires a high degree of cultural intelligence from the student as well as the supervisor:

'To students, I would say that it helps a lot to understand the background and culture of your supervisor, in order to communicate effectively, and to understand what he is trying to tell you. What I would say

> *to supervisors is: understand that the student is used to working in a different way than what he is experiencing and that could raise issues.'*
>
> *Research student, Saudi Arabia*

The concept of cultural intelligence was established in the book *Cultural Intelligence: Individual Interactions Across Cultures* (Earley and Ang 2003; see also Livermore 2011), in which the authors define cultural intelligence as an individual's ability to adapt flexibly to a new cultural setting. This means being aware of, sensitive to and respectful of the values, beliefs, attitudes and communication (vocal and non-vocal) of people from different cultures, and using this behaviour with empathy. Of course, a degree of common sensitivity plays an important part here, and a large amount of good can be done with a friendly manner and an open mind. Cultural intelligence is also about observing and noticing what is occurring at a verbal, vocal and visual level, and adapting one's behaviour accordingly. Cultural intelligence comes first and foremost from the motivation of an individual to want to find out about other cultures and behaviours, and to want to do their very best to build a successful relationship with another:

> *'I think it's quite simple. Find out as much as you can about your student. The more I know about them, the easier supervising them is.'*
>
> *Research supervisor – Engineering*

At the most basic level a supervisor may wish to find out as much as they can about the individual (regardless of culture), since many values (that are often said to be cultural traits) can be revealed in individual responses. Questions like these are all very useful openings and can open up different areas of cultural conversation:

- What's home like?
- Where exactly do you come from? What was it like living there? How is living in the UK different?
- Can you tell me a little about your family and friends or colleagues?
- Do you have family with you? How old are your children? How are they adapting to the UK?
- Do you have family at home for whom you are responsible – parents, extended family? How do you keep in touch with them?

- What was your previous education like?
- What's the most interesting thing about our respective countries?
- Who's been the biggest influence on your career so far?
- What's the biggest surprise so far about the UK?

These questions help to open discussions and enable both parties to learn more about each other. As with designing the alliance, the supervisor has to lead this conversation, disclose some information first, and let the student know that this curiosity is not a judgemental test or intended to be intrusive.

In parallel with this process, supervisors may wish to conduct some research of their own about a new student's culture and country. Many supervisors we spoke to recognized the value of doing this. Indeed, for some it was the most important piece of advice they would offer another supervisor. The benefits of doing this are twofold: firstly, to gain valuable information that may help the supervisor manage the relationship more effectively, but also (and probably mainly) to show the student that the supervisor is paying attention to their needs and individual characteristics. As such, a simple understanding of the following issues may yield great dividends.

Supervisory Enquiries about Understanding Another's Culture

- What is really important within your student's culture?
- What does their culture value, and what values does their culture embrace?
- How are these values comparable to those of your own culture and society?
- Where are there likely to be challenges between differing values?

There are a number of comprehensive works on cross-cultural relations, ranging from the management-focused, such as *Managing People Across Cultures* (Trompenaars and Hampden Turner 2004) and *Cultures and Organisations: Software of the Mind* (Hofstede and Hofstede 2005), to those focused on business etiquette, such as *Kiss, Bow or Shake Hands* (Morrison and Conaway 2006) and a number of websites and mobile apps such as CultureGPS,[4] and wise researchers may wish to study the cultural background of their colleagues in more detail. We wouldn't be the first to observe that tensions can arise from minor, almost unrecognized, cultural differences as well as from major ones.

In terms of supervisor preparation, a little prior research – even anecdotally from colleagues – can go a long way to establishing some basic parameters: what to be aware or wary of. But as with all such issues, the benefits of potential insight may easily be counterbalanced by the costs of assumptions, generalizations and caricatures. Regardless of such caveats, it is clear that certain cultural factors (such as decision making and relationships with authority or educational superiority) may generally be more important than others (such as eating habits), for while these may cause significant cultural offence in the wrong situation, they are unlikely to have a major impact within a purely research-based relationship.

Supervisors may wish to consider some broad cultural traits of a student's home country while remembering that there may be immense cultural variety within a particular nation. It is useful to consider the ramifications of any value clashes between the student's culture and the supervisor's culture and style and British cultural and academic life. For example, a student arriving from a culture that prizes community and co-operation may well find the nature of British and academic life more challenging than those who've been raised in a more individualistic culture. There are of course more dimensions to culture, but the dichotomies set out in Table 5.1 seem to be key ones that can have an impact on supervisory relationships in this context.

Table 5.1 Cultural dichotomies for supervisors to consider

Universalism Value is placed upon rules and obligations. Fairness comes from universal application of laws.	⇔	**Particularism** Each circumstance and relationship dictates the rules an individual lives by.
Individualism People believe in personal achievement and freedom. Individual must make their own decisions and take care of themselves.	⇔	**Communitarianism** The group is more important than individual achievement. Loyalty to the group is extremely important.

4 See www.culturegps.com/About.html (accessed 18 June 2014).

Specific People keep work and personal life separate. Although relationships are important, people can 'be professional' and work together without having a strong relationship.	⇔	**Diffuse** There is an overlap between work and personal life. People spend time outside work with colleagues, and this is essential for work effectiveness.
Neutral People make a concerted effort to control their emotions, and don't often reveal how they are feeling.	⇔	**Emotional** In these cultures it is normal and welcomed to show emotions, even spontaneously.
Achievement Achievement-oriented cultures value performance and demonstrable action.	⇔	**Ascription** People believe that titles, power and position matter, and these will define behaviour.
Uncertainty-tolerant People from low uncertainty-avoidance cultures accept and feel comfortable with unstructured situations and changeable environments.	⇔	**Uncertainty-averse** People with a trait of uncertainty averseness try to minimize the occurrence of unknown and unusual circumstances and to proceed with careful changes through step-by-step planning.
Masculinity Masculine cultures value competition, assertiveness and materialism. Such cultures often have more dramatic differences between gender roles.	⇔	**Femininity** Feminine cultures place more value on modesty, caring, sharing and quality of life. Gender role differences are often much less pronounced.
Long-term Orientation Such societies attach more importance to the future and foster pragmatism, persistence and capacity for adaptation.	⇔	**Short-term Orientation** The values promoted by these cultures and societies are related to the past and the present, and include steadiness, respect for tradition, preservation of face, and fulfilling obligations.

Sources: Adapted from Trompenaars and Hampden-Turner (2004) and Hofstede and Hofstede (2005).

Supervisory Enquiries or Discussion Points about Cultural Diversity

- Where would the UK sit in each of the cultural dichotomies described in Table 5.1?
- If appropriate, where would your home country sit in each of these cultural dichotomies?
- What experiences have you had of working with colleagues and students from different countries and cultures, and where would these countries sit in each of these cultural dichotomies?
- Where do you think that your research student's culture or society would sit, and what challenges might that pose to the doctoral process and supervisory relationship?

In our research for this book, supervisors and students alike mentioned the need for sensitivity from all parties when it came to elements of cross-cultural understanding. Supervisors may therefore also wish to examine protocols and norms related to the following communicative traits, and maybe even compile examples of misunderstandings resulting from them:

- smiling and facial mannerisms;
- eye contact (What is enough, and what is too much?);
- body language (for example, crossing arms/legs means different things in different parts of the world);
- spatial proximity (How much is enough, and how much is intrusive?);
- bodily contact and touching (such as handshakes);
- hand gestures (thumbs up to show approval is not a universal signal);
- head gestures (nodding to show agreement is not a universal signal);
- positions when meeting;

- modes of greeting;
- formality of meetings.

There is of course a duty here for both parties to learn about, observe and thus accommodate the other. Both parties need to consider, as a result of their cultural investigations, what specific accommodations they are going to make, how specifically they may have to compromise, and what types of situations may cause the most relationship stress.

One final point about cultural awareness is to offer the challenge that if UK supervisors in UK universities accommodate the needs of their culturally different students too much, then perhaps they are diluting and reducing the quality of the international experience. However, we are not advocating that a supervisor or student must alter every facet of their behaviour to accommodate the other, simply that making small changes and efforts can have dramatic results. Or, put more eruditely in the words of the poet Khalil Gibran: 'A little knowledge that acts is worth infinitely more than much knowledge that is idle.'

Culture Shock

Whenever someone moves from one environment to another, there is likely to be an element of culture shock. This phenomenon was first named by Canadian anthropologist Kalervo Oberg in 1960 (see Furnham 1997). He describes a number of aspects:

- strain – resulting from the effort needed to adapt;
- sense of loss and deprivation – relating to friends, possessions, status;
- feeling rejected or rejecting members of the new culture;
- confusion – about roles, expectations, values and identity;
- surprise, anxiety, indignation or disgust at discovered differences;
- feeling impotent – inability to cope.

Anyone experiencing any of the above is unlikely to be able to function at the high intellectual level a doctorate requires. What's more, the greater 'distance' travelled between cultures (not geographically, but in terms of the dichotomies described in Table 5.1), the greater the debilitating nature of any cultural shock may be, as these two examples illustrate:

> *'I gathered some information regarding the PhD programme and [my university] before I came over. However, knowing in the head is quite different from actually experiencing it. The hardest part is acclimatizing to a different culture, a completely different living style and a new studying mode.'*
>
> *Research student – Arts and Humanities, China*

> *'I felt on my own. I didn't understand why this was, and I didn't know what I should be doing.'*
>
> *Research student – Social Sciences, West Indies*

It should not be assumed that this kind of reaction is limited to those who have travelled to the UK for doctoral research. An experienced supervisor I spoke to told the story of a student from within the UK who struggled significantly, largely because his limited prior experience didn't include many things most of the research group took for granted. In addition, culture shock can also apply to students who are studying in their home country, but within an institution that has its origins and ethos from another nation or culture (as detailed in Pyvis and Chapman 2005).

Culture shock is, in essence, a predictable emotional response to a change in circumstances. The extent to which people struggle with this will differ, but the wise supervisor will bear it in mind when considering an international student.

Supervisory Enquiries about Cultural Adaptation

- Do you remember when you first joined the department you're currently working in?
- What specifically was difficult to adapt to?
- What specific incidents or actions helped you to settle in?
- Do you feel 'at home' there now? Why, or why not?
- What support did you need even as a fully independent scholar?

In educational research, the concept of culture shock has been refined and labelled 'study shock' (see Scheyvnes et al. 2003; see also Taylor and Beasley 2005 for a comprehensive overview). Study shock may comprise a mixture of some or all a number of experiences: differing expectations, differing learning styles, differing cultural and linguistic educational issues and tensions concerning intellectual exploration and productivity. International researchers may experience both culture shock and study shock, and some may also experience the 'status shock' of being labelled a 'student' when returning to university after time away.

One assumption we encountered repeatedly in our conversations was that the greatest shock for UK academics, assumed to have been educationally raised or acculturated to the 'Western' traditions of challenge and argument, came from supervising students who had been raised in an 'Eastern' academic tradition valuing consensus and harmony (see Wu 2002). Anecdotally, we found that these assumptions were often borne out by reality, though it seems that these situations were more common where supervisors used group meetings as a supervisory mechanism. We found that study shock frequently resulted from the speed and spontaneity of academic discourse, which is perceived as a linguistic issue but may be more complex:

> *'When my supervisor asks a question, I need to think. I find it hard to speak my mind at that time.'*
>
> *Research student, China*

Cortazzi and Jin (1997) highlight the differences in questions asked between 'Eastern' students (those they claim ask spontaneously) and Chinese students (who 'value thoughtful questions that they ask after sound reflection'), but we found that this was true of many of the students (regardless of nationality) we spoke to – the reasons relating to intellectual, linguistic and confidence issues.

Another shock factor we encountered was the necessary learning style shift from either conservative and reproductive or wholly analytical (as is often rewarded at undergraduate level regardless of nation) to a learning style that, at doctoral level, must be speculative and enquiring. It may be of interest for a student and supervisor to discuss how the student best likes to learn. There are many learning styles models and frameworks available (for a pragmatic treatment of experiential learning styles models, see Hutchinson and Lawrence 2011), although there is an acknowledgement within the sector (see Apfelthaler et al. 2007) that many learning styles inventories and tools were based on work carried out in only a limited range of cultures, such as the UK. Apfelthaler (and, more generally, Palfreyman and McBride 2007) also notes the difficulties faced in translating traditional educational models into practical and applicable recommendations that would improve the educational environment for international students. There are notable exceptions to this trend (see, for example, Oxford and Anderson 1995), but there has traditionally been an undeniable 'Western' bias in the vast majority of learning styles literature. For these reasons, an honest and open discussion between student and supervisor may serve just as well as a 'model-based' enquiry – and we will revisit this aspect of doctoral study in Chapter 8.

In one of the most comprehensive studies of cross-cultural doctoral supervision, Winchester-Seeto et al. (2013) proposed four major areas of challenge for cross-cultural supervision – mismatched expectations, maintenance of a positive relationship, effective communication and issues outside the thesis – and eight 'intensifiers' – separation from the familiar, language, cultural differences concerning hierarchy, other cultural differences, stereotypes, separation from support, time and the return home – that tend to exacerbate any existing cultural supervision challenges. The students and supervisors who contributed to this book talked of similar major and minor challenges and shocks.

All of these linked 'shocks' can, like any other form of stressor, in small doses be a positive ingredient and result in increased confidence and personal growth. For this to be the case, though, the student must have the necessary coping mechanisms, and the supervisor can play an enormous part in helping the student to develop these, academically, personally and even socially. We will now discuss a few of the key cultural and study shocks that seem to be more debilitating, and some simple supervisory strategies for helping students to cope.

CONFIDENCE

A change in context can result in a loss of confidence even when someone is secure in their relationships and abilities. So when these are both in the process of being established (or when they are both uncertain), confidence issues caused by the new context can be even greater:

> *'I was unsure just how different things [in the UK University] were. No one tells you – you just must work it out. I made lots of mistakes.'*
>
> *Research student – Social Sciences, Hong Kong*

Yet academic confidence is essential for independence, and the skill of the supervisor at the early stages lies in recognizing that they are on home territory and in thinking through what the candidate will need in order to feel confident as quickly as possible. We will explore this issue more in Chapter 9.

SELF-CONFIDENCE PERCEIVED AS ARROGANCE

The UK academic system, which requires debate, challenge and self-assurance, can be debilitating to a new student who is trying to find their intellectual feet, regardless of the traditions of their academic expectation:

> *'How can I challenge my supervisor? He is a professor and I am just beginning!'*
>
> *Research student, Singapore*

> *'I was amazed at the students at the seminar I first attended. So confident in their views. This did not seem proper to me.'*
>
> *Research student – information withheld*

It is important for the supervisor to provide a solid base from which the student can start to challenge and enquire safely. We explore this issue in more detail in Chapter 10.

SENIORITY AND DEFERENCE

Sometimes reticence to challenge and academically criticize is linked to issues of respect for seniority. Okorocha (2010) observes that 'in Asian culture you do not contradict your seniors or embarrass them in public', and quotes the story of a supervisor who advises their student to prune an extensive draft and leave some material out. At the candidate's upgrade meeting the examiner asks why the material is so scant, and the student says nothing for fear of embarrassing the supervisor. We found similar issues concerning status deference and confusion about what constituted 'respect':

> *'In my home, respect [for] seniors is everything. I fear my language will be disrespectful if I question my supervisor.'*
>
> *Research student – Sciences*

Since (not least at the viva), the student will need to learn to mount a confident and assertive defence of their Thesis, unless a supervisor helps the student to address any issues concerning seniority (practical guidance is provided in

Chapter 10), this may be a major challenge culturally if the examiner has high status, age and wisdom.

In the UK academic tradition difference is easily assumed to be a necessary part of even the most basic academic discussion. But where deference, especially to wisdom, is prized and prioritized by a student, such argument can easily slip into agreement. Hence, the simple supervisory question 'Do you agree?' may not yield anything other than 'Yes.' When agreement is reached, supervisors need to consider what this really means. We explore this issue in more detail in Chapter 10.

POWER, EQUALITY AND EQUITY

Linked to the issue of deference is the power imbalance associated with the label 'supervisor'. While some supervisors (depending on their preference, as discussed in Chapter 4) may take a more egalitarian role, for many students there is a keen perception of strong status inequality:

> *'I find things are not so good [with my supervisor]. But he is my supervisor. What can I do?'*
>
> *Research student – information withheld*

Supervisors must be aware of the possible effects of their status and do what is necessary to mitigate any debilitating effects of this. Thushari Welikala (quoted in Trahar 2011) says: 'One of the things that my supervisor did not attempt to do was to hold a supervision over my learning. This does not mean that the relationship was neutral and there were no traces of power, politics and authority.'

Depending on cultural background (see the cultural dichotomies presented in Table 5.1), gender may also play a role here – although it was not something that explicitly came up at all in any of the conversations or questionnaire responses from students or supervisors. However, other factors did prove intimidating:

> *'My supervisor [was a] great man, but always sat behind his big desk. He had many of his books and papers on his shelf. There was always a distance between us. This was intimidating.'*
>
> *(Male) post-doctoral researcher – Medical Science, Egypt*

Supervisors may wish to consider any aspects of the supervisory setting that might denote power and status, and minimize these if they present a barrier.

One supervisor we spoke to said that the most helpful thing he'd learned to do was simply to conduct his supervisions away from his office, as it provided a neutral space in which his students didn't feel they had to be deferential. However, with regard to equality, one supervisor revealed an interesting dimension which turns the usual diversity debate on its head:

> *'My two [international] students need more help, not intellectually, but with their language and the feedback on their written work. I have other [native English-speaking] students and don't give them as much time. Pragmatically, I know this is necessary, but it does seem unfair.'*
>
> *Research supervisor – Engineering*

FORMALITY

For some students we spoke to, the shock of the informality of the British system was linked to issues of status and deference:

> *'When I arrived I referred to my supervisor as "Professor". He laughed and told me to call him [by his first name]. I found this strange indeed.'*
>
> *Research student – Engineering*

> *'Remember that as strange as you find it to call him by his first name, he will find it strange to be called "Professor". If you explain that you find it strange – perhaps bordering on disrespectful – he will be more accepting of your politeness.'*
>
> *Research student – information withheld*

At the very core of communication is the cultural perspective from which the message is transmitted, and to which it is received. At a very basic level, when a supervisor invites a new doctoral researcher to call them by their first name, the intention of demonstrating equality or informality (or a multitude of other possible meanings) may be 'heard' as insulting, unacceptable, weird, overly familiar, silly, or almost any other reaction imaginable. The problem lies in being able to interpret or empathize enough to gain a sense of what the message might sound like to the recipient (see Lewis and Habeshaw 1997).

INTELLECTUAL POLITENESS

International students can often struggle with British 'politeness' of expression. This can be because the British system is too circumspect:

> *'Students should be polite in expressing their opinions. While it works [in Germany] to say "this is nonsense", a more polite formulation will get you further [here].'*
>
> *Research student, Germany*

Or it may be because it is too direct, as one supervisor of a Japanese student told us:

> *'I mailed my student to ask him look at something. His answer was polite. A few days later, I went to see him and he'd not started it ... [and] this irritated me. Later I asked him [about the incident]. He said he wasn't ready to do it – but he'd not wanted to say "no" for fear of seeming impolite. Still, I'm not sure how I should have handled that.'*
>
> *Research supervisor – Sciences*

A particular cross-cultural block here applies to students who consider that giving a 'wrong answer' means losing face. It is important in such situations for the supervisor to engage the student in conversation about which norms are academically acceptable and which are not. This could be part of the normal supervisory dialogue or for a student who wants to approach other academics and researchers, and it could also relate to face-to-face and electronic communications etiquette. We explore this issue fully in Chapter 11.

AMBIGUITY OF INFORMATION

The open-ended nature of communication and doctoral research proved to be a challenge to some researchers we spoke to. This a particular problem in situations involving joint supervision:

> *'The big difficulty is to get used to not knowing things. My two supervisors told me different things. I worried about who was right for a long time. Then I discovered they both were not correct. So then I worried about that.'*
>
> *Research student, Ghana*

Supervisors have a role to play here in helping students to acclimatize to what is normal academic practice, but they also have a duty to answer questions clearly when a clear answer is required. Supervisory strategies we encountered that seemed effective included:

- encouraging students to prioritize their questions and focusing supervision meetings on the important ones;
- encouraging students to come to supervisory sessions with questions and several possible answers, instead of just questions;
- separating out questions (one supervisor suggested the use of coloured sticky notes) into those that are discretely answerable (such as university policy and administrative information), reasonably clear (such as methodological protocols) or totally open-ended.

All these tactics revolve around increasing the student's proactivity and ability to function in an uncertain environment. We explore this issue more fully in Chapter 7.

LACK OF STRUCTURE

Associated with the shock of ambiguity is the lack of structure many supervisors (especially those adopting the hands-off, liberating coach and academic partner styles) may provide:

> *'The thing that I'm finding hardest to get used to (other than the weather!) is the way that there is no pressure or structure. No one tells me when to do anything and there are no deadlines or targets. It's just vague. I know that this is the academic way – but it's hard to cope with.'*
>
> *Research student – Sciences, Mexico*

This situation can be exacerbated if the student is under external funding or time pressures:

> *'My government funding says that I must return after three years. My permits run out and I must go home. My supervisor knows this. But he doesn't seem to have a plan to help me [finish on time].'*
>
> *Research student – Social Sciences*

This issue is not explicitly a cultural one, and is more about the difference in expectations between what students need individually and what supervisors feel they should provide. Here, a designed alliance conversation is required. The supervisor must be careful not to promise unrealistic levels of support, but if the student is being reasonable, then meeting them halfway and at the very least providing feedback in a timely manner may help. If the student is part of a strong research community, many issues of structure and expected targets can be learned by peer osmosis. Many of the problems here are often the result of the isolating nature of the research degree.

ISOLATION AND INCLUSION

Manathunga (2007) discusses supervisors facilitating growth by ensuring that students are included in a supportive research culture. We found instances of supportive cultures, but often the opposite was reported:

> *'It was lonely. I lived by myself and I had some friends who were also doing [a] PhD, and were always working like me. I saw my supervisor infrequently. I remember being lonely. I should have made more time to meet new people and try new things.'*
>
> *Post-doctoral researcher – Computer Sciences*

Supervisory Enquiries about Research Culture

- To what extent do any of your students feel included as part of a 'supportive research culture'?
- What could a 'supportive research culture' mean in your environment?

Note that just because your department runs a seminar series doesn't mean there is a supportive research culture.

Students who are subject to external expectations may feel that they don't have time to get involved in other activities and sometimes need supervisory guidance that working all day every day is not helpful. However, linguistic competence and unrealistic expectations can lead to a situation where a student's workload leads to increasing isolation, limiting their intellectual growth. Supervisors have a key role to play here. This may be as simple as asking a student about how their weekend was (or their plans for the upcoming one). It is relatively easy to pick up whether a colleague is socially involved or happy or not – and if not, appropriate action can be taken. This needn't necessarily entail the supervisor inviting the student to join their social circle or asking them home for tea. It may be as simple as letting the student know that it's academically important to have work–life balance, and that the supervisor gives 'permission' for this – even though none is required.

A design conversation here may be useful too, perhaps involving the supervisor listening carefully to whether the student talks about 'doing a doctorate' or 'being' a researcher or research student. Linguistically, it is our frequent experience that students who 'do' a doctorate also have balance in their life, as presumably they 'do' other things too. A student whose self-identity is borne out by their research (to 'be a researcher') is often far more prone to isolation and wild mood swings when the research doesn't progress according to expectations.

CULTURAL TRANSFORMATION

One of the major cultural shocks we found when we spoke to research students was not the newness of the UK or the UK system, but their own surprise at how much the UK system had changed them. For instance:

> *'I hadn't realized how much I had changed, how much I'd learned to debate and construct an argument and how much I learned to challenge the accepted view until I returned home and saw my grandparents. They said it was if I was not a real Chinese any more.'*
>
> *Research student – Social Sciences, China*

The word 'metamorphosis' is often used to describe the doctoral journey (see, for example, Burnapp 2009), and we personally often have metaphoric metamorphic conversations with our students about academic tadpoles and caterpillars becoming intellectual frogs and butterflies. It is important that supervisors, as part of the design process, help their students to understand that this transformation is as important a part of the doctoral experience as producing the Thesis. This can cause tension within a student, especially if acclimatizing to the UK system clashes fundamentally with the student's established cultural value set. Again, this can be resolved by the supervisor if the relationship is strong and well designed. More than anything, though, it requires a huge deal of hard work and tenacity – perhaps as much as the intellectual endeavour itself. Recently, I was working with a group of international doctoral researchers and asked them each individually to write on a sticky note what they considered to be the most helpful character quality or attribute for doctoral study. Six wrote 'hard working', five wrote 'perseverance'. One wrote 'warm clothing and perseverance'.

This section merely scratches the surface of what is a hugely complex and highly charged issue. Even at the most basic level there seem to be a lot of variables for the well-meaning supervisor to remember. Yet if these cultural variables are ignored and the supervisor does not consider how different cultural filters can skew the academic norms, then much of the intellectual effort the supervisor devotes to supervision may be wasted.

Supervisory Enquiries about Cultural Backgrounds

- Do you bear in mind your supervisory style and adapt your actions in light of students from culturally different backgrounds?
- Do you have a fundamental understanding of the culture, educational systems and learning approaches in your supervisee's home country?
- How does your cultural background (and your student's) affect the supervisory process?
- Where appropriate, are you providing opportunities for students to create new intellectual approaches by combining their own cultural approaches to research with the currently acceptable ones in the UK? Have you considered the reaction of examiners to any cross-cultural intellectual approaches you develop?

The assumptions each party makes about the other's cultural and educational background is, to some extent, irrelevant provided those assumptions don't cause a problem in the relationship. This is particularly the case since there is often a considerable confusion between causation and correlation when national or cultural character traits are raised. As one supervisor pointed out:

> *'It's interesting that you ask whether a trait is cultural. I mean, a guy in the group here is Russian and he's quite blunt with his opinions. But is he blunt because he is Russian, or is he blunt because he's blunt? I don't know, and I don't worry too much. I just treat him as Vitaly.'*[5]
>
> *Research supervisor – Computer Science*

Finally, then, it's vital for both parties to get to know each other as individuals, but never to forget that the concept of 'the individual' can differ considerably

5 Vitaly is a pseudonym.

from culture to culture. Since individuals differ and change over time, students and supervisors must learn to know each other culturally. However, as usual, what is required by both parties is an appreciation that the other is making an effort to listen, tolerate and encourage. However, even if all the supervisor and student do is to start thinking about and discussing cultural issues, this can only enhance the quality of the experience for all concerned:

> *'Contrary to what it is usually suggested, I think that to write a doctorate one should not only be very dedicated to work independently, and to have a good command of his/her own time, but also to understand deeply the potential of the supervisors, department and college. It should also be noted that the multicultural approach and the case of equal opportunities do not work every time, so one should be prepared to deal even with these cases, understanding that there is no perfect system of Education, nor perfect academic environment. These issues should be simply considered as another challenge to deal with.'*
>
> *Research student – Arts and Humanities, Russia*

Once the basic needs of the student have been addressed and linguistic issues resolved, the alliance designed and cultural differences clarified, the next step is to ensure that the supervisor is fully aware of the student's academic experience to date.

Step 5: Establishing Academic Experience

> *Experiences have no end, and one always gains from them.*
>
> *Arabic proverb*

In most cases a student's curriculum vitae (or record of qualifications) will have been seen by the supervisor prior to the student's arrival in the UK, and at the very least the individual's previous academic qualification level will have been discussed. However, academic experience includes a mixture of attributes, only some of which would appear on a curriculum vitae, so it is vital for the supervisor to ensure that both parties have a conversation about the student's intellectual level, knowledge and skills relevant to the topic under investigation.

Such a conversation should include general (ethics and contextual) and specific field knowledge, and academic skills such as literature searching and correct referencing should be included in this conversation. The intent here should be developmental, not accusatory and assuming deficiencies on the part of the student. We found a number of examples where such questioning had been taken as implied criticism or scepticism, such as:

> *'I never expected I would have to face so many administrative problems in my faculty, and worst of all, I didn't expected my previous academic qualifications to be questioned.'*
>
> *Research student – Social Sciences*

Failure to hold academic experience conversations can lead to situation where students feel that supervisors are unaware of their capabilities, and supervisors may assume that students are intellectually deficient simply because they are finding adapting to the UK or the language challenging. Similarly, a lack of familiarity with normalized UK research tools and techniques must not be assumed to be indicative of a lack of academic ability. Sadly, this is sometimes not the actual experience of international students:

> *'Please, remember international students are not fools.'*
>
> *Research student – Social Sciences, Chile*

In many ways, having an academic experience conversation with a new student is simple if the alliance has been designed, but it can lead to explorations of whether the student understands how to engage in an intellectual debate in a way that complies with UK norms, and whether the student understands the conventions for appropriate citation, the avoidance of plagiarism, and intellectual professionalism. Supervisors may wish to consider the research output from the student's culture. In some intellectual cultures the practice of accrediting and citing published work is less common. Thus, different approaches across cultures can result in international students being accused of plagiarism (Denicolo and Pope 1999) and penalized for behaviours which had previously been rewarded. We will revisit this aspect of scholarly integrity in Chapter 8. Much of this conversational work can be done through simple questions from the supervisor, such as 'What do we need to know about you academically/educationally/technically?' or 'What is good research practice?', but sometimes it is easier to have this conversation after asking the student to complete a small piece of written work, which if conducted 'properly', should adhere to acceptable UK academic norms. These ideas are explored more fully in Chapter 7.

Supervisory Idea to Facilitate Academic Experience Conversations

Ask the student to draw map of their intellectual journey up to this point and get them to talk through it with you. Find out the expertise gained from each level and project. What aspects did they enjoy more? What do they regret? What responsibilities did they have? This approach is particularly effective with more mature students. The wise supervisor may wish to refer to this expertise or experience regularly.

Such an activity may offer interesting leads to discussion of training needs and help to provide a palatable introduction to tools such as the *Researcher Development Framework* (see Chapter 2).

One of the key advantages of such tasks and conversations is that they bring into sharp focus the status shock that can be suffered by students who come to the UK to conduct research which will build upon their areas of professional expertise. As we discussed in Chapter 3, we've met surgeons, consultants, clergymen, clergywomen and military officers, all of whom have been highly skilled:

> *'In my country I am an expert – but I didn't know the academic rules here at all. Suddenly it felt like I knew nothing again.'*
>
> *Research student – Social Sciences*

International doctoral candidates may also have had considerable academic experience prior to registering for a UK doctorate, but where previous education has occurred in a foreign system, the mismatch of qualification levels and perceived knowledge and capabilities can produce tension and a challenge to both supervisor and student.

Perhaps one of the key blocks for the student to overcome is inherent within the label 'student'. The word 'student' implies burgeoning (and hence incomplete) knowledge, lack of control, and also that there will be a 'teacher' who will have control and knowledge. Many educational authors prefer to use the term 'doctoral researcher' instead, as 'student' signifies the 'institutional power relationships at work in the supervisory relationship' (Kamler and Thompson 2006). In the conversations we've had in higher education over the last decade we are often amazed by the dismissive way highly intelligent, articulate and talented people belittle their efforts and qualifications by adding a limiting prefix – as the word 'just' in this example shows:

> *'Back home [in my company] I am respected and manage a team and have large financial responsibilities. Here I am just a student.'*
>
> *Research student – Psychology*

While 'student' is far easier to say than 'doctoral researcher' (and indeed, we have used the label 'student' throughout this book), perhaps supervisors may need to consider the labels they use and the way these labels are interpreted. A supervisor who is seeking to build an academic partnership may wish to be especially careful, since it is difficult to change midstream from the proprietary label 'my student'.

Step 6: Defining Academic Expectations

> *No matter how far you have gone*
> *on a wrong road, turn back.*
>
> *Turkish proverb*

Finally, supervisors need to complete the embarkation process by exploring the expectations and motivations of all parties. Of course, supervisors should be relatively clear about their own expectations and motivations (as covered in Chapters 3 and 4), and we've suggested that motivations are a necessary topic for conversation pre-arrival. Before the student and supervisor commence the business of serious scholarship, they must examine and clarify the responsibilities and expectations of both parties:

> *'Perhaps supervisors should arrange a couple of meetings at the start, discussing the way PhD study is conducted in the UK and give a clear understanding of what it entails. Also, maybe he or she can try and understand where the student is coming from. It may be a huge change culturally besides other things, which can be quite daunting. I mean, a genuine effort on part of the supervisor to connect with the student at some level is always encouraging.'*
>
> *Research student – Sciences, Mexico*

This conversation should examine three elements from three angles: those of the student, supervisor and any stakeholders, including the institution and funding agency. The elements are defined by what both parties consider success to be with regard to the outputs and outcomes of the project, the research process and environment and the supervisory relationship. Of course, it is unlikely that all these will be completely met, but it is important to start with a declaration of what these are, or are perceived to be. A successful and fully enhanced doctoral experience in the holistic sense comes when all of the conditions in Figure 5.2 are met.

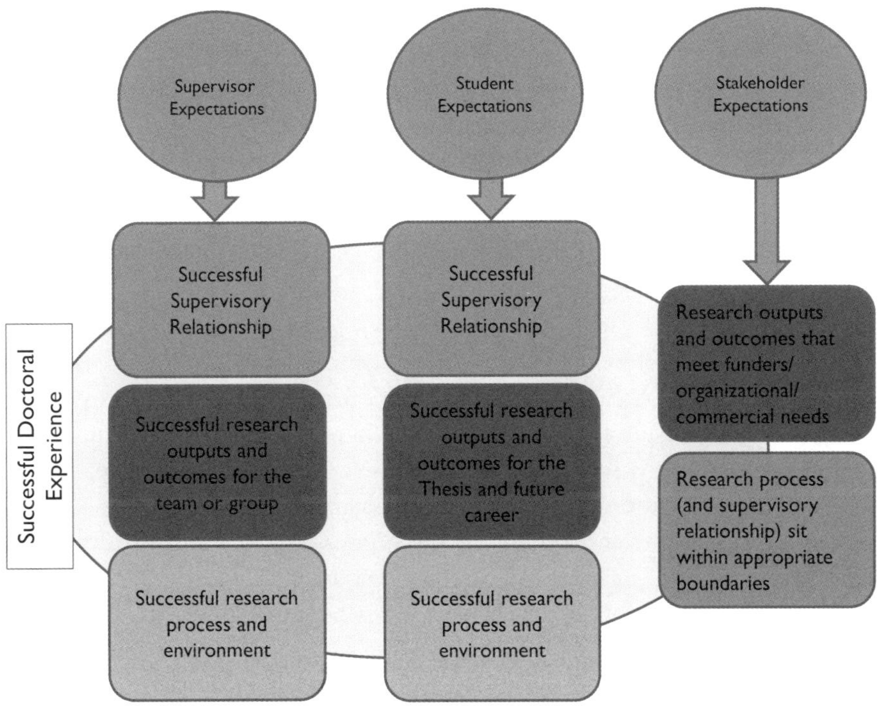

Figure 5.2 Successful doctoral experience

As part of any conversation about academic expectations, it is necessary to establish and perhaps negotiate which party must take responsibility for which roles and functions. There is of course no correct answer to the question of which member of the doctoral team has responsibility for what. Even where the institutional guidelines clearly state that a certain task is the responsibility of one or another party, often the practice on the ground is very different. Sometimes this is a positive aspect of supervision:

> *'I've read the rules and I know my supervisor is meant to keep a record of each of our formal meetings. Yet I find it very helpful to take this job. It helps me to remember what we had agreed and to stay focused.'*
>
> *Research student – Biology, Scandinavia*

But sometimes this confusion is a source of frustration for one party:

> *'My supervisor doesn't do what it says in the [departmental] handbook. What should I do about this?'*
>
> *Research student – Social Sciences, Iran*

And sometimes it frustrates the other:

> *[What do you find hardest about supervising your international student?] 'Her lack of proofreading. I'm not her editor, but most of our time is spent doing corrections that a proofreader could do.'*
>
> *Research supervisor – Social Sciences*

A supervisory relationship where both parties are clear about the formal rules of engagement is likely to progress to one where the informal and unspoken rules are raised and discussed more readily, so a conversation about formal expectations is an important part of the design process. Again, due to the (perceived or real) power imbalance in the supervisory relationship, this is one area where a supervisor must lead and consult the student in order to find an agreed style and level of supervision which is truly mutually acceptable and beneficial:

> *'I'm told to challenge and to question my supervisor. Even if I am polite this is difficult. He holds all the cards.'*
>
> *Research student – Biomedical Sciences, India*

The lack of a genuine conversation about expectations sometimes results from more than just a power imbalance. Many students we speak to believe that their supervisor holds 'all the cards' in terms of knowledge about supervision, subject expertise and the requirements of the system, both nationally and institutionally. However, this perception often leads to confusion and frustration for one, if not both, parties. As one researcher told us:

> *'When I came I was sure that my supervisor would know how to supervise and would have the information I needed – not on my subject, but about the UK system. [How do you feel now?] Now, not so certain ....'*
>
> *Research student – Engineering*

To an extent, this perception of the home knowledge being correct and omniscient is nothing unusual, in effect it's a natural extension of the 'do as the Romans do' paradigm. However, when combined with a perceived power imbalance (the teacher who teaches and the student who learns), it can become damaging if the desired end product in question is an independent scholar. Overlay this with a cultural dimension, and here lies the root of the vast majority of issues and problems we encountered while researching this book. Catherine Manathunga (2007) puts it well when she writes: 'Culturally diverse students may feel that they have very little power in the supervisory relationship not only because the supervisor has greater authority as the teacher, but also because the supervisor and student may have very different cultural expectations about how supervision should work.' Yet if one digs into this issue even briefly, it becomes very clear that these perceptions of power and systematic omniscience can be deeply flawed:

> *'We're expected to know how to supervise and manage people well – but I only saw my supervisor twice in my entire first year. There's no culture of support from above me here [in this institution,] and the training I was given at the start merely outlined the regulations.'*
>
> *Research supervisor – information withheld*

To conclude this chapter, it is highly worthwhile to focus on the perceptions of power and expertise both parties may have. It could be argued that both parties may be perceived to have certain information (cards they hold), while the reality may be different. In some cases the student and supervisor may have some information, but this needs to be fleshed out with a sensible series of conversations over the first few weeks of the doctorate.

Let's examine the 'cards' held by the supervisor first (see Table 5.2).

Table 5.2 Knowledge and expectation 'cards' that may be held by the supervisor

PERCEPTION **Cards the supervisor is perceived by the student to hold**	**REALITY** **Cards actually held by the supervisor***	**POTENTIAL** **Cards the supervisor may not fully hold at the start of the project**
Their version of the supervisory norm	Personal research track record and experience	Omniscience about 'correct' supervision
Their version of the disciplinary norm	Knowledge of techniques and approaches that have worked generically with previous students (where appropriate)	Pragmatically useful knowledge about how to supervise their new student
Their version of the research methods norm	An understanding of their own disciplinary and supervisory motivations	Understanding of the student's culture
Knowledge of institutional rules and norms		Specific understanding of the details of this project
A full and proper understanding of what the doctorate actually is		

* In addition, the supervisor may actually fully hold cards from the 'Perception' and 'Potential' columns.

It is the supervisor's job here to ensure that the student is fully aware of what cards are held, and not to allow assumptions to go unchallenged.

Let's now view this from the reverse perspective (see Table 5.3).

Table 5.3 **Knowledge and expectation 'cards' that may be held by the student**

PERCEPTION **Cards the student may be perceived by the supervisor to hold**	**REALITY** **Cards actually held by the student***	**POTENTIAL** **Cards the student may not fully hold at start of project**
Aligned motivation (doing the doctorate for the academically 'right' reasons) Their version of the disciplinary norm Their version of the research methods norm Sufficient knowledge of institutional rules and norms	Personal motivation for doctoral study A culturally influenced set of expectations about supervision, education and the doctoral process The experiences and events (culturally, educationally and professionally) that have led them to this point	Knowledge of how (up to this point) they might work best Specific understanding of the details of this project An understanding of what the UK doctorate actually is Knowledge of institutional rules and norms Personal logistical focus (timelines etc.)

* In addition, the student may actually fully hold cards from the 'Perception' and 'Potential' columns.

Again, it is the supervisor's responsibility in the early stages to ensure that the alliance is sufficiently well designed that the student feels able to declare their cards and express their true expectations and motivations. After all, doctoral supervision is not a competition. Only when both parties know the full set of cards the other holds can the relationship develop to reach its full potential, and it is the subject of building the relationship that we move to in the next chapter.

Chapter 6
Building the Relationship

If you want to go quickly, go alone.
If you want to go far, go together.
Swahili proverb

While researchers must acknowledge that they do not know the precise results of a research project because they have not yet done the research, they *do* know at the outset that they aim to have an answer to a number of different questions, many of which are formulated at the very beginning. They may not have a full vision for the project, but they will have an emergent vision and a reasonably clear set of values. The same can be said for the supervisor, who will know that at the beginning of a research project it's not only possible, but imperative to lay out the parameters of the project.

In exactly the same way, at the beginning of a supervisory relationship it's not only possible, but imperative to develop an understanding of the vision both parties have for that relationship and to appreciate the value system within which the relationship will operate.

A vision for a relationship is perhaps a slightly odd concept; however, our contention is that any professional relationship begins with both parties having ideas, expectations and hopes for what that relationship will look like or what it will become. When a doctoral candidate first meets their supervisor, both parties will have expectations for the next three years, as discussed in Chapters 4 and 5.

However, beyond this, does the supervisor expect the relationship to come to a natural end with the submission and completion of the Thesis? Or is the hope of the supervisor that this perhaps rather shocked new researcher will become a valued colleague and co-investigator in due course? To some extent the answer to this question depends on the style of the supervisor (see Chapter 4) and the motivations of both parties (Chapter 3). Earlier we told the story of a doctoral candidate who, early in the doctoral process, was referred to by his supervisor as 'my colleague'. Such an epithet is indicative of a vision for that supervisory relationship which extends beyond submission and completion of the Thesis.

Supervisory Enquiries (and Later Discussion Points) about Relationships

- At the start of any project, what vision do you have for any post-doctoral relationship with your student?
- How far into the doctoral process do you know what the long-term relationship is likely to be?
- What do you think the relationship will be like in six months, three years, five years or ten years?
- You had a great student – how did you help facilitate that 'greatness'?
- In three years your student says they had a *great supervisory relationship*? What did either party do to help that relationship develop?

It is not our contention that supervisors must have a desire for a long-term professional relationship from day one, or even that such a long-term relationship is a necessity. However, if a supervisor is to recoup any investment from their supervisory efforts, it makes sense that the student should not simply graduate and disappear. We return to this issue in Chapter 12.

Recently I was talking to the supervisor of a doctoral candidate who was about to submit his Thesis. When I asked whether she envisaged this relationship continuing beyond the completion of the doctorate, she commented that she hoped they would stay in friendly contact, but she had known from the outset that the candidate had embarked on the doctorate to develop his professional career. As his career path was outside academia, there had never been a vision for an ongoing professional relationship after he had completed his Thesis.

However, what is essential is that the student and supervisor build on the initially designed alliance and work together over time to build a productive working relationship. This is not a difficult task as long as the initial expectations of the student and supervisory roles have been explored – and at some level it simply requires some understanding and openness from both parties:

> *'Empathy and approachability is very important for the student to feel secure especially when he is homesick and the supervisor is mainly his most trusted person.'*
>
> *Research student – information withheld*

There are very pragmatic reasons why a strong working relationship may help, even without a long-term vision of a successful relationship. For instance:

> *The student whose tutor provides enlightened feedback on work submitted, or the researcher whose supervisor invites him home for Sunday lunch is most unlikely to complain about photocopying restrictions or lack of lab space. Conversely, those students who feel that those who teach them have no interest in them complain about everything and even the most excellent facilities can only ameliorate the position.*
>
> *(Humfrey 1999)*

Moreover, there are correlations between completion rates and the duration and frequency of doctoral meetings, and shorter doctoral completion times are also linked to whether the student develops a 'close working relationship' with the supervisor (Seagram et al. 1998). And at a fundamental level, 'even students who are independent prefer a relaxed rather than tense atmosphere' in their supervision meetings (Kam 1997).

At some level it is important for both supervisor and student to remember that they are in an adult relationship and the other party is a human being with their own needs, wants, agendas, vision and values. Strong relationships (especially those between individuals whose intellectual and cultural identities are emerging) are those that continue to be designed and those in which *both* parties take a responsibility for the state of the relationship. Of course, there are issues inherent in this statement – not least any cultural expectations a student may have about a 'supervisory' relationship. Also, this process requires the supervisor to be sufficiently self-aware to recognize that the design process must be two-way, so they must consequently elicit contributions from even the most reticent student:

> *'The most difficult thing is working with diverse student personalities, motivations and needs. Every student is different and the combination is not always ideal. I always say to myself, "How can I best help this particular student?" But the answer is not always easy and I have often felt dissatisfied with the result, and I suspect so have the students. In the end, I think that it is best to just let students be who they are and guide them, sometimes gently and other times more forcefully. But I think, for students, the hard part of having me as a supervisor is they have to deal with me too. I have high standards for myself and for them. And sometimes that is not ideal for them. So, more and more, I have stepped back where possible and let students come to me.'*
>
> *Research supervisor – Linguistics*

Primarily, the process of both researcher and supervisor constructing, deconstructing and reconstructing their own roles and their perceptions of each other requires honesty from both parties. If there is honesty and reciprocity in the relationship, then the roles will develop to become complementary, and then evolve symbiotically. A lack of trust and honesty will either produce immediate dissatisfaction or some sort of artificial role-play, which is likely to end painfully for at least one, if not both of them. The possibilities of an honest and open relationship with a supervisor are often culturally shocking, but also refreshing for international students:

> *'Be open-minded, because the relationship with the supervisor is much more relaxed than in my home.'*
>
> *Research student, Chile*

However, on top of the honest, designed adult relationship we advocate, it must also be remembered that this is a relationship with a purpose: to help nurture and foster an independent scholar. The balance between a close working relationship and independence is a hard one to negotiate, and much is determined by whether the supervisor's default style is liberating coach or academic partner:

> *'I'd say the hardest thing is the independence that is required. In my country I'd always been taught and been told how to work. Here it is very different, and this is frustrating. Though I'd also say to never fear asking people for help. Achieving both of these at once is difficult.'*
>
> *Research student – Medicine, Egypt*

Because this balance is difficult to negotiate, an idea we often propose to both research students and supervisors is that both parties would benefit from feedback on their input to the relationship, and open discussion about it.

Student and Supervisor Discussion Questions about Relationships

- What are the strengths of this working relationship?
- What do we need to do to improve this relationship?
- How useful is my input as a supervisor? How useful is my guidance?
- How are you feeling about the way we're working?

On top of a mutual acceptance that a well-defined and designed relationship is highly advantageous to both parties, and following the initial design phase (set out in Chapter 5), building a supervisory relationship requires at least three elements, (and ideally a fourth):

1. time;
2. empathy;
3. listening;
4. mutual research projects and interests.

We will briefly examine these in reverse order. These aspects require effort (at first), so they take time, but investment in them pays large dividends in the long term, and ultimately time savings through avoidance of misunderstanding and grievances.

Mutual Research Projects and Interests

Professional relationships are far more likely to be strong and productive if the protagonists are engaged in a project where there is a clear and tangible end product that demonstrably benefits both parties. Certainly, I received far more input and insight from my own supervisor when we were writing papers together then when he was reading my Thesis drafts. Shared research products require the supervisor to place a great deal of trust in their student (since a joint publication, for instance, has both their reputations attached to it), but demonstrating this trust can be enormously empowering for the student. This idea is explored further in Chapter 9.

Shared research outputs are often supervisor-led as (regardless of culture), so it can be difficult for a student to suggest such endeavours. However, what is frequently surprising to us is that research students often have little idea of what is on their supervisor's research agenda at any given time. This is particularly the case in disciplines without a strong research team ethos.

We often see that dynamic and inspirational leaders are very team-focused, collegiate and inclusive in their use of language. They talk about 'our endeavours' and refer to 'what we're doing' (as opposed to 'my team' and 'my project'). This trend continues in supervisors who are able to walk the fine line between collegiality and allowing the student to function independently. Essentially, we believe that a student should be able to reach the end of the process and say: 'This is *my* thesis and *my* Thesis, but we did it together.'

If a student is to be immersed in a strong research culture, then perhaps this needs to start with discussions about what the supervisor is involved in and what trials and tribulations they are facing. Several supervisors told us that they deliberately keep their own work out of the supervisory arena, not as an intellectual property protection issue, but so that the student does not feel that their supervisor is hijacking the conversation. Obviously, then, care must be taken, but a clearly shared sub-project within the Thesis can help both parties to build an effective relationship. A social science academic told me with some delight about a doctoral candidate in her research group who had recently submitted her Thesis and they had secured funding for her to continue post-doctorally. The academic told me how startled the candidate had been to be asked for comments on a draft paper written by other members of the research group. This was the point when the tables were turned and the years of investing in a very able candidate were about to pay off as the fledgling researcher was to begin taking more responsibility within the team as a whole. This is the point many supervisors long for. Whether it comes before or after completion of the doctorate, the time when the doctoral candidate begins to invest in projects other than their own signals the possibility of true collaboration.

Listening

There are many sayings and proverbs from all around the world to the effect that active and empathic listening is as influential as erudite and clever talk. There are issues here, though, for research supervisors who are on a limited time budget, and students who may feel that they are inappropriately burdening their supervisor with non-technical issues. To build a strong relationship requires listening, and listening is something that can be learned and practised. It is interesting that the Chinese calligraphic symbol for listening combines the elements of ear, eye, focus, importance (royalty) and compassion (heart)!

- **Ears** – In order to listen more, maybe we need to question more and talk less. (Note that this is easier for those adopting the liberating coach style than for those serving as critical teacher.)

> **Supervisory Enquiries about Listening**
>
> - In your supervisions, who does what proportion of talking and listening?
> - How much of your own talk is 'telling' or 'asking'?
> - When are your 'suggestions' taken as something more absolute?

- **Eyes** – Active listening involves showing another person that they are truly being listened to.

- **Focus** – Active listeners focus their attention on the person who is talking. Focus shows concern, but is difficult to achieve in the ever-connected world of smartphones and emails, let alone with the distraction of one's own academic agenda. One student told us that he had initially believed that his supervisor was 'wasting' his time, because the supervisor would spend the first 20 minutes of an hour-long supervision reading what the student had brought with him. The student had realized that this was not the supervisor's fault, but the student's, and had recalibrated his own working week as a result so that he sent written documents to the supervisor three days before a meeting. This allowed the supervisor to read and digest the work, then focus fully on the supervisory meeting.

> **Supervisory Enquiries about Focus**
>
> - What gets in the way of your supervisory focus? What can you do to minimize any distractions and ensure you focus appropriately?
> - What do you need to do to ensure that your student does the same? What groundrules might be necessary for supervision meetings?

- **Importance** – True listening acknowledges that what the other person says is important, even if the recipient may personally regard it as wrong, irrelevant or ill considered. Treating a student's comment as valuable and important can do much to build intellectual confidence. Treating a contribution as important is not the same as sycophancy, and obvious errors should be corrected. However, in an environment where there is often no right or wrong, just different approaches and ideas, it is important to show that contributions are valued and not just routinely challenged.

Supervisory Enquiries about Intellectual Encroachment

- How often do you find your own intellectual agenda encroaching upon your student's?
- When is such intrusion a positive force (opening up possible collaborations) and when is it a negative one (constricting a student's independence)?

- **Compassion** – Effective listening involves paying attention to verbal and non-verbal messages and listening not just to facts, but also to the feelings being communicated. Again this requires focus, challenging one's assumptions and an acceptance that differences offer rich intellectual seams to be mined. If my supervisor had focused all her comments on her passion for the topic (as opposed to mine) or the intrinsic value of the research, I suspect two things would have happened: my enthusiasm and confidence would almost certainly have waned, and possibly more significantly, I would have felt increasingly that I didn't fit with her idea of what a successful researcher should be. As it was, she understood my perspective and was sufficiently emotionally intelligent to accept that it was different from hers. She frequently expressed her belief in me, particularly when I had doubts, resulting in not only a successfully completed doctorate, but also great communication.

Empathy

Do not measure (others) by your own yardstick.
Russian proverb

In some ways, a designed and strong relationship revolves around both parties (but especially the supervisor) knowing what the other party needs. This cannot be taught, but can usually be learned over time, mainly by paying attention, asking open questions and setting a foundation upon which honest disclosure can build. Supervisors and students alike pointed out to us that this was often a challenge as some academics 'don't do the human stuff too well'.

To keep this very complex issue simple, a supervisor needs to have a feeling for what the student needs at any point. These needs may be research-led and technical, career-focused and aspirational, or pastoral or process-based (timescales and logistics). Phrased even more simply, in any given exchange the supervisor needs to make a decision to focus on the *task* (research and Thesis) or the *person* (pastoral, career and relationship issues). Every supervisor should recognize that both are necessary, but the wise one will know when to focus on one and when to switch to the other.

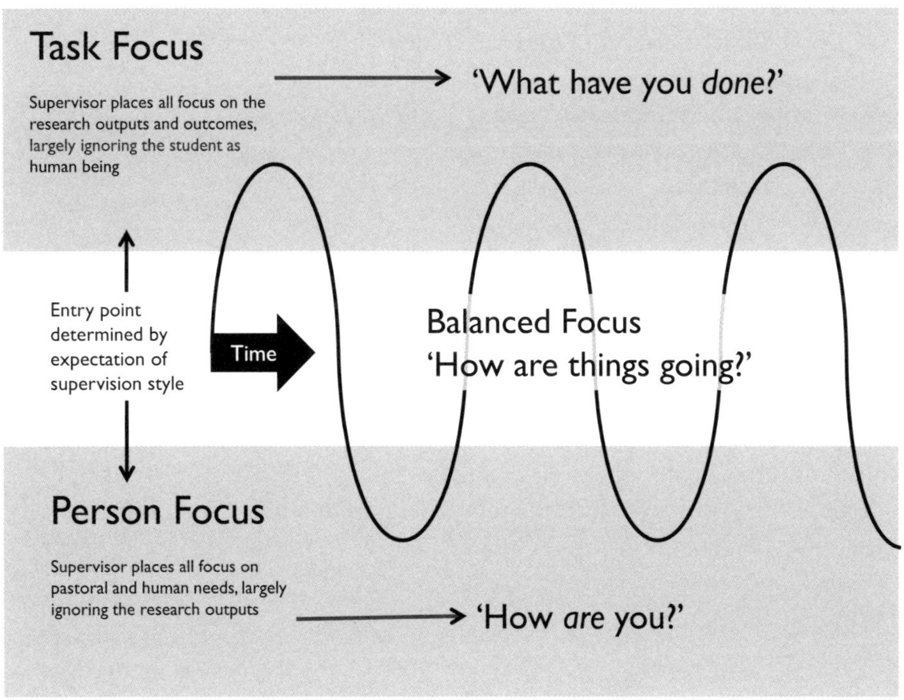

Figure 6.1 Supervisory focus

There is plenty of literature and advice that suggests that supervisors should be aware of the time pressures on international students and should pay particular attention to helping them keep to schedules and deadlines. Supervisors with a predilection for the project manager style (and indeed the critical teacher one) will place their focus here more readily. Supervisory sessions will revolve around the questions 'What have you *done*?' and 'What are you going to do *next*?' Such an approach can facilitate independence, but can feel impersonal and lacks the long-term advantages of a strong collaborative approach. Sometimes, in an attempt to provide balance, a supervisor will overcompensate for their natural style and focus too much instead on the opposite driver. This is the personal approach favoured by supervisors adopting the academic partner and liberating coach styles, who instead may ask the question 'How *are* you?' or 'How are we getting *on*?' Of course, the student can choose to answer either type of question in any way they wish, but the unspoken tone and underlying agenda are usually clear to them and they will respond accordingly.

Neither approach in and of itself is suitable or fit for purpose, and what is required is balance. Skilled supervision on the journey to the point of independence is therefore a careful combination of these two approaches. Perhaps, then, a sensible way forward is for the supervisor to begin a supervision session with the attitude that they will allow the student to lead. This may start by asking the opening question 'So, how are things going?' This question allows the student to focus on task, process or individual concerns – whichever seems most pressing to them at the time. It then allows the supervisor to steer the conversation to provide balance if necessary:

> *'I notice that we always talk about the data. Is that OK with you? You know that we could talk about [for example] how this fits into the broader project if you want to?'*

This allows the supervisor to be accessible in any way the student wants, but also allows the student to lead the relationship into other areas if they want to.

Time

A supervisory relationship that incorporates a good balance between academic and pastoral elements is almost certainly going to involve some contact outside formal supervision meetings. Often this will take the form of departmental or research group socials, and an informal chat in these situations is often all that is needed for a postgraduate to feel that the supervisor sees them not just as a researcher, but also as a person. However, these events don't take place every day, and there needs to be regular human contact in order for the relationship to feel comfortable for both parties.

Of course this sounds simple, but most doctoral supervisors need to fit meetings with their students in among many other commitments, so supervisions need to be conducted efficiently and sometimes quickly. As we've discussed above, both quality of meeting and quantity of contact are important, and part of any designed expectations conversation involves negotiating about such parameters. The primary trap the relationship can fall into here is that the drive for efficiency means that the supervisor tends to hold meetings with their student which focus solely on problems with work. This may not prove effective in the long term. Applying the acronym TEA below to every meeting, regardless how brief, will ensure that the person never disappears behind the mask of their work:

- **T**une in – First, connect with the student. Notice how they seem – are they relaxed and happy, nervous, flustered, stressed? If you haven't seen them for a while, ask what they have been up to. Give a little information about yourself to set the tone and allow them to feel connected.

- **E**xchange – One of the best aspects of supervision is the creativity that can emerge from organic conversation. Regardless of whether the student has come with a problem or with some results, make it your habit to ask them first for their ideas about how to move forward. But remember that this is an exchange: they may well feel insecure if you don't give your own opinion or thoughts. By asking for theirs first, you provide the opportunity to acknowledge and give credit for good work, or to encourage independent thought, thus reinforcing the expectation that such self-governance is required.

- **A**lign – Before you part, ensure that you both have the same understanding of the actions involved. Often this will involve more than a simple check such as 'Great, so are you OK with that?' or 'You know what to do now, right?', which will frequently elicit the answer the student feels you want to hear rather than necessarily the accurate one. Simply asking the student to outline *what* they are going to do and *how* they are going to approach this may provide an accurate picture of their understanding.

Ultimately, the supervisory relationship is like any other: it needs effort, design and mutual trust. And of course, despite the key individuals originating from different cultural contexts with different definitions of individualism, the supervisory process and relationship is one involving two adult human beings. In the rarefied academic air and context, it's easy to forget this:

> *'Different topics, different individuals, different expectations and abilities. I would be reluctant to generalize to "international" versus "home" students, because my experience tells me that you have to treat each individual as an individual. International students may have a flexibility and maturity that comes about from living abroad that may be lacking in some UK students. All of them have enjoyed sharing something of their life and background with me and I think that this has led to happier relationships and communication. But I have learnt that there is not one way to supervise PhDs.'*
>
> *Research supervisor – Arts and Humanities*

Perhaps a challenge to the content of both Chapters 5 and 6 is that it requires supervisory effort, and supervisors are already very busy people. However, it is our honest contention that investing time in the basics of the relationship will increase efficiency in the long term, meaning that the relationship will work and therefore decrease problems and grievances in the long term.

Once the basics are covered and the relationship is established on a solid foundation, then the serious business of doctoral level scholarship can begin. The doctoral process is, of course, a holistic one where different skills and attributes can be brought to bear on different areas of the study. Over the next six chapters we will cross-reference and examine each of the Dublin Descriptors in turn and examine how the designed alliance of supervisor and doctoral researcher can work together to develop a candidate who:

- can demonstrate a systematic understanding of a field of study and mastery of the skills and methods of research associated with that field;
- can demonstrate the ability to conceive, design, implement and adapt a substantial process of research with scholarly integrity;
- has made a contribution through original research that extends the frontier of knowledge by developing a substantial body of work, some of which merits national or international refereed publication;

- is capable of critical analysis, evaluation and synthesis of new and complex ideas;
- can communicate with their peers, the larger scholarly community and with society in general about their areas of expertise;
- can be expected and able to promote, within academic and professional contexts, technological, social or cultural advancement in a knowledge-based society.

Chapter 7

Laying Firm Intellectual Foundations

The first of the Dublin Descriptors – that a successful doctoral candidate will 'have demonstrated a systematic understanding of a field of study and mastery of the skills and methods of research associated with that field' – can be seen as the establishment of the basic skill set required of a researcher at doctoral level in the relevant discipline. This chapter will encompass general research approaches and skills beyond the more technical and specific, including an understanding of why these skills and methods matter, and where the research fits within the field. This is what differentiates the doctoral researcher from the craftsman or technician.

> *A bad workman never finds a good tool.*
>
> *French proverb*

The broad requirements are that the researcher know their field, and can define its scope, as well as understanding the skills and methods within it, including discerning which are the most appropriate to use, and which are not.

Supervisory Enquiries about Research Skills

- Can you recall learning the basic skills of research? How did you learn them? Were you taught them, or did you learn by observation or experimentation?
- How much bibliographic research do you now conduct yourself? Are you up to date with the necessary tools and techniques? How much do you rely on the input of your students here?
- How much of your time do you spend on hands-on research? Are you up to date with the necessary tools and techniques?
- Which of the research and bibliographic skills come naturally to you? Which do you have to put conscious effort into?

Systematic Understanding of Field of Study

We frequently use the analogy of a sand-filled hourglass to describe a piece of research. The top of the hourglass is wide, where the context of the research is considered: the field of study, the relevant existing literature, the rationale for and definition of the scope of the current research. The neck of the hourglass narrows, as does the focus of the piece, where the precise details of the research methodology, results and analysis are discussed. Then the hourglass broadens once again as the work focuses outwards to the contribution the research will make and the impact it will have.

This chapter considers the top of the hourglass – the context and input. Later chapters will address the other parts of the hourglass.

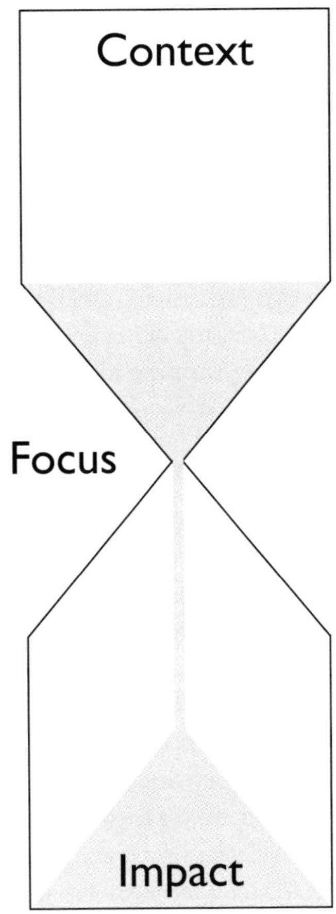

Figure 7.1 Thesis structure represented as an hourglass

> *'I get my students to do two things in the first couple of weeks. I want to get them into the lab so I can see whether they know the right techniques and to check on their general approach. I also give them something very open-ended to find out how they handle that, such as to write a short report on current trends in their area. I want them to be able to function without me – but I need to see that they do things in the proper way.'*
>
> *Research supervisor – Biology*

As a supervisor comes to know their student as an individual (see Chapters 5 and 6), one of the areas worth focusing on is how much experience the student already has of the field of study and the context within which they are working. Some students come to a doctorate with relatively little knowledge of the field, others with significant up-to-date understanding. Regardless of the student's current knowledge, among the first skills a doctoral candidate must develop or hone are bibliographic skills and critical reading.

Bibliographic Skills and Critical Reading

The foundation of this skill set is knowledge and use of library resources relevant to the research area. It is likely that incoming candidates will have many of these skills, but it is worth supervisors verifying this to their satisfaction. This can be especially important for international students, who may be unfamiliar with national or institutional procedures and resources. It will be a worthwhile investment of time for supervisors to familiarize themselves with what training and resources are available in order to be able to point students in the right direction at this early stage.

Incidentally, I have lost count of the number of times I have been met with amazement when I have talked of the willingness of university subject librarians or information specialists to talk with doctoral researchers. Yet it should be unsurprising that library professionals have great skill and knowledge of the resources that are available and how best to access them.

Supervisory Enquiries about Bibliographic Knowledge

- Do you know who the subject librarian or information specialist is for your discipline in your university library? Have you had a conversation with them?

- Would you consider asking them to spend a little time with your incoming doctoral researchers, perhaps orienting them in the library? (And would this be appropriate?)
- Are you confident you are up to date with the resources available in your university as well as those available online?

Beyond this basic mastery of locating resources, something considerably more is required to make use of them: the ability to read and comprehend with some discernment as a prelude to defining a research question – being able to say 'not that' as well as 'yes this' on a suitable scale. This is the essence of systematic understanding of a field.

In order to achieve this, students need to develop their first real research sense: what the British colloquially call 'nous', meaning to read not only what they've been directed to, but to intuitively chase references and to read around and outside the subject. In addition, it is necessary to begin to exercise judgements about the sources and the sorts of questions they may pose. One recent example I came across was a student of international law who didn't pause to consider that a paper published by a Jewish author in a Jerusalem-based journal might potentially have an agenda when writing about the legal status of Palestine.

Supervisory Ideas about Dealing with Academic Literature

As an initial exercise before approaching the idea of a literature review, ask your student to produce a critical analysis of a single paper. This will most likely be selected by you, but can be negotiated with them. On this occasion, emphasize that the review needn't be written in fluent academic prose. You could even suggest it be in note or bullet-point form, because it is the ideas that are important. Give them some key points to note:

- What is the central message of the paper?
- What is good about the research?
- What has been left undone?
- What questions do you have about the research?
- What is the author's bias? (Do all authors always have bias? Do you?)

The aim is not to seek the 'right' answers, but to convey the idea that everything needs to be read with a degree of criticality. It may add a dimension to this process if you prepare your own answers to these questions, but do make sure to focus on the student's contribution, at least in the first instance.

The idea of reading with discernment needs to be imbued from the start of the doctorate, and continued throughout the process. This skill will need to develop into full critical analysis, which is addressed in Chapter 10. But the importance of maintaining an up-to-date awareness of the wider literature in the field needs to be borne in mind and included in supervisory discussions throughout the doctorate. This applies not just to the text-based, discursive and literary disciplines, but the technical and hard fact-based sciences as well. Again, this sounds obvious, but it is surprising how little time is actually spent doing this.

This can have obvious advantages, as well as some that are less obvious. As a doctoral candidate, in the context of a graduate research group, I once loaned my copy of a paper to be discussed to a senior academic. When she returned it to me, she thanked me for the loan and commented as an aside, 'I thought your notes were well taken.' This affirmation of my responses to the text did more to increase my confidence in my ability to engage critically with the literature than she could have imagined.

Supervisory Ideas about Reading Groups

Where possible, could you encourage your students to become part of a reading group, or could you organize this? It's likely that you will need to facilitate it in the early stages, but ideally it should become something that more experienced research students can eventually facilitate, which is itself an additional developmental process for them.

There are a number of potential approaches here:

- Ask all members of the group to read the same paper then engage with the sorts of analytical questions set out in the task above.
- Ask one student to prepare their analysis of a paper and circulate this in advance. The rest of the group then engage in a discussion of the

analysis, rather than the original paper. Questions here might include: Are your notes well taken? Are your contributions valid?

As the process continues, the students can nominate the papers to be read. They clearly need to be of sufficiently general relevance to the rest of the group for it to make sense, but they need not be directly related to their own research projects since the purpose is to ensure that your students are regularly hearing academic opinions other than yours, and that they are building their confidence and capability in conversing in academic and scholarly English while also reading with discernment.

One potential challenge here is the reticence of some students, particularly those not accustomed to the 'Western' education system, to challenge the ideas of those perceived as 'superior' (see Chapter 4). Our experience is that this is often extended from present academics to authors of published work, with the sentiments 'If Professor X wrote it in a published article, it must be true' and 'How can I possibly challenge Dr Y's words?' being very common. Within the safety of a designed alliance, these attitudes must be challenged if the doctoral student is to succeed.

Supervisors can encourage their students to challenge the ideas they are presented with in a number of different ways. Observing how other academics do it is one way – although it must be confessed that this may be too great a leap for someone who is struggling to overcome culturally defined deference. A bright, outspoken, confident academic who loudly decries a colleague's work in friendly but colourful language may be seen as too brash and disrespectful to be a useful role-model. Within the designed alliance of a student's relationship with their supervisor, it is possible to strike an appropriate balance, and even to discuss the student's reaction to the ways work is discussed within the department or research group. This process is consistent with a critical teacher or a liberating coach style of supervision. These ideas of challenge will be explored further in Chapter 9.

As well as developing the linguistic, analytical and critical skills of the student, being an active part of a research group will also, if well facilitated, have a practical outcome in terms of building a supportive research community – with all the associated pastoral benefits. However, it should be noted that a facilitated reading group where the more experienced students lead and everyone takes a turn to suggest a paper and the group share the debate is potentially very different to the group supervisions that occur in larger team-led research departments. The process needs to occur in addition to supervision, not instead of it.

This kind of process will not only build confidence, but will help to maintain scholarly integrity as the student develops a healthy relationship with the literature under examination. It also provides a sound basis on which to build research design, which we will discuss further in Chapter 8.

As useful as it is to discuss literature with a research group or more widely, at some point the student must focus on material that is truly relevant to their own work and produce some kind of critical review:

> *'I was asked to write a short literature review. I had no idea what this was.'*
>
> *Research student – Biomedical Sciences, Malaysia*

As it forms part of almost every piece of research-based writing from the earliest stages onwards, it is hard not to assume that everyone will know what a literature review is and what its purpose is. However, the dozens of occasions when I have met both international and UK doctoral candidates who have had the same response as the Malaysian student quoted above are testament to the fact that this knowledge can't be taken for granted.

Supervisory Enquiries about the Literature Review

- How would you define a literature review?
- What would a great doctoral literature review look like – and how would it differ from something you would accept from an undergraduate?
- In terms of their candidature, when would you ask a student to write a literature review? What would be the purpose of this piece?

Doctoral students frequently talk to us about two apparently opposite problems when they consider the literature in their discipline: 'Nothing has been written about my topic' or 'There is so much that I don't know where to start.' Of course, the reality is that these are two aspects of the same problem – that the scope of the literature search has been inappropriately defined.

The scope of the literature review needs to be defined in order to provide an adequate foundation for the research to be undertaken. Often an initial literature review is intended to do just this, to find out what is already out there, to understand where the field is strong and where there are gaps. This necessarily encompasses a wide range of different types of literature in order to ensure a sufficient range is discussed.

It is clear to those who have been working within academic research for any length of time that not all literature is of the same status. However, the wise supervisor will remember that academic 'nous' or the 'nose' for literature which provides an instinct about what is useful and citable and what should be viewed with some caution is not simply common sense, but must be learned. When an international researcher begins their journey into literature, with so many things being strange (as outlined in Chapter 5), a little guidance early on about what is 'good' in terms of sources may be very timely. Figure 7.2 offers one way to discuss this with research students, to help them identify the different types of literature that they may come across and wish to use.

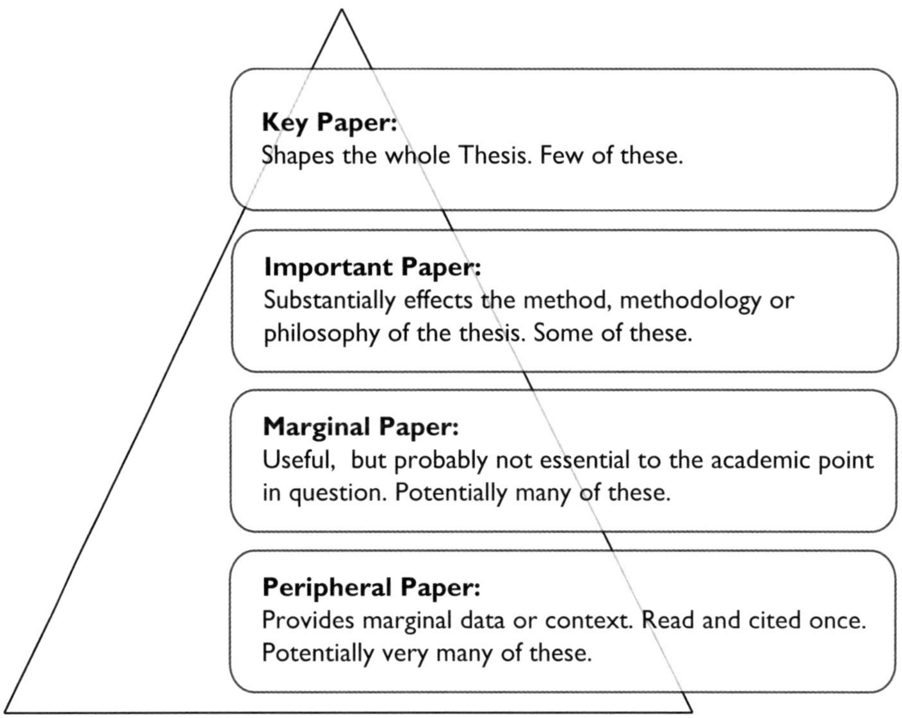

Figure 7.2 Categories of literature referenced

There is of course a deeper and wider base to this pyramid of all the material that is in the public domain, most obviously Wikipedia, which may be apparently of relevance but actually of little real value because of its lack of academic rigour.

Supervisory Enquiries about Literary Hierarchies

- Other than your supervisor, who were the key authors in your field when you started research, which were the key papers, and how did your work compare to theirs?
- How did you discover which these keynote papers were?
- How could you facilitate this discovery process within your students?

Supervisory Ideas about Literary Hierarchies

- Ask your student to describe what makes 'good' literature? What characteristics does it have? (How do impact factors influence this?)
- Which papers are keynote for your research?
- As the student's understanding of the literature grows, look together at the range of publications and encourage the student to decide which pieces fit where in the pyramid in Figure 7.2.
- What do these choices mean for the type of Thesis the student will create?

To gain a systematic understanding of a field of study means not only appreciating the established 'truth' in the accepted theoretical work, but also grasping the areas of ongoing discussion and debate among researchers. Such understanding may require the researcher to look beyond the confines of their own speciality, or their supervisor's, to see how their work fits into with the wider discipline. As we mentioned above, the notion that the doctorate must be placed in context is vital, but again, this awareness often comes too late to the student, whether for cultural reasons or due to technical unfamiliarity with academic parlance and norms.

For many students, both international and UK, the value of their research is not something that will occupy their thoughts until towards the end of the process. However, it is also true that an appreciation of the significance of what a student is researching can enhance their understanding of the field. I had a Damascene moment in the second year of my doctorate when I was listening to an obligatory guest lecture on a topic I believed to be irrelevant to my speciality. Suddenly I saw the relevance of a piece of theory to my work, and of my work to that piece of theory. The conversation I had with the guest lecturer (a researcher of international renown) led to the swapping of data and my receiving an acknowledgement in her next publication. More significantly than this, my appreciation of the field deepened and broadened in one moment of clarity.

Mastery of Skills and Methods

One of the delights of research for many academics is the actual mechanics of the work. This may be one of the reasons why academics who take on senior administrative roles within a department or university often relinquish those roles at the end of (usually) a fixed term with alacrity, keen to get back to doing 'real' research.

There are many and various skills involved in the actual mechanics of research, but they have one feature in common: they must be mastered before they can be used effectively. Whether it is the analysis of ancient texts, the sequencing of a particular strand of DNA, the gathering and interpreting of statistical data or anything else, these skills are those of a specialist, and must be meticulously learned.

There is more than one way to approach a research question, and it is rarely the case that there is one single right way to conduct a piece of research. More commonly there are just different ways that offer a variety of possibilities. Students who become fixated on finding 'the answer' or 'the right way' often find themselves frustrated. And this frustration can exacerbated culturally when there is a background of dogma in education. What there must be, of course, is a justifiable decision as to which approach will be taken, but this may feel like a huge – if not impossible – challenge for the research student to face.

Supervisory Enquiries about Comparative Approaches

- What are the essential skills and techniques in your discipline?
- Which are the ones you use most often in your research? What other possibilities are there?
- How do you select the methodology you will employ for a given research project?
- Do you know what previous experience your student has in the key research skills?

Supervisory Ideas about Comparative Approaches

Encourage your student to compare two possible approaches to a question and to provide a reasoned argument for using one rather than the other. You could repeat this a few times where it is reasonable that they might select different approaches in different contexts. Obviously it is important here to choose situations where genuine alternatives are available.

When a supervisor asks their student to compare and contrast two methodologies, the ostensible purpose is simply and purely a methodological one. However, beneath this aim is a deeper one – for the student to understand the publishable quality of academic work, to engage with it critically, and actually to voice an opinion. Making such a choice requires sophisticated learning skills, those of synthesis and evaluation of information; it is worth making this explicit to international doctoral students who may not have been accustomed to being asked to use such skills and apply them in such a way in their previous academic environments.

Even when it seems that there is a relatively obvious way forward, it is important for doctoral candidates to understand why they have chosen a particular method. Between us, we have had many conversations with doctoral candidates who, on being asked why they had adopted their approach, responded along the lines: 'Because that's what my supervisor told me to do.'

The principal and possibly most important characteristic attribute of a successful doctoral candidate is their ability to contextualize their work and to place this high-level knowledge and understanding into a framework that gives it a purpose. Put more simply, a technician must understand and be able to use one technique. A doctoral candidate must understand at least two (if not considerably more), be able to understand and decide which one is better suited to the nature and purpose of the study, and then be able to defend that decision.

In order to make an evaluative decision about which tools and techniques to use, it is necessary to consider the purpose of research in itself, and of the specific research to be undertaken in particular. As with many aspects of this chapter, this thought process may come so naturally to experienced academics that they are likely to pay it little attention. But a student who has just arrived in the UK may either have considered this deeply as part of their decision-making process concerning whether to pursue a doctorate, or (more commonly in our experience) may have not considered it at all.

Supervisory Enquiries about Research Value

- What would you consider 'research' to be?
- What is the value of research in your field?
- How would you describe the nature, purpose and value of the particular piece of work you are supervising?
- How will you ensure that your perception of the nature, purpose and value of your student's research is at least appreciated, if not shared, by your student?

Irrespective of issues concerning the impact of research, research must make a contribution to the field at least, and likely to the academy or to society more generally, in order to be valid. Therefore, a successful candidate must be able to appreciate the scope of what they are doing, must be able to read critically, to question the received wisdom in the field and have sufficient literary and information skills to appreciate that (regardless of field) there are always multiple methods, each have advantages and disadvantages, and all of them can be improved.

Supervisor and Student Discussion Points about Research Value

In practice, a conversation focusing on the following questions is not usually part of the supervisor–doctoral candidate engagement. However, we believe that it could add significant value to the experience:

- What is research?
- What is research *for*?
- What makes for *good* research?
- What is *doctoral* research? (How is this different to the bachelor's, master's or professional research and development?)
- What is *this* research for?

It is important to devote sufficient time to the development of the skills required for the conduct of good-quality research. That is what this chapter has been concerned with. But some of the skills will only really develop with time and experience. Likewise, the ability to scope and understand the significance of the research and its likely findings will only be fully possible during the course of undertaking research worthy of a doctorate. Therefore, it is time to move on to consider the conception, design and implementation of the research process.

Chapter 8
Scholarly Construction

The second of the Dublin Descriptors states that a successful doctoral candidate will have 'demonstrated the ability to conceive, design, implement and adapt a substantial process of research with scholarly integrity'. The ability to construct an achievable, viable, tractable research question is a rare skill. Few have this skill naturally, and it is frequently an iterative process, demonstrating the ability to ascertain what in the area is important, disentangling the chaos of related issues by trial and 'error'. This chapter examines this skill, as well as the ability to select appropriate methods and techniques to answer the research question effectively; to design, possibly by tweaking selected methods in order to suit the question or questions perfectly. Of course, there is a need to put those methods into practice and carry the research out with honour and reliability, upholding the standards both the academic and wider community hold to be significant. This is a learning experience for anyone, but for a doctoral candidate from an educational system where questioning of any kind is not encouraged, this is represents a significant challenge.

The Ability to 'Conceive'

Knowledge without wisdom is like water in the sand.
Guinean proverb

Early in my time as a research student, the wise head of department said with substantial passion: 'Intelligence isn't about having all the answers. It's about asking interesting questions.' Initially I was rather intimidated by this. What if I didn't ask interesting questions? What did it say about me if my questions weren't interesting enough? Would I be able to conceive a suitable research project?

This academic had a reputation among the graduates in the department for being an inspiring and supportive supervisor for his PhD students. He also took opportunities to chat with other research students and was frequently to be found asking questions and encouraging others to ask questions. He affirmed this practice often by loudly proclaiming 'Well, that's an empirical question!' while beaming with joy at the interesting enquiry that had piqued his curiosity.

Soon I found that I felt more intelligent in his presence rather than being intimidated by him. I was being encouraged to ask as many questions as possible, and to focus on the ones that were interesting.

Supervisory Enquiries about Research Conception

- How do you conceive research projects?
- Where do your ideas come from?
- How do you know which questions are worth pursuing?
- How could you encourage your international students to formulate interesting questions?

To conceive a project – whether it is the whole doctoral Thesis or a smaller component part of it – is about more than simply asking questions – otherwise most small children would be expert researchers! But sometimes a question captures a child's imagination and they set about working out how to find the answer.

People often observe to us that many from non-UK educational systems are unaccustomed to asking questions. This comment comes from both supervisors, who find the lack of questions frustrating, and from international students, who are wary of engaging in an interrogative process that is contrary to the way they have been trained to learn. So how can the supervisor help an international student navigate this treacherous path?

Supervisory Ideas about Intellectual Conception

- Give your student a notebook, emphasizing that this is theirs, and that you won't ask to see it. Encourage them to use this notebook to jot down any and every question that occurs to them.

- When appropriate in terms of the project, ask your student to choose three or four questions from the notebook they think might be worth following up and to bring those questions to your next meeting.
- When you meet, ask them which they think is the strongest question or offers the most potential for their research.

The important aspect of this is for the student who is diffident about asking questions to understand that by asking questions they are not challenging their supervisor, but probing the field of academic study. By changing the emphasis here, many students who are hesitant to question those they feel are superior may become more confident in conceiving their own research questions and projects.

The Ability to 'Design'

Simply asking the questions, however interesting those questions might be, does not guarantee a great research project. Rather, it is a key academic skill to look at the question and to discern a way of answering it empirically.

Of course, the supervisor will have substantial experience in the research design process. The traditional way to encourage a student to develop this skill would be to get them to 'have a go'. It is wise to take this procedure slowly, designing and trying in small steps, then critiquing the conception, design and implementation of an original research project, either by pointing out problems (the critical teacher style) or by asking questions (the liberating coach style) to encourage the student to think about their research from a range of perspectives. But how the supervisor does this will have a huge impact on the confidence of the student and effectiveness of the learning process.

Supervisory Enquiries about Research Design

Look at the questions below. What impact might they have on a budding researcher:

- 'Do you really think this is going to work?'
- 'How will you get over the problem of X?'

- 'I can see a problem with this – can you take some time after this meeting to think about what that might be?'
- 'What do you think I'm going to say the problem with this is?'

Although these types of questions are intended to prompt a student to think further about their work, it's likely that the student has already thought about them as far as they believe they are able. Therefore leading questions tend to provoke a stress response rather than an intellectual exercise: the student loses face by having a mistake pointed out rather than being inspired to consider a solution.

- What sorts of questions would be helpful in your discipline?

The challenge faced by the supervisor here is to strike the balance between allowing the student to try out research design processes and sharing their own experience with the student. It would be a callous move to see a fatal flaw in a research design and to allow an inexperienced researcher to plunge headlong into what can be foreseen to be a dead end at best.

However, clearly the supervisor does not need to know all the answers. One supervisor told us a story about a colleague. This colleague had been struggling with a research problem for over ten years when he decided to give it to a doctoral candidate as a challenge. The student, perhaps unsurprisingly, failed to solve the problem, but became very skilled in the process at designing experiments and understanding the results of each one, thus successfully attaining his doctorate.

Supervisory Ideas about Creativity and Problem-solving

If you feel your international student is struggling with problem-solving, the following techniques may help.

- Ask your student to imagine how they would approach the problem if they had infinite resources and no limitations of any kind.
- Ask your student to imagine the worst research project ever.

These tactics help to turn around a student's thought processes and can result in some productive creative thoughts.

- Sit with a student and encourage them to brainstorm ideas about a project while you take notes. Try not to comment on the value of the ideas or to ask too many questions about a single idea, but simply record the thoughts so that the student can evaluate them and explore them more fully later.

The Ability to 'Implement'

No man can perfectly empty a pot with a ladle.
South African proverb

Once a research project has been conceived and designed, it must be put into practice or the research will only ever be a good idea. Doctoral study requires the student to do something, to try something, even if they are not 100 per cent confident it will work. The ideas must be implemented, meaning that the project must become tangible, and therefore manageable.

When we run project management sessions, we frequently refer to the work of Stephen Covey, and especially to his first principle: begin with the end in mind. This is a tricky concept for researchers as, by definition, they cannot know the end result of their project – if they did, it wouldn't be research. However, managing a doctoral project means having some idea of what the desired outcome is, what will be 'good enough', what the student's intended result is.

Supervisory Enquiries about Research Vision

- When you set out on a new research project, how do you envisage what the end result will be?
- Funding agencies generally want an idea of the outcome when looking at a proposal – how do you decide how to fill in that part of the application?

Once the end point is established, the planning phase is simply a matter of working out how to get from 'here' to 'there' in the time allowed.

Cultural and educational differences aside, the variety of ways human beings approach planning is wide. Between the three authors of this book, our individual approaches to planning and implementation of a project have differed although our backgrounds and experience are relatively homogenous. So rather than looking for the 'right' way, the challenge for the supervisor is to consider how best to help their student approach this in a way that works both of them.

Supervisory Ideas about Planning

- Ask your student to describe the way they approached a particular – but non-academic – task such as coming to the UK to study. Notice whether they talk with joy about the planning phase. How spontaneous do they appear to be?
- If your student appears to relish planning, this will almost certainly translate into planning research projects carefully, and if there appears to be a problem in implementation, it will almost certainly be a result of a lack of understanding or confidence rather than a failure to organize.
- If your student appears to enjoy spontaneity and their eyes glaze over at the mention of project management, this will frequently translate into an enviable flexibility in response to change, bursts of activity interspersed by periods of conscious or subconscious processing and collection of information, and a mad dash towards the deadline.

Which of these reflects your personal approach? What does this approach give you in terms of benefits for your research? What are the pitfalls?

Inherent in the implementation phase is an element of risk. Within the supervisory relationship a wide range of hazards must be negotiated.

For the supervisor, there is the real risk that their own reputation may be tarnished if the student fails to complete the doctorate successfully. But for the student, particularly one who has sacrificed a good deal by relocating to the UK for doctoral study, the very idea of failure is unthinkable.

Supervisory Enquiries about Risk

- How much is your international student risking by following this course of study? What is at stake for them?
- What do you have to lose if it all goes wrong?
- What impact do the answers to these questions have on your approach to supervising this student?

Of course, the majority of doctoral candidates do pass, but this doesn't mean that there is no risk within the process. Most of the time when the phrase 'risk assessment' comes into a discussion, it's not the whole project that's at risk, but part of it. When a supervisor puts the conception, design and implementation of a research project into the hands of a doctoral student, the responsibility shifts.

In the time before a supervision meeting, students could, as a matter of course, conduct their own risk assessment of any ideas they are about to present to their supervisor. This could be done formally with a pro-forma designed by the supervisor to be appropriate to the specific area of research and used for all their students, or it could be as simple as considering what the potential problems with the approach are. Some questions worth posing in a risk assessment are:

- What could possibly go wrong with this approach?
- How could this approach be sabotaged?
- How would someone criticize this approach if they were determined to be negative?
- How could the results gained from this research be considered invalid?
- What could happen that would render the whole project a failure?

And for each of the above enquiries:

- What would the consequences of this be?

- How bad would this be?
- How likely is this to happen?
- What will you do if the risk is realized?

Bearing in mind the impact of and response to failure, even perceived failure, when the student is more invested in the process than many UK students, it's not surprising that some international students become risk-averse, lacking in confidence to act innovatively or even independently. However, other students who are not experienced in research practice, when given an unprecedented level of autonomy, may aim to do something that is particularly high-risk simply because they are not aware of what 'safe' practice is.

If a student applies these questions to their own work and brings the results of their thinking about the risk of their research to their supervisor when proposing a new research design, they may well have pre-empted some of the constructive criticism the supervisor might offer. A discussion of the implications of the risk assessment can then ensue, with the student's prior thinking informing the discussion as much as the supervisor's greater experience. In addition to the increased effectiveness that results from this, where there is new material for the supervisor to bring in regarding suggested challenges, this can happen as part of a shared risk assessment dialogue, rather than a one-way hierarchical critique.

Clearly, for a project to be implemented successfully, it must be completed in a timely fashion. Submission deadlines for international students are frequently more rigid than for UK students because visas expire, funding is limited and often there are careers to return to. As discussed in Chapter 4, there are times when a supervisor needs to be a project manager.

As I write, I am in the process of juggling two significant but unrelated projects. In order to decide how to use my limited time effectively, I have had to make a number of different decisions: When is the deadline for each task? What is the relative importance of each task? What does each task require of me? So when I note that although both projects are important and have similarly pressing deadlines, one requires more of me intellectually than the other, I know that I must work on that one when I am functioning at my best, whereas the other can be fitted in at times of the day when I am less effective.

Supervisory Enquiries about Efficiency and Effectiveness

- How do you manage your own time on a day-to-day basis, week-to-week and month-to-month?
- What works particularly well for you? What have you tried that didn't work?
- What tips and techniques could you share with your students?

Supervisor and Student Discussion Points

- What is really important to your student?
- What is of primary importance to the project?
- When is the final deadline? How flexible is it?
- What is the next deadline? What needs to be done to meet that deadline?
- When during the day is your student most effective? Are they an early riser, or do they relish working into the night?
- When do they 'slump'?
- What do they need in order to be able to be effective – a variety of tasks, exercise, coffee?

It often helps to have a shared conversation about this, and do be prepared to share your own working preferences – as well as the reality that we can't always have things our own way!

Of course, research ideas don't always come to anything: experiments 'go wrong' or simply don't answer the question they were intended to. This is sometimes to do with the nature of research, but often to do with simply making mistakes. The human error factor is significant in research, and being able to say 'I made a mistake' rather than 'My study didn't work' is a giant leap towards the ability to address problems. Few people find it easy to admit mistakes, but it shouldn't be forgotten that some international students may find this extremely uncomfortable due to a culturally driven resistance to losing face.

Fall seven times, stand up eight.
Japanese proverb

Researchers need, among all the other skills they possess or must develop, a high level of resilience. This is often thought of as a character trait: one is either resilient or not. But the supervisor can play a significant role in helping to develop resilience in a research setting.

Bearing in mind that some (both international and UK) students have come to doctoral study from an educational context where, provided they do as they are told, they will succeed, the impact on a student's self-belief when something goes wrong can be substantial. And when they are struggling with confidence, it is almost inevitable that they will struggle to develop the creative processes necessary to conceive and design research.

When we work with postgraduate students who teach undergraduates, one of the concepts we often raise is the notion of experiential learning. David Kolb's (1984) representation of this as a cycle (see Figure 8.1) is helpful in the research design process too.

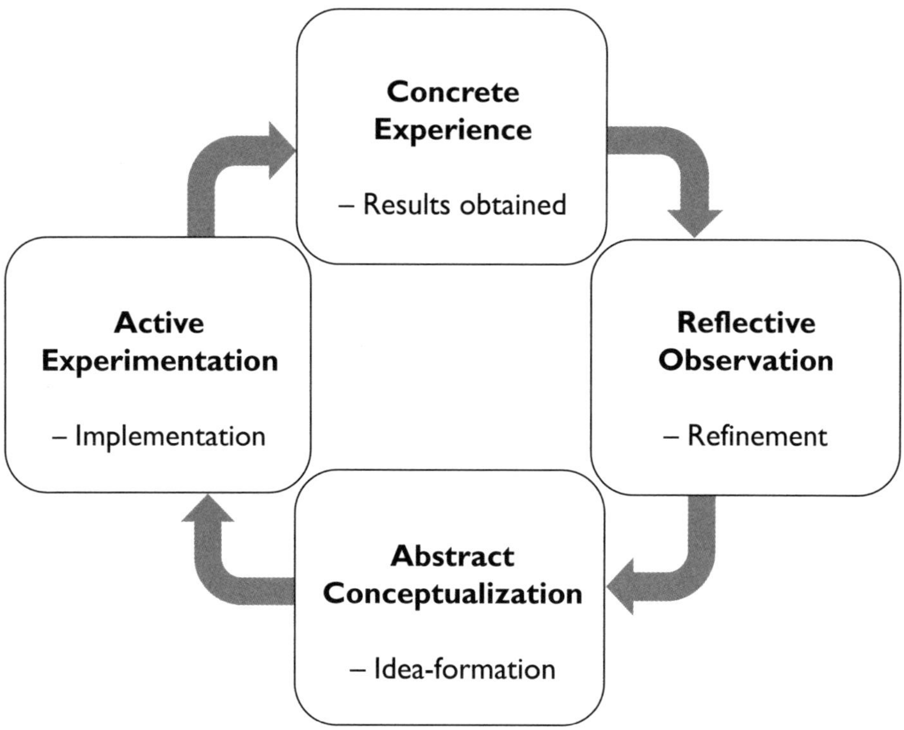

Figure 8.1 Adaptation of Kolb's Experimental Learning Cycle
Source: Based on Kolb (1984).

Developing the skill of research design, implementation and adaptation in many cases follows this pattern. An idea is formed in *abstract conceptualization*, implemented in *active experimentation* and a result obtained as *concrete experience*, which in many cases is not what the researcher originally envisaged. It is necessary to work with the result in *reflective observation*, to reflect on it in order to work out what went well and what went badly, and to plan to do something differently next time in order not only to achieve the hoped-for results, but also to demonstrate the highest levels of scholarly integrity.

Supervisory Enquiries about Experiential Learning

- Which stages of Kolb's Experimental Learning Cycle are you most comfortable in? Which do you struggle with?
- What about your student?

If you're unsure about your student's preferences and issues here, notice which elements of a short pilot project seem to energize them the most.

There are many ways the supervision relationship can come into its own here and aid the learning. A student is likely to gravitate naturally to one of these stages, and often a lack of confidence will result in becoming stuck.

Supervisory Ideas about Formulating Concepts

When a new piece of empirical work is in the offing, you could provide a question sheet for your student to complete prior to meeting with you. This could be really simple, provided it is clear that you expect the answers to be full. The following are examples of questions you could include.

- What is the question you want to answer in this phase? What information do you need to answer it?
- Which models or theories are relevant here?
- What are your options for finding this information?
- What variety of techniques could you use?
- Which option will you choose first, and why?

The notion here is that by providing an 'exercise' for a student to complete while not in the supervisor's presence, the student is allowed time to process the questions and their implications. A pro-forma demonstrates that the questions aren't challenges to their intellectual ability, but an articulation of questions all researchers must ask themselves. At the same time, it establishes that the student is responsible for thinking through the foundation of the research. In order to minimize paperwork, we would suggest keeping the questions general so that the same pro-forma can be used over and over again with different students and with the same students in different phases.

A discussion – either in person or by email – about the answers to these questions can give a student confidence that they have planned sufficiently. If they lack self-assurance, it may be worth the supervisor referring to the risk analysis questions detailed above, hopefully demonstrating to the student that the inherent riskiness of research is managed and they can move on to active experimentation with confidence.

Once both the student and the supervisor are happy that the empirical work has been adequately planned, there is nothing more be done but to launch in and do something. It can often help to encourage the student to talk about what they are doing – particularly if their work is taking them away from the department. This will generally help them to feel connected.

Supervisory Ideas about Progress Recording

- If your student enjoys engaging with social media, could they use this platform to actively record their progress?
- Could the postgraduates in your department set up a discussion forum so they can post comments about what they're doing, thus keeping in touch with each other's progress?
- If your student is away from the department on fieldwork, could you encourage them to write a blog detailing their work and their experiences?

Keeping good records of exactly what is done is great research practice and has been acknowledged as such for years. In my experience, laboratory-based scientists are well practised in keeping a 'lab book', and those whose research doesn't rely on laboratories could learn a good deal from this procedure. But it's not necessary do this with a physical book. The ideas above allow the supervisor to examine what the student is doing, but the primary purpose is record-keeping.

Many people get stuck at the juncture between the active experimentation and concrete experience stages, where the need arises to acknowledge what the result of the empirical work has been, and the reflective observation stage, where it is necessary to consider what the implications of this result are. Frequently this is a time of disappointment and feelings of failure if the work hasn't answered the questions the student wanted to address.

Within the UK academic setting, much as we all like to think that we are independent and self-reliant, there are frequent 'failures', and the plain truth of the matter is that while some adults are naturally confident and resilient, some need a little encouragement in order to get back on the research bicycle.

An additional challenge here is that introverted personality types are more common in academia than they are in the general population (Briggs-Myers and Myers 1980), and this tends to be compounded by a perception of the necessity for individual success. One of the manifestations of this is the tendency to isolate oneself, particularly in times of disappointment. Of course, when a student comes from an educational or cultural background where 'failure' is unacceptable, the implications of admitting that a piece of empirical work has not yielded the results that were hoped for mean that the situation is even more complicated.

Supervisory Enquiries about Dealing with Setbacks

- How do you know when your student has had a setback of some kind? Some will tell you, but many won't be so forthcoming.
- What does it mean if your student 'goes quiet' and doesn't contact you as often as you would expect? Is there likely to be cause for concern?

While a short period of private 'grieving' over a disappointment may well be appropriate, if this is extended, it can tend to lead to a significant drop in self-confidence. Supervisors can help their students to deal with disappointments in a way that is constructive, reflecting objectively on the results and – crucially – adapting the plans with a view to moving on.

Supervisory Ideas about Reviewing Experience

When you know your student is doing some empirical work (because you've discussed its planning and risk assessment), why not set up an agreement that they will email you on a given date to let you know how it's going?

If you sense that they are likely to tell you what they think you want to hear, why not ask them to answer specific questions, such as:

- How did it go? What did you find? Was the result what you expected?
- What was good about it? What was difficult about it?
- Given the opportunity, what would you do differently another time?
- What do you think the next step should be?

By asking questions like these you're making it clear that you expect some things to have been difficult or unexpected. If you can set these questions up as standard even before the work has been done, it will help to reinforce the message that research is littered with pitfalls and that this does not (necessarily) reflect on the individual student and their overall chances of success.

When you know your student has had a setback of some kind, make contact and encourage a meeting soon afterwards. This could be simply to check in with them and see how they're doing, or it could be to encourage them to focus on what they have learned from the experience and to plan for future integration of the learning into the research.

Several international students commented that because of research setbacks, they had hidden from or avoided their supervisor. If they were encouraged to experience setbacks not as failures but as opportunities to learn offering valid opportunities for them to discuss their work and progress with their supervisor, the whole process might become a little easier.

Supervisory Enquiries about Disappointment

- How do you share your own disappointments (such as rejected papers or grant proposals) with a student when they occur, and make your response to these setbacks transparent?

Leading by example is great, and sometimes that example needs to be explicit.

Generally, the response to a fully frank, honest assessment of what has happened will lead naturally back to the beginning of the learning cycle: planning what to do next. By asking the student to assess what the next step should be, the supervisor allows the student to put all the wisdom they have accrued into action and build on it as the cycle continues.

Throughout this chapter we have assumed that all the work done will be completed 'with scholarly integrity', as articulated in the Dublin Descriptor that provides the title of the chapter. It is essential for the supervisor to keep watch for transgressions of this integrity in the planning, risk assessment and empirical phases, and to challenge them when they arise. Depending on the nature of the transgression, it may be that a fairly gentle challenge could be appropriate, simply pointing out the problem and asking for a solution. With regular contact and discussion of the content of work, problems will be seen early on and the danger of plagiarism avoided.

In Chapter 7 we suggested the possibility of research students reading papers and discussing them together for mutual benefit. That principle applies here too, as it is always easier to see the flaws in another's work than to spot the problems in one's own.

It would take little effort for a group of research students in cognate research fields to bring along their experiment designs, systematic literature search criteria, questionnaires and so on to show one another. An individual student could bring their own work and present their questions, approach and rationale for doing whatever they're about to do, and allow other students to critique it. Our experience is that when a person knows that their own work is about to be subjected to critique, they are likely to be gentle and constructive in critiquing another's efforts. If required, the following questions provide a framework that can be useful:

- What are the good points about this approach?
- What kind of results do you think this will offer?
- Are there any visible gaps in what the approach will provide?
- Is there any flaw you think might endanger the validity of the project?
- What do you suggest doing that would solve the problems you have identified?
- What single change would you make to improve this?

The conception, design and implementation of research represents the core of what a research student will be doing throughout the duration of their candidature. In terms of their experience while registered at a UK university, the relationships international students have with their supervisors with regard to this aspect of the doctorate are crucial.

The skills required to conceive, design and deliver a project are highly prized in any field, and are requirements for skilled research assistants or laboratory technicians. In the next chapter we will investigate how supervisors can support doctoral students in making significant contributions to the academic field.

Chapter 9
Making an Intellectual Contribution

Copying everyone else all the time,
the monkey will cut his throat.

Zulu proverb

The third Dublin Descriptor states that a successful doctoral candidate will have 'made a contribution through original research that extends the frontier of knowledge by developing a substantial body of work, some of which merits national or international refereed publication'. When we ask postgraduates about the purpose of a doctorate, the idea of making a contribution to knowledge is usually high on the list. But the fact that it's the easiest purpose to recognize doesn't necessarily mean it's the best understood. Indeed, our experience is that in discussions with students, it's often quite poorly understood, in terms of detail at least:

> *'I did not, I think, grasp what was meant when I read what was a PhD.'*
>
> *Research student, Sri Lanka*

For supervisors, it is of paramount importance that students have a clear idea of the requirements here. Such an understanding will form the foundation of the developing intellectual independence. Getting it right early on should lead to the potential for much lighter-touch supervision later in the doctoral process, such as the liberating coach style of supervision described in Chapter 4.

Making an academic contribution is likely to be the aspect where most supervisors feel best able to support their students. It needs to build in and on the systematic understanding of the field, including critical ability and research design. But making a contribution goes significantly beyond these, and is about the production of real research outputs, which are results and then the analysis of those results. It is also the part of the doctorate that concerns production: writing a Thesis for submission.

What does this idea of intellectual contribution mean for students, and for their supervisors?

Encouraging Independence

This third Dublin Descriptor requires the student and their supervisor to believe that the research is of sufficient quality to warrant being written up for publication. There needs to be a degree of confidence-building within this process: the student needs to become sufficiently confident in their own competence to share their work. They need to have confidence in the project, how it's researched, their results, and fundamentally their role as the chief agent in all these matters. This confidence then needs to be married with understanding and with evidence of what level and standard is required for their work to represent a contribution, and so merit publication:

> *'Confidence is necessary, but don't come with an "I am the best" attitude.'*
>
> *Research student – information withheld*

How can supervisors support their students in this necessary process of developing their own intellectual confidence? What (additional) issues will there be for international students? And what time-efficient approaches can supervisors use to achieve these ends?

Encouragement may need to take different forms for different students, and may well need to be given in different forms by different supervisors, as discussed in Chapter 4. This latter point may be key: if the encouragement doesn't feel authentic, then the student won't believe it, so it will serve no positive function. Indeed, it may well undermine the student's faith in what their supervisor says, possibly extending to other matters as well. Encouragement therefore requires empathy from the supervisor in order to discern the needs of the student, and authenticity for their message to be believed. Some of these issues are expanded upon below when we discuss feedback on written work in more detail.

To be effective, encouragement needs to be heard. We frequently encounter postgraduate students who feel they do not know what their supervisor thinks of their work. When this is discussed with them, it often transpires that they've been told on a number of occasions that everything is 'OK', yet they still maintain that they don't know their supervisor's opinion of their work. There are potentially two problems here:

1. the supervisor's meaning of 'OK';

2. the student's understanding of 'OK'.

Does the supervisor mean 'It's OK. It's exactly where it needs to be,' or 'It's OK. Just OK. Barely scraping along. A low pass at best'? And, irrespective of what the supervisor means, which of these does the student 'hear' – or rather, how do they interpret the phrase? There is the potential for this sort of gap in mutual understanding in any supervisory relationship, but the potential is likely to be greater where international students are involved.

Whichever meaning the supervisor intends or the student understands, it's likely that the information given by such phrases is too minimal anyway. 'It's OK' lacks any detail about how the work is 'OK', what about it's 'OK' and what needs to be done to maintain or improve its 'OK-ness'. In their communication about the work – its progress, level, achievement, quality, 'publishability' – both supervisor and student need to try to use a few more words and be specific.

Supervisory Ideas about Specificity

When you think your student's work is 'OK', perhaps you should consider saying:

- 'Your work is right on track/good/excellent.'
- 'Your work is OK (right on track/good/excellent) because it ....'
- 'Specifically, X aspect of your work is OK (right on track/good/excellent), but Y aspect of your work needs ....'

In addition, how could you encourage your students, when you tell them their work is OK, to respond by asking questions like:

- 'And is OK what you'd be expecting at this stage?'
- 'Do you mean "OK for this point" or "OK for a completed doctorate"?'
- 'Are there parts/aspects that are not OK?'

Much benefit could be gained by modelling these practices when you receive feedback from colleagues in front of your student.

The challenges of developing the sort of dialogue illustrated in the box above may be manifold. At the most basic level there will be individual preferences as to how to package this sort of information and how to process it. Some people respond best to comments which acknowledge the personal effort they have put into a task, others prefer their feedback to relate solely to the result of their labours and feel uncomfortable with anything else. This difference is not so much culturally as individually determined, but the issues may be more acute, and potentially less visible, where international students are concerned. For example, it can be a huge obstacle if there is a requirement to seemingly challenge the words of a superior:

> *'It was very frustrating. Even at the end, I couldn't get her [student] to challenge. I ran out of ideas in the end, it was too much effort. I know this was my failure.'*
>
> *Research supervisor – Civil Engineering*

Supervisors therefore need to ask themselves whether they are sure that their students could actually ask questions about statements in the manner illustrated above. Hopefully they will be developing skills and experience in criticality, but at the start such criticality is focused externally on published research only. The supervisor's task, then, is to encourage such criticality in relation to the process of supervision, and thence to the development of the student's own work. There are a number of techniques that can be employed to help with this development, some of which are illustrated below.

Supervisory Ideas about Developing Feedback

- To explore the process of reviewing feedback comments, but on material neutral to the student, give your student a paper you are reviewing for a colleague (or other appropriate context) and ask them to review your comments. This could encourage interrogative practice as your student asks clarifying questions: 'What did you mean here?', 'What does this comment refer to?' or 'What action would you expect the writer to take in response to this comment?'
- To develop the critical practice of interrogating your feedback on the student's work, ask your student to reframe your feedback comments. Where appropriate, they might also suggest specific actions to take as a consequence of the comments given. The aim throughout is to check the student's understanding of your comments, and also to

clarify mutual understanding of the comments and of the material being commented upon.

- An interim step in developing the student's skills in interrogating their own feedback might be to involve a second supervisor, and for the student to review one supervisor's comments jointly with the other supervisor.
- A deeper process might be to ask your students to give you feedback on the supervision they are receiving (or a specific aspect of it). You can then model the process of supportive interrogative questioning of this feedback to clarify meaning and understanding. As well as developing the skills being discussed here, this technique can also have clear benefits for the supervision being given, and also the supervisory relationship – provided you are prepared to listen to and, where appropriate, act on this feedback.

A pivotal moment in my own experience of being supervised occurred when my supervisor interrupted a supervisory meeting as he'd received some review comments on a paper he'd submitted. He invited me to go through them with him, which made me feel like a colleague, thus building our relationship, and I saw him responding to feedback and could learn from this model.

Spoken encouragement is often weaker than that which is visible. A supervisor can tell a student that they believe in their work, or they can demonstrate this belief. This can be done in many ways, depending on the choice of supervisory style adopted, as detailed in Chapter 4.

Supervisory Ideas about Demonstrating Encouragement

When might you have the opportunity to:

- introduce your student to your colleagues, and introduce their work as *their* work;
- invite your student to participate in a seminar, symposium or journal you are involved with;
- ask your student's opinion of your work (a draft paper, conference proposal, funding bid or even an undergraduate lecture)?

These sorts of approaches will potentially move the relationship towards the gatekeeping or liberating coach style, and so to relationship-building.

These demonstrations all echo the same practice as that in the story above – by treating a student as a colleague, you can clearly communicate that you believe in their ability to make a contribution through research worthy of publication. One of the clearest benefits of a supervisor showing or demonstrating encouragement and belief in a student's abilities rather than just stating it is that actions tend to translate across linguistic and cultural boundaries more clearly than words do. Behaviour is one clear way supervisors can overcome some of the problems inherent in international supervision.

We hear time and again from postgraduate students who are trying to understand what constitutes a 'contribution'. Many researchers tend to begin their research with a belief that they are seeking to change the world, discover 'the answer' or something similar. This is an impossible ambition, within the doctorate at least, which then hopefully leads to a brief sense of the impossibility of such achievement – 'hopefully', because otherwise the student either has no grasp of what level of research is required, or they have an ego that is likely to lead to much bigger problems in the future. At this point the supervisor must provide the encouraging external push towards *appropriate* self-belief.

As well as the encouragement of feedback and behaviour, the student also needs tangible evidence of quality research and practice against which to compare their own efforts. In this way, both student and supervisor can then consider any work produced alongside such evidence to see how good it really is relative to how good it needs to be:

> *'The thing I found hardest [to] understand was why my supervisor told me that my work was good at the start and then a few weeks later told me that I needed to do much more to make it good enough.'*
>
> *Research student – Engineering, China*

A starting point for the process of understanding what is required should be developing a shared understanding of what the finished doctorate needs to be for it to be 'fit for purpose' in context:

- What is good enough?
- Specifically, what will meet the assessment criteria of the doctorate with reference to previous successful Theses?
- What level of writing is required?

Some agreement needs to be reached about what constitutes 'good enough' for the doctorate. This almost certainly needs to be considered and discussed explicitly, since there can be numerous issues involved. The timing of these discussions is also likely to be important, since perspectives may well change during the process of research, especially in the early phases, as idealism potentially gives way to realism. Fundamentally this is an issue of efficiency: any work beyond 'good enough' may be seen as wasted, since a doctorate is all that can be awarded and no grades are available. As such, any work or ambitions beyond what is 'good enough' need to be carefully justified and agreed by both parties, otherwise completion times may be extended and potentially poor professional habits developed.

Student and Supervisor Discussion Points about Success

It's important to consider with your student their motivations, and your own for supervising, as discussed in Chapter 3. Beyond these motivations, two useful questions to discuss are:

- Do either you or your student regard anything other than the successful award of the doctoral degree to be an essential outcome – publications, experience and so on? If so, is this realistic, and is it agreed between all parties concerned?
- Are there any other parties whose definitions of 'good enough' need to be considered – sponsors, employers (current or future), the host institution and so on? If so, how can these be ascertained and clarified?

The purpose of developing and maintaining a shared understanding of what is 'good enough' in the context of the doctorate is to allow all parties to be clear about what the work should focus on and what's superfluous. This can enable the supervisor to help keep the student on track, steering them away from a distracting conference paper or teaching role, for example. It can equally assist the student in deflecting a supervisor from trying to steer them towards additional experiments, studies or reading that go beyond what's required to obtain the doctorate.

'Good enough' can also be a useful interim measure, be it of reading, critical analysis, experimentation, evaluation of results or writing. The question to be posed before any critique is: 'What's good enough for this stage in the process?'

'Good enough' therefore needs to be related to the context:

- What's good enough to pass the degree?
- What's good enough to constitute a contribution?
- What's good enough to merit refereed publication?

These questions can be explored with reference to the relevant assessment criteria and previous Theses. It is likely that the student will have received such information at some point in their institutional induction process, when they are perhaps least able to comprehend their real meaning and are also more likely to be distracted by much more pressing concerns of housing, settling in, understanding their role and so on. Formally, the regulations are unlikely to be revisited explicitly again except in the context of examiners' assessments at the viva stage. But if the student and supervisor are seeking to understand what constitutes 'fit for purpose', then surely the criteria by which the student's work will be assessed would be a sensible starting point?

Supervisory Ideas about the Doctoral Examination

You could ask your student to review the doctoral assessment criteria they will be subject to. These are likely to include the institutional regulations, and potentially also department/school/college-level additions. They might then produce their own characterization of what these require to allow a suitable discussion for you both.

If you or a colleague are involved in the process of externally examining another doctorate, could your student 'interview' you about what you are looking for, what sorts of questions have arisen and why? Clearly there are issues of confidentiality here, but these should be relatively easy to accommodate.

While the regulations might be a relatively dry way of understanding what is fit for purpose, looking at previous Theses can provide a much more visceral illustration:

> *'When I arrived, we [student and supervisor] talked about generally what the PhD was. She told me to be ambitious, but to remember also that I should keep perspective and that it wasn't a lifetime work, but a PhD. She gave me two past Theses to read to let me know the size of my task. This was helpful indeed.'*
>
> *Research student – Education, Japan*

However, it's our experience that the majority of the doctoral students we encounter have never read a whole doctoral Thesis, especially one from the institution which will award their degree. Reading a doctoral Thesis from cover to cover will help the student to understand what will be required of them to pass their doctorate. This is true of any student, but for an international student who may, as a result of being a product of a different education system, have a different understanding of the nature of a doctorate, the exercise is invaluable.

Supervisory Ideas about Understanding the Thesis

It can be a powerful task if you suggest (or assign) a Thesis for your student to read. There are a number of possible choices of Thesis to make:

- You could select a recent good one that you supervised. This might make it harder for the student to criticize, but it will mean you know it well and may be able to put them in contact with the author if appropriate.
- You could choose a recent good one supervised by a colleague. This may be less directly relevant to your student's topic, but possibly offers more comfortable neutral territory for you both. Could you ask your colleague to have a chat with your student about it too? This would give them a second opinion, and save you needing to be so familiar with the content.
- You could opt for a 'just good enough' one to show the standard that has to be achieved, although it is worth emphasizing that it's always wise to aim a little higher than this. However, this activity does make the point that anything vastly above what's required to pass may be wasted effort.

- You could choose the Thesis of someone who is now quite notable in the field to show that it's a training piece, not a magnum opus.
- You could focus on your own Thesis. This can be a powerful way to establish trust and dispel some of the student-perceived hierarchy. It may, however, be difficult for both parties to engage effectively with this document.

The topic of the chosen Thesis is also important. Clearly it needs to be close enough to your student's area of study to be relevant. But if the topic of the Thesis in question is too close, then your student may not read the Thesis so much as follow up the references. This is a useful task, but not the main point of this activity, so it should be avoided.

The point of reading a doctoral Thesis is to help the student see what is needed in practice to meet the UK's, the institution's and potentially the department's or discipline's requirements, and to understand the relationship between these requirements. As such, it can be useful to structure this process and follow it up with careful discussion.

Student and Supervisor Discussion Points about the Thesis

Questions that can be discussed following the reading of a Thesis could include:

- What about the research is original? How substantial is it?
- What about the Thesis merits publication? You could then suggest that your student find out whether any of it has been published, and if so, where. There is a potentially useful follow-up activity here to explore the standard of writing required for the doctorate by comparing the Thesis and any papers published from it.
- What 'shape' is the Thesis and what structure has it adopted (for example, a general field, detailed context, analysis, research, conclusions, relevance to the field)?
- How has the Thesis been critical? How does it show evidence of each of the Dublin Descriptors or the assessment criteria?
- If the student were examining this Thesis, what questions would they ask at the viva?

If additional key papers are to be read alongside the Thesis:

- How does the writing differ to merit publication?
- Are the papers equivalent in their content, structure, originality, analysis or writing?

A final stage in the process of considering past Theses may be to aim to speak to the author. This can allow very specific questions to be posed, such as: 'Why did you select (only) these case studies?', 'Why did you choose this methodology?', 'What did you leave out?' or 'What were you challenged on in your viva?' For a doctoral student, the chance to engage in this level of discussion can be invaluable in developing an independent understanding of what is required to produce as Thesis that is 'fit for purpose'. This is particularly easy to facilitate if the author is still working in the department, but not impossible if they're in another location.

Developing Independence

Belief in and understanding of independence matter in the development of a doctoral researcher, but fundamentally this part of the Dublin Descriptor concerns the doing of research and the production of a Thesis. It is, however, likely that this 'doing' will also lead to greater belief in and understanding of independence, hence there needs to be a push to get on with the 'doing', even when belief and understanding might still be emerging. If this is to be developed by students themselves, then the supervisory style may need to be that of liberating coach. The key role for the supervisor is to provide the motive force to ensure that research is conducted that can extend the frontier of knowledge, so that there can be a doctorate and to ensure that a Thesis of the required quality is written to explain the research and make the argument to be advanced. We have already explored the gaining of knowledge of what is required, so what skills do postgraduate students need to be able to meet the standard of 'good enough'? Broadly speaking, there are three skill areas to be addressed:

1. disciplinary research techniques

2. analysis and argument

3. writing/Thesis construction.

Much of the technical disciplinary knowledge and ability to conduct research should have been developed through the course of the work covered in Chapters 7 and 8, but it remains important that this is checked and, if necessary, new skills learned. The practicalities of how supervisors develop these elements will need to vary with their preferences and those of their students, as well as the nature of the context, discipline or skill, and some approaches are discussed below.

Supervisory Ideas about Skill Acquisition

The balance for the supervisor needs to be between time efficiency in the short and medium term and the appropriateness of the technique to the situation. Which approaches would work best for you, and which fit with your supervisory style as discussed in Chapter 4?

- Demonstration – Whether by the supervisor or another researcher, demonstration of a technique or approach is a simple method for conveying it. But it's very likely to then need to be followed by practice on the part of the student, which may need to be supported and discussed (project manager and critical teacher styles).
- Joint work – An alternative to demonstration and practice is to undertake the task jointly with the student. This can encourage greater confidence, not least by communicating a level of belief, especially if this can be done as part of someone else's 'real' research. Thus, if convenient, can you conduct some of your research jointly with your student? As well as offering a very effective technique to help the student develop their skills, this can also you a time benefit in that you are also conducting your own research work (liberating coach, academic partner and gatekeeper styles).
- Critique – By presenting a methodology description for criticism and critique by your student then discussing this, you can help them develop knowledge and understanding of a technique without having to use it. This can be a decent alternative early in the process and/or where it is simply not viable to either demonstrate or use the technique (critical teacher and liberating coach styles).
- Co-teaching – A student who is encouraged to undertake a teaching role (although this may detract from the doctoral research schedule) can develop their own understanding of approaches and techniques that might then be of use in their research (gatekeeper style).

Each of these approaches may require a considerable upfront time commitment from you, albeit offering potential medium-term efficiency by developing your student's independence. However, a possible alternative is for your role to be taken by, for example, a trusted post-doctoral researcher. Although this does have potential advantages, it also carries risks and costs – not least a possible perception on your student's part that they are not getting their 'value for money' in terms of fees paid and the distance travelled to be supervised by you.

Choices about the skill development techniques used and the precise way they are employed will need to be influenced by the student's previous level of exposure. An experienced international researcher may well have a highly developed skill in a particular technique, which may mean it is harder to show them an alternative way of doing the same thing or a different technique that might actually be better suited to the task. It might also be the case that the student is already more proficient in the technique than the supervisor. Whatever the precise nuances here, it's important that the supervisor checks that the student is able to conduct the relevant research at a level that is fit for purpose:

> *'There must be an overarching argument in a Thesis. Otherwise it's just data. A significant contribution to a paper, perhaps, but not to the field. You need to do something with it.'*
>
> *Research supervisor and doctoral examiner – Biological Sciences*

The distinct feature of being a researcher – especially a doctoral researcher – and of producing a contribution to knowledge is not merely the production of results, but the analysis of them in order to support an argument. Realizing this and understanding what's required to achieve it is possibly the core skill to be developed. It will again be built on the experience of looking at other previous work at a comparable level, but specifically focusing on the mechanisms by which the results of the research are analysed and the way these two are combined to make and defend an argument – the thesis of a Thesis, as it were.

When should the thesis be defined? In our experience, the simple answer is the sooner the better. Given that it's the defining point of the research being conducted and the literature being read, once the thesis is defined, everything else can then be assessed against it. This does not mean that it needs to be fixed, but that it is changeable in specific terms. If a student knows that their thesis is 'X causes Y under conditions A, B and C', then when their research results indicate that condition C isn't relevant, they can amend their thesis accordingly. They can also know that the literature they're reading is relevant (it supports or contradicts an aspect of their thesis), or that it isn't (it doesn't do either of those things) – in which case they can stop reading it and move on. Accordingly, if encouraged to define their own thesis, a student can become increasingly independent of their supervisor and their guidance – a liberating coach approach. This can be especially powerful where there has been considerable early reliance on the supervisor's judgements, or where the student has come from a system in which such independence has not been developed.

The nature of the thesis developed may vary depending on the discipline and project, but the broad principles will be the same. The following are true of various types of Thesis:

- An extended series of studies still need to be linked by an overarching thematic thesis.
- Investigating new material with existing techniques still requires a thesis to sustain it as a contribution through original research, rather than a functional application of known work.
- Anthropological study and grounded theory both need a set of ideas to determine what's studied and where, even if the answers remain unknown and the thesis needs to emerge after study.

This same element of a central underlying argument applies to all forms of doctorates; it will emerge in the linking write-up of the PhD by Publication and in the accompanying Thesis for a Professional Doctorate or a PhD by Practice. Indeed, it is the single, central element that makes all forms of doctorates equivalent.

While the need for a thesis is self-evident, when it needs to be developed is less clear. Our experience of working with numerous doctoral researchers suggests that it can be addressed relatively early in the process, even perhaps towards the end of year one of full-time equivalent, and generally before any confirmation or upgrade process. If this definition is possible, it can provide a degree of clarity and certainty, as well as an understanding of the nature of the contribution being made, to support the independence of the student.

Supervisory Ideas about the *thesis* (Rather than the Thesis)

At an appropriate, relatively early stage, could you challenge your students to define their thesis, in so far as it is known at the present stage? In order to mitigate what could be a rather challenging task, there are steps towards this:

- Have them look at examples of published work or doctoral Theses, and ask them to isolate the thesis as a single sentence. Is it clear from the work? Is it original? Is it sustained throughout the piece and supported by the evidence presented?
- Can they now develop their own thesis in a similar form – one sentence, with one positively stated thesis? If need be, suggest the use of placeholders for ideas that are not yet clarified – for example, 'under certain conditions', 'impacts [either positively or negatively]'.
- Have them present and defend this thesis to ensure it is sufficiently robust in its construction, given the stage the research is at. This could even take the form of a mock viva for additional practice value.
- Use this thesis as a touchstone for all future work, perhaps revisiting it briefly in each supervision meeting, to ensure it remains as robust as possible for the stage of the work and that all work is leading directly towards it.

The process of identifying the thesis of a Thesis will also lead to consideration of the construction of the Thesis – the structure of the supporting document. The shape and construction of a Thesis will be a discipline-specific endeavour. It will also differ between types of doctorates (professional doctorates, by practice, by publication and so on), but there will be broad general agreement about the necessary contents of a Thesis, such as those set out by Paltridge (2002). Beyond these, the structure, ordering and weighting of Thesis elements remain more subjective. The determination of what's required, and in what order, is probably one of the last steps a research student needs to make towards appreciating their own contribution to knowledge.

Supervisory Ideas about Thesis Structure (1)

Ask your student:

- What Thesis elements are required to support the thesis and to meet the doctoral assessment criteria?
- What is the relative importance of these component elements, and how do they need to work together to advance a coherent argument in support of this thesis?
- Are there defined standards of Thesis (and other forms of scholarship) structures that must be adhered to in our discipline(s)?

Since this level of consideration is not likely to need to be individual to any particular project, this sort of activity can also fruitfully be engaged in by a group of postgraduate students together, perhaps at departmental or similar level. Such a process could also include a review of the Thesis archetypes presented by Paltridge (2002).

Supervisory Ideas about Thesis Structure (2)

After the general groundwork has been laid, you can usefully assign specific tasks to your students enabling them to develop their own sense of what is an appropriate structure for their own Thesis, since they will be the ones who will have to defend it.

- Have them consider a number of different models of presenting research, possibly from different disciplines or areas within a discipline, and distil from them the key elements.
- Consider some successful doctoral Theses. What are their structures? What aspects are most and least effective in supporting the thesis? Would any of these models, or aspects of them, work for the present study? (This activity can usefully include the one above about reading a Thesis to understand what is generally required for the doctorate.)

The aim of this series of activities and discussions is to develop a clear understanding of the thesis that is being argued, and a skeleton structure of the final Thesis that will most effectively support this. With these two essential building blocks in place early on, the doctoral researcher will possess the strongest basis for actually being independent, through understanding what their contribution will be and how their substantial body of original work will extend the frontier of knowledge. Having this clarity is crucial to removing much of the uncertainty that is common among doctoral researchers, and often especially so in those from different educational contexts.

With the building blocks in place, the final component of this Dublin Descriptor is the production of the piece of writing – the writing of the Thesis. This is not the place to go too deeply into techniques for producing, developing and improving academic writing – there's plenty of good material already available about this.[1] However, there are aspects of the writing process we can usefully consider here. Perhaps the first is to revisit the concept of 'good enough'.

Student and Supervisor Discussion Points about Written Outputs

- What level of writing is good enough for a doctorate?
- How much writing, exactly, should merit national or international refereed publication?
- How many journal articles should come from a Thesis? Or should the whole Thesis be intended as a published monograph?
- Which journals are to be targeted?

These questions need to be tailored to the context, and should not be unrealistically aspirational.

Essentially, supervisors and students should have a conversation about the expectations about writing, and the supervisor should bear in mind their student's previous writing experience, linguistic competence and confidence.

1 See, for example, Bolker (1998), Brewer (2007), Dunleavy (2003) or Murray (2011). And, specifically on writing a Thesis in a second language, see Paltridge and Starfield (2007).

It could be a useful exercise to encourage doctoral candidates to take notice of the writing, as well as the content, of the publications they're reading. In reality, it's not the case that standards of writing are uniformly stellar in the highest-profile journals and of lesser quality in those more likely to be within a first-time author's reach. Our experience is that some rather questionable writing practices are to be found in both! This can encourage doctoral students that they can at least meet, if not surpass, the standard of written academic English they find in published research. Their writing may well be 'good enough' already.

Writing is important from the earliest stages of a doctoral candidature. It can be a crucial means of developing defensibility and robustness of thesis argument and support for it, as well as clarifying the very ideas being expressed. When the research needs to be presented in full written form, there are few places to hide, so this can represent a necessary form of honest communication between student and supervisor.

But there are challenges here. Words and identity are closely bound together for researchers. So when the words are unclear – when the academic language isn't good enough – then one's identity can become unclear too. If I can't communicate my ideas, then do my ideas have any value? And if my ideas lack value, then do I? This can always be a challenge, but is likely magnified when the writer is a non-native speaker of English. Phillips and Pugh (2010) consider that writing in English all the time may even create a sense of losing part of an individual's personality. Even if the problems aren't this great, specific strategies may still be needed to encourage reluctant writers to begin writing, and considerable care will need to be exercised when giving feedback on written work.

Supervisor and Student Discussion Points about Written Work

If there are concerns about writing, it is crucial that you get to the heart of the problem with your student, possibly through asking key questions such as:

- What's causing the writing problem? Is it knowing or understanding the ideas/concepts/story of the research, or is it being able to articulate these?
- Writing can necessitate a breakdown of the work. If X needs to be written/understood before Y can be engaged with, what needs to be written/understood before X can be addressed?

- What are the writing issues your student faces, and what level do you need to achieve together? Is this achievable? If not, can you consider engaging an English-language editor? If this is to occur, you must be aware of who is editing the work, therefore ensuring there is no concern that the final work is not your student's.

We find that a majority of postgraduate students in the later stages of their research tend to wish they'd started writing earlier. This is often echoed by post-doctoral researchers and others in academia. To some extent this is probably a consequence of being under pressure towards the end:

> *'I would write from the beginning. If I could go back, I'd write from day one.'*
>
> *Post-doctoral researcher – Physics, Czech Republic*

But there are stronger reasons to justify writing in the early stages – namely that it is through the process of writing (or forming thoughts into coherent sentences and phrases) that ideas are formed, tested, and also can be examined, critiqued, challenged or even be recognized as being 'OK'. The box below sets out a few techniques we've picked up from students that they've found to be helpful in getting down to writing, which supervisors might usefully suggest to their students.

Supervisory Ideas about Encouraging Writing

- Daily target – Set your students a daily (and that means every working day – no excuses) writing target that is manageable and achievable, such as 50 or 100 words. You may need to support them in developing this as a habit. Small, frequent writing outputs make it easy for you to provide feedback and input, and mean that no day will ever end with your student feeling that they have achieved nothing.
- Write little and often – Encourage your students to write up aspects of the research *process* and so begin to build the necessary writing momentum. Examples here might be descriptions of the research/study/experiment, accounts of the findings (without the need to analyse) or reflections on other scholarship.

- One sentence – Whenever your student does any research – a result gained, a paper read, a conversation had, a subject interviewed, an experiment failed – they should write one sentence of Thesis-worthy (that is, defensible) text about how this informs their thesis (which, of course, is well defined and specified already – see above).

The purpose of any of these approaches is to encourage your students to begin their writing and to build up writing momentum. Furthermore, right from the start, stress that writing is something to share with you, so that these pieces of writing can serve as discussion points.

Many of these writing ideas need not be time-consuming for the supervisor, and institutional support is often available. Once good writing habits have been established, the core effort is the student's, and it will ultimately be an efficient use of their time in terms of producing a Thesis. However, some of the discussion and sharing stages can also be made more efficient by encouraging students to have other research students as writing buddies to edit and critique early drafts of each other's work. A slightly more formalized version of this could be organized at research group, departmental or school level, where students share their written work and are questioned on it by others in the group, with one of the participants (not the writer) acting as a rapporteur. This allows the whole group to develop an understanding of peer review, of defensibility, and hopefully it will also help to refine the research ideas and develop a research story:

> *'I got some comments [from my supervisor] on my first pieces of writing. Some of their words were vague and some were blunt and critical. I wasn't sure what to do [with the feedback]. Was it good enough or not?'*
>
> *Research student – Social Sciences*

In tandem with creating written outputs, the most important element of student development is receiving feedback. Whether such feedback comes from the supervisor (and clearly much of it should) or from others involved in the process, care needs to be taken. This is especially true of feedback on writing, given the issues of identity already discussed and the potential daily insecurities that non-native speakers may already feel about their language. To these ends, effective feedback must be:

- **Bespoke** – Feedback should always be specifically tailored to the student, to the piece of work being addressed, and from the person giving it. It should also be appropriate to the time or stage of the doctorate.

- **Task-focused** – Separate work from identity when criticizing. Avoiding the word 'you' will help to focus your attention on this.

- **Actionable** – It should be about something that the student can specifically change, thus encouraging them to engage practically with it.

- **Precise and objective** – Make clear what is 'good enough' or not 'good enough' about the work, with reference to applicable standards rather than just based on opinion. It should also be clear what aspect(s) of the doctorate it addresses – including whether it's an issue with the ideas or the writing.

- **Positive direction** – It should indicate a positive direction of travel – detailing what needs to be done to improve or maintain the quality.

- **Complete** – Feedback can be a challenge to digest at the best of times. Hence, it should ideally not necessitate further questioning – it should be complete in itself. Thus, the only questions that should need to arise will concern ensuring that the feedback given is understood, rather than in clarifying what the supervisor means.

- **Manageable** – Large blocks of feedback can be too much to digest, especially where language or other cultural issues are at play. Hence, little and often is more likely to be effective. This may also be the most time-efficient for both student and supervisor, since it will encourage brief interactions 'now' rather than necessitating longer ones 'later'.

- **Sincere** – Feedback is a trust process, so it's crucial that it's delivered in a manner that communicates the supervisor's sincerity in giving it as part of the joint pursuit of achieving doctoral success.

- **Responsive** – All feedback should ideally be in response to a specific request from the student for it, in a particular form, about a specific piece of work and clear elements or aspects of it.

Student and Supervisor Discussion Points about Offering Feedback

- What are our expectations concerning feedback?
- How is feedback given and received in your culture?
- How would you like to receive feedback?
- How often, and in what form, should feedback be expected? On what scale?
- How far in advance should work be submitted?

Encourage your student to always submit specific feedback requests with any work they ask you to consider. What specifically do they want feedback about? Which parts, and what aspects of them? What form of feedback do they want, and (within reason) by when?

Deliberate mechanisms can be used to foster the giving of effective, constructive feedback, and these can be linked directly to some of the techniques already discussed for encouraging writing. For example, working on small chunks of writing can foster timeliness of feedback. It also means that feedback can more effectively be formative, as opposed to when it is given on large pieces of prose long after they were written. Also, aiming to address specific questions in the feedback, whether asked by the student or set by the supervisor, can to help focus discussions: for example, 'Is the narrative clear?', 'Is there sufficient evidence for this point?' or 'Is the way I've written about X's work critical/respectful enough?'

> *'He [the supervisor] kept my chapter for nearly three weeks and all it had written on it was "You have some good ideas in here."'*
>
> *Research student – Social Science, Iran*

Although this discussion has specifically focused on feedback on writing, the same principles apply to all aspects of the research process. So this returns us to the ideas discussed at the beginning of this chapter, of developing the student's critical abilities in response to effective encouragement. These discussions can now be informed by having a clear, shared understanding of what represents 'good enough' in the context of producing a Thesis that is fit for purpose.

The process of becoming an independent researcher is at the heart of the doctorate, and it's likely to be a long and potentially painful one. That's why we've devoted more attention to it than some of the other aspects. But all aspects are essential, not least the ability to critically analyse, evaluate and synthesize new and complex ideas, which is the topic of the next chapter.

Chapter 10
Sophisticated Thinking

In the previous chapter we focused on the output of the doctoral process being the production of a Thesis to make a contribution. This chapter concerns elements a doctoral student needs to engage with and conduct within that research process.

The fourth Dublin Descriptor states that successful doctoral candidates must have 'proven themselves capable of critical analysis, evaluation and synthesis of new and complex ideas'. This concerns three linked but separable aspects which collectively represent the core required thinking processes doctoral students must engage with. They reflect the definition of critical ability and awareness cited in Caruna and Spurling (2007): 'the willingness to question material encountered, to form opinions and be assertive about expressing viewpoints, in other words to be aware of the contestability of knowledge'.

Act honestly and answer boldly.
Danish proverb

Potential difficulties here arise from the step-up required from previous stages of higher education, and these difficulties may be magnified where the international dimension of the student's prior education is factored in. There are a number of studies that examine the question of whether there is a cultural difference in critical reasoning ability, and notwithstanding the homogenization issue, there seems to be no conclusive evidence one way or the other. For instance, Nisbett (2003) suggests that East Asians process holistically and based on experience, whereas 'Westerners' think more analytically and abstractly. However, Nisbett's findings are contradicted by Lee and Johnson-Laird (2006). Nevertheless, taken together, the ideas of critical analysis, evaluation and synthesis could be said to represent the core ways of thinking at a doctoral level. They could also be said to be reflective of a certain 'Western' (loosely characterized as following a Socratic method of dialogue and critique) academic conception of thinking – of higher intellectual processes.

Supervisory Enquiries about Academic Thinking

Consider your own thinking processes:

- How do you move from reading to writing your own original work?
- What stages do you go through? Can you isolate the steps?
- Which do you find easiest/most challenging?

Capable of 'Critical Analysis'

The critical analysis required of doctoral students involves the significant step of moving beyond reporting findings, results or reading to investing their own judgements, and overlaying these judgements onto material that already exists. It will require them to be dispassionate – not attached to one approach, open-minded, not defensive. Critical analysis also requires delving into detail: breaking down the whole into its constituent parts in order to identify and assess each part's relevance and contribution.

Critical analysis needs to be applied to various elements within the doctorate:

- methodology;
- approaches;
- ideas/literature;
- findings (one's own, others');
- drafts of the thesis and of the Thesis.

Engaging in the required level of critical analysis is likely to pose one of the greatest challenges for those who have been educated in a non-critical educational environment. There is real potential at this stage for the full force of academic culture shock to hit – and it can be every bit as hard as the more general forms of culture shock the international student may already have encountered (as dealt with in Chapter 5).

Supervisory Enquiries about Critical Analysis

- What does critical analysis mean to you? How does what you require from your research students differ from what you ask of master's students? Does it differ from what you expect of colleagues/or yourself?
- How/when did you first master the skill(s)? When did you realize you had mastered them?
- Did your own supervisor introduce these skills to you? If so, how – by deliberate instruction or osmotic example? And how did you feel about this at the time?
- Have you explicitly addressed critical analysis with previous research students? What have they struggled with?

How is it possible to inculcate an ethos of critical thinking while being understanding about how difficult and counter-cultural this might be for the student? Even for those not experiencing academic culture shock, there is still a challenge since this is the first stage of doctoral students becoming independent researchers in their own right – of pitting their opinions 'against' those of others in the field:

> *'My supervisor is critical of me. This makes me feel bad, and so I don't want to give him work and I put it off. This makes me guilty. My supervisor does not make me feel good.'*
>
> *Research student, Nigeria*

There are two main approaches to addressing this. The supervisor can be very direct, and directive, while encouraging a student to fend for themselves, intellectually – the critical teacher style:

> *'I ask my research students to write two or three questions a week for us to use in our meetings. This is very useful if a student has limited critical capabilities.'*
>
> *Research supervisor – Arts and Humanities*

Alternatively, one can take a gentler approach, communicating understanding of the difficulty – the liberating coach style. In all likelihood, your approach will be some mixture of the two.

Supervisory Ideas about Critical Thinking

Could you introduce critical thinking exercises right from the beginning of the research process?

- At the first stages of reading, perhaps assign a small number of papers (two, three or four?) to be read on a similar theme. Ask your student to draw up a table comparing and contrasting specific aspects, such as methodology.
- Ask the student to produce a one-paragraph critique of any research they come across, specifically requiring them to characterize the strengths and weaknesses of the question(s) posed, the methods used, the result achieved and the analysis of these.

When I started my doctorate, fairly early on I needed to wrestle with the intellectual underpinnings of the discipline, and my approach was largely reportage. Hence, my supervisor – the single best thing she ever did for me – plucked two books from her bookshelf. Each represented a fully formed, detailed, and utterly distinct philosophical tract attempting to characterize not only the theoretical basis of the discipline, but also its justification. Her guidance was simple: 'Read these, and then tell me what you think.' After considerable time spent immersed in each book, I was welcomed into the world of critical thinking, because the books were essentially irreconcilable. To accept part of one required some level of rejection of the other, which had to be justified. Inevitably, I sought justification in other writings, but always had to come back to being pitted between these two. In this way I navigated my own way through the history and philosophy of the discipline. I emerged from the process, approximately three months later, slightly scarred (and scared!), but at the very least with an appreciation of the level of critical analysis necessary in order to complete my doctoral thesis. This was an effective process, but with hindsight I'm not sure it was necessarily an efficient one. It was also a very ambiguous task, which might have exacerbated my discomfort had I been from a culture less comfortable with ambiguity.

Supervisory Ideas about Criticism of Literature

A potentially more efficient method of introducing this deeper critical analysis of scholarly work might be to introduce (or perhaps negotiate with your student) a set of questions, or pro-forma, to be used in preparation for a supervision meeting:

- What are the most memorable papers you've read since our last supervision?
- What have you learned from them?
- What are you incorporating into your own research from them?
- What are the best aspects of their research? What are the limitations?
- Which is the best paper of all of them? Why?
- Write a summary of the themes covered in all the papers you've mentioned.

This could be submitted before the session, so you can review it beforehand, or it could become something your student automatically does, without the need for explicit review or discussion.

There are a number of different aspects of the doctoral process where the skills of critical analysis will need to be employed. In selecting methods to be used and in circumscribing the focus of the study, critical analysis is essential since it provides the justification for what to do and how to do it. But the skills should also be employed in supervisor interactions, most explicitly in dealing with feedback. Generally, the supervisors we've talked to have expressed frustration with doctoral students 'doing as they are told'. Rather, it's an aim of most supervisors that the feedback they give should be taken in context, weighed against other information and acted upon advisedly:

> *'In my country the professor is boss. He says – you do. Here it is very different. I can challenge and be critical. Well, I know I should, and I know I can, but it is hard.'*
>
> *Research student, Turkey*

While critical analysis skills need to be addressed and developed in different ways in different contexts, it may help the student to have parallels between the discrete contexts highlighted. In this way, learning from one context may enhance development in others.

Supervisory Ideas about Critical Analysis

The choices here will depend very much on the discipline, type of research and the individual researcher, but, for example, when first engaging with critical analysis of work, as a supervisor you may wish to begin with the choice of method used, asking your student to answer questions such as:

- What alternative methods could have been used?
- What advantages and disadvantages might they have afforded?
- How would you propose moving forward?

In selecting case studies or other subjects of study, ask your student to answer questions such as:

- Which other objects could have been selected (in addition to those chosen, or instead of them)?
- What would be the advantages and disadvantages of adding more data?
- If you had to replace one of those chosen by the author of the paper with one of your own, which would it be? How would you justify this decision to the author?

Since the purpose here is to introduce the process of critical analysis on potentially less challenging ground, it is a moot point whether applying this idea to the feedback you give your students is a good place to start or is the final point in their development. However, the idea is still the same. Once you have given feedback (ideally written, so there is an agreed record to work with) on a specific piece of work, ask your student to critically analyse your feedback by answering questions like:

- What was the most useful aspect of the feedback? What was the least? In each case, why?
- If you were grading this feedback, what grade would you give it? What would your accompanying comments be (bearing in mind that they should aimed to helping the supervisor's feedback improve the next time)?
- Do you agree with all of the feedback? Are there any parts of it you would challenge or modify? If so, which parts – and specifically, what would you challenge or modify about them?

If the process of applying the techniques of critical analysis to the supervision itself is especially challenging for the student – whether for personality or cultural reasons – it might be necessary, or at least useful, for the supervisor to model the sort of process that is needed. Indeed, it might even be useful for the supervisor to become clearer on what is needed too.

Supervisory Ideas about Critical Leadership

Is there something your student could teach you – and/or other members of the research group – to do? Ideally, this will draw on some prior expertise of the student and will not be related at all to the research process. The important thing is to put the student in the lead role. (One example we came across in the course of interviewing researchers for this book was a Japanese researcher teaching an entire research group how to make sushi.) The process modelling is then akin to the Socratic method of teaching, consisting of you, or the other members of the research group, asking questions throughout – and specifically critical analysis questions. It's important to establish what answers are impermissible, such as 'I don't know' or 'Because that's the way it's done/the way my supervisor does it.'

Once the student is comfortable with the process and the sorts of results it achieves, it should be a relatively easy process to ask them to reverse roles and question you about the feedback you are giving them on their work.

While critical analysis will always lead to evaluation, it's important that time is reserved just for this analysis. Shifting too early to evaluation (and even to synthesis) risks there being insufficient depth of analysis. This danger can be especially acute for individuals who prefer to think about the big ideas rather than being comfortable with addressing details.

Capable of 'Evaluation'

At some point critical analysis has to shift to evaluation. In essence, evaluation is the output or consequence, or even the 'So what?', of critical analysis. It is the process of making comparative judgements, whereas critical analysis is the process of making essentially internal qualitative judgements. Evaluation needs to result in choices about what of the analysed material will be used, whether for the final decision, perhaps as to the methodology to be followed, or for contribution to the later synthesis, and so to the development of new ideas and contributions to knowledge.

Unseen merchandise cannot be evaluated.
Corsican proverb

Because evaluation is a further step in the process of asserting judgement on work, it presents the new researcher with a further challenge. It is essentially the first stage of producing defensible arguments, or at least establishing the foundations for them. Where students feel further threatened by this – where they may perhaps feel their identity is being put up for consideration, since identity and ideas are closely bound up, it may be worth investigating the nature of the identity being sought by them in engaging in the doctoral process.

Student and Supervisor Discussion Points about Intellectual Evaluation

- What distinguishes a researcher from a lab technician or archivist (or other equivalent position relevant to your discipline)?
- When someone has obtained a doctorate, are they sufficiently qualified as a researcher to evaluate other researchers' work?
- How do you feel about evaluating other people's work?
- How do you feel about other people evaluating your work?

Sometimes the challenge lies in whether the student is prepared to engage in evaluating material over which they do not yet feel sufficiently authoritative. Where this is the case, one strategy is to begin the process on ground where they either feel more at home or possibly where they feel they have an advantage over their supervisor.

Supervisory Ideas about Evaluation (1)

You could ask your student to evaluate a key aspect (perhaps the contribution made or the methodology used) of a paper that is:

- about something they have experience in, even if not directly relevant to their research – for example, this might draw on their own previous professional experience if relevant, or perhaps a source they used during their master's or bachelor's dissertation, or similar.
- written in their native language (if this is not English) – this will bring forward material that you as supervisor might not directly access, and allows the student to feel a degree of superiority, or at least to have some 'home advantage'.
- addressing an issue from their own country/region/context – this also capitalizes on the positive dimension of the student having some 'home advantage' over you.

The purpose of these 'easing in' approaches is, of course, to enable international students to feel comfortable with the requirements of evaluation inherent in their doctoral study. Once these initial steps have been taken, it will be important to direct their attention to the evaluation of their own doctoral process. This is another important area for supervisory input and guidance.

Supervisory Ideas about Evaluation (2)

Establish a routine of having your students address a set of evaluative questions for every piece of work they do. This may be especially relevant for practical research work, such as experiments, fieldwork and so on. The questions could be pre-set by you, or jointly agreed as part of their development.

Questions might include:

- What went well? What didn't go so well?
- What of this was predictable? Was any of it predicted?
- What happened that was unexpected? How could you reduce the chances of this in the future?

This sort of evaluative practice is likely to be most relevant to aspects that will likely be decided upon at this stage – those that won't require further synthesis and creation.

Evaluation always has to be 'against' or 'with reference to' something. There must be some standards by which the material under consideration is being evaluated. For some elements there will be a degree of comparative evaluation – which methodology is likely to yield the best results in the most efficient way? But for other potentially more developmental aspects, the evaluation may well have to be conducted with reference to the research itself, its purposes, and ultimately with the thesis being argued.

We have already addressed the process of research students developing a clearly identified research question, then developing from this their own, defensible, thesis – the argument they will defend in their Thesis (see Chapters 8 and 9). These are the obvious, ultimate evaluative standards to be referred to.

Supervisory Ideas about Evaluation (3)

Depending on the stage in the process, choose one of the options below.

Ask your student to draw up a clear, written version of their research question, or if appropriate, of sub-questions. Then, during any evaluation process, have them make explicit reference to this, possibly as the final summary piece:

- How might this action help you to answer that question?
- What sort of answers might it produce?
- Does the information obtained suggest any need to alter the question or to ask further questions? Or does it answer the question to the extent that you need to develop a new question?

Alternatively, ask your student to have draw up a clear, written version of their thesis. Where appropriate, this might consist of more minor hypotheses for interim studies, but it is always worth bearing in mind the overall thesis of their Thesis. For any evaluative process, ask them to make explicit, direct reference to this, possibly as the summary piece:

- How does this inform your thesis? If it doesn't inform it at all, is it relevant?
- Does new evidence support your thesis? If so, how? This question is not intended to be critical, but to help your student to build their argument. It will also help them to develop defensibility by rehearsing their arguments for how the material supports their thesis.

- Does new evidence suggest any amendments, additions, expansion or narrowing of your thesis? Is the resultant thesis definitely more robust than the version it replaced?
- Does new evidence in any way challenge your thesis? If so, how? How will you rebut this, build the argument and develop defensibility.

In the early stages, the sorts of evaluation ideas suggested above, as with so many of these supervisory activities, will require some explicit supervisor input and guidance. But the purpose is to develop a student's autonomy in their evaluative skills so that they will routinely engage in this form of evaluation autonomously throughout their research work. As always, the aim is to develop their research capabilities, as appropriate to their needs, experience and context.

Capable of 'Synthesis'

For those thinking processes where evaluation does not signify the exit point, the next stage will be the synthesis of the evaluated elements of whatever has been critically analysed. Such synthesis is the output or 'So what?' of evaluation. It is here that the new ideas are created, so synthesis will be an essential part of the Thesis construction process, especially concerning the elucidation of the thesis of the Thesis (the core argument of the final submitted work, as discussed in Chapter 9).

As the very heart of the intellectual creation process, it is also likely to be the single most demanding aspect of the international student's developing identity as an independent researcher, and the one where emotions influenced by unfamiliarity with the 'Western' academic approaches are likely to show themselves most strongly.

Student and Supervisor Discussion Points about Academic Synthesis

Discussion is a supportive way of exploring the issues, and identity impacts, involved in synthesis of ideas for knowledge creation. These questions build upon those suggested above for evaluation:

- What will the research in your doctorate be for? What will it produce?
- What can you derive from the critical analysis and evaluation processes you have already engaged in? What purpose did they serve?
- How do you feel about being the creator of new knowledge?

These discussion points strongly echo many of the issues implicitly raised in the discussion of the student's contribution to knowledge in Chapter 9.

The idea of synthesis is to take a number of component parts and weave them together to create a new whole. The component parts could be varied in nature: published work of other researchers, the results of a student's own investigations, or questions springing from either. But these components are not presented individually, but as one coherent argument, woven together from the different threads. This is the 'creation' part of research, and is the culmination of the critical analysis and evaluation processes.

Supervisory Ideas about Academic Synthesis (1)

Select a published paper, relevant to your field, which you feel demonstrates the synthesis of ideas particularly well. Once you have chosen one, you can use it for several doctoral students over a number of years. Ask your student to read it and then attempt to reverse-engineer the synthesized argument to get to the heart of how it was built.

- What is the argument rooted in? What is the context?
- What are the theoretical foundations, the literature relevant to this argument? How have these been used – what has been taken from which pieces?
- What is the main resultant argument?
- How is it justified? How defensible is the justification?
- What are the outcomes – both main and subsidiary – of the research? Can these be traced back to particular 'input' pieces of research?
- How do all of the elements relate to one another?

The second stage of this exercise, if you feel it would be useful to really drive the point home, would be to ask the student to produce a graphical representation of the synthesized argument. This will inevitably show the dependent relationships between the component parts of the paper and provide a model for the student to follow.

Another challenge of synthesis is the need to see the bigger picture, to spot connections and linkages between ideas in order to construct the larger whole. This is a major movement away from the attention to detail needed for critical analysis. It is where the entire thinking process leads to the development of the overall thesis, which emerges from this cycle of critical analysis, evaluation and synthesis, albeit iteratively.

Supervisory Enquiries about Academic Synthesis

- Do you prefer to focus on the detail of analysis or the big picture of synthesis?
- How do you achieve a balance between these two in your work?
- Do you use any techniques to address challenges with one or the other?

It is important to understand one's own preference and perspective before engaging with someone else about it, since each individual is likely to find some processes easier and more automatic than others. It will be useful for supervisors to build on this self-understanding to inform communication with research students about how they engage with the requirements of, in particular, critical analysis and synthesis.

Supervisory Ideas about Academic Synthesis (2)

Where students find it easier to stick to the details of analysis and evaluation rather than seeing the larger whole, you might try asking them to communicate their thinking in alternative modes which could foster a wider perspective, such as by producing concept maps or rich pictures (often used in software development).

Another approach is to press for frequent references to the larger perspective, for example with questions like:

- Why are we reading/reviewing/looking at this?
- What does this mean for the question/hypothesis/thesis we are currently addressing?

Alternatively, a simpler approach would be to nudge your student with 'So what?' This is the underlying question throughout, but it shouldn't be posed in this 'raw' form until you have established a sufficiently comfortable and robust working relationship.

Although these questions can be asked in supervision meetings, they might be more usefully addressed more regularly in a student's working processes. In such cases, you could suggest that one of them is addressed briefly at the foot of every page of writing, or even after every paragraph written. Although possibly slightly extreme, this sort of mechanism, simply by repetition, can then reduce some of the reluctance to engage with larger ideas.

A further stage in this process could then be to summarize the answers to these questions as a separate piece of work to the core analysis. This holistic approach may lead to a more effective synthesis piece.

The output or product of synthesis is very likely to be something that needs to be subjected to critical analysis, then evaluation, and further synthesis, to ultimately construct Thesis-worthy ideas. Such ideas need to be able to develop, and to be accumulated, and to evolve. These iterations may themselves pose further challenges for researchers. The temptation may be for a student to see the work as finished after a single cycle, or to be even more reluctant to analyse their own produced ideas than they were to address other people's. As throughout this chapter, there are clear potential cultural blocks or barriers here.

Supervisory Task Ideas about Intellectual Quality

Chapter 9 (concerning the third Dublin Descriptor) introduced the concepts of 'good enough' and the doctorate being 'fit for purpose'. You could use the outcomes of these discussions to encourage your student to examine their own ideas:

- Are their ideas fit for purpose?
- Are their ideas good enough to pass a doctoral examination?

If this format is too abstract or is too large a leap, then there are alternative ways of tackling the same issue. Different questions might be:

- If you were a doctoral examiner, what would your comments on this idea be?
- Identify the two greatest strengths of this idea, and the two points on which you think it is most vulnerable to challenge?

Either of these approaches leads the student back into the critical analysis phase.

As we have said at various points, there can be scope for greater supervisory efficiency if the sorts of activities covered throughout this chapter can take place with clusters of research students, whether from a single research group or department, or possibly even organized centrally (at department, school, college or institutional level). Indeed, there may be a training unit or body that could facilitate such sessions. Regardless of where they occur, the aim would be for the students to present their work, and have others begin the critical analysis process with them, so helping the student to move towards independent analysis of their own work. However, a balance needs to be struck between developing the skills involved in defending arguments and being open-minded in critical analysis.

So far we have focused on the core elements of research – the skills required, research design, making a contribution, and in the present chapter, critical analysis, evaluation and synthesis. The next stage is to consider the need to communicate this work to others, which is the topic of the next chapter.

Chapter 11

Spreading the Message

To spread the news is to multiply it.
Tibetan proverb

The fifth Dublin Descriptor stresses the importance of communicating research, stating that a successful doctoral candidate must show that they can 'communicate with their peers, the larger scholarly community and with society in general about their areas of expertise'. Often when working with supervisors and the issue of communication arises with reference to international doctoral students, their primary concern seems to be the ability of the student to use correct English. It's notable that this concern is also raised frequently by international students, suggesting that it's at least as pressing for them as it is for their supervisors. While we recognize that this is a valid concern – of course it is – there's a danger that, by focusing on grammar, vocabulary and pronunciation, an issue of more consequence will be missed.

Earlier we discussed the problems that arise from a lack of mutual clarity about the expectations of the two parties. It is important that both student and supervisor are clear who has responsibility for the written and spoken outputs resulting from the research undertaken. As Halai (2011) points out: 'many students think that it is the responsibility of the supervisor to edit their language'.

However, this chapter is less about the use of the English language than it is about conveying ideas and expertise from one person to their audience, whoever that audience might be. This chapter will inevitably also deal with preparation for the PhD viva. We will address this at the end of the chapter, while recognizing that the viva incorporates many of the skills addressed in Chapter 12.

> *'For a new student there might be an intimidating language barrier at first. Often you can understand a lot more than you can actually express as a foreign student. So it's always good to have a little patience.'*
> *Research student – Arts and Humanities, Denmark*

Having said that, it would be unwise to ignore the language issue altogether. One of the joys of working in the higher education sector is that it's so cosmopolitan – people move around the world relatively freely, and it's extremely unusual to find a department which is totally monolingual. Therefore, it is inevitable that academics will be working with colleagues and students who do not share a first language; and that the range of competence in English will be broad.

As we discussed in Chapter 5, supervisors could usefully spend a little time looking at their non-native speaking students' abilities as shown in their IELTS scores. The quote from the Danish student above expresses quite eloquently a common issue: that an international student's understanding can often surpass their ability to produce language. Likewise, a student's ability to read in English may exceed their ability to write in perfect prose; the individual scores that make up the overall score a department will look at highlight these subtleties.

Supervisory Enquiries about Language and Power

- Which language do you use to converse with your non-English as a first language students?
- What works about this? What are the problems?
- What impact does language have on your relationships with students?
- Does this reinforce any power imbalance?

A focus on language – words, phrases and punctuation – can be unhelpful as it draws attention to aspects which can usually easily be sorted out by a competent proofreader towards the end of the process if the underlying ideas are clear. A great deal of supervisory time can be taken up if every piece of submitted work is marked for grammatical accuracy. This was highlighted by the words of a doctoral student who told me that he had become despondent because of his supervisor's constant focus on his grammatical errors. His supervisor had noticed this, and reined himself in from spending too much time on it, assuring the student that they would find a proofreader at the end. The student wrote:

> *'Now my supervisor does help me with comments on the use of the English when I ask. I like it, but we agreed to proofread my Thesis at the end of PhD, using outside resources.'*
>
> *Research student, Palestine*

The Dublin Descriptor that provides the focus of this chapter is not about technical use of English; it is about the sharing of sophisticated thoughts with a number of different audiences. It concerns the ability to be sufficiently confident in the nature and content of one's own work that the ideas within it can be shared successfully with others. When true communication has been achieved, all parties end up with the same understanding of the communicated message. And language in itself does not equal message.

Ideas can and should be shared in a number of different ways. Within the UK academic context, it is common for them to be shared in writing, both in the Thesis and in publications, in public speaking at conferences, in seminars, lectures and through the media, in conversation, both formal (for example, at the doctoral viva) and informal in a variety of networking contexts, and increasingly in engaging with the wider community. Each forum for communication has its own challenges, but there are many skills they have in common. A supervisor adopting the gatekeeper style (see Chapter 4) may excel in identifying and promoting the opportunities a student may have to exploit these different forums.

He who gets close to a good tree will have a good shade.
Spanish proverb

International students frequently tell us that they knew of their supervisor's reputation before coming to the UK to study with them. This is a significant demonstration of the supervisor's success in communicating about their research and can therefore provide a helpful model of what is required.

However, as we have said above, leading by example can only go so far, unless that example is explained and deconstructed. In essence, it's not always sufficient for a supervisor to do what they normally do in the hope that their student will learn from it by osmosis. Particularly when a student hails from a non-UK education system, and if they are struggling to adjust, it may be important for the supervisor to be explicit about their own practice.

Supervisory Enquiries about Communicating Research

- What would you consider to be your major strengths in communicating research?
- What difficulties do you experience?

- Do you find it easiest to communicate your expertise by writing papers, by giving talks, by teaching, in conversation?
- Which audiences do you regularly communicate with about your expertise? With which don't you communicate as regularly as you might?
- Which audiences do you find easiest? Which ones present the greatest struggle, and what do you do to address that?

I was in a taxi recently, and in the course of conversation the driver asked me the purpose of my visit, which was to give a presentation. Without pausing for breath, he asked: 'So, in one sentence, what are you going to say?'

The conversation went on, but the impact on my performance of that simple articulation of my main message was significant. I was more focused than I might otherwise have been; and I am confident that, having articulated the message to one audience simply and clearly, I was able to transmit it more effectively to a different audience.

Supervisory Ideas about Summarizing a Message

- Try asking your international student to summarize their own understanding of a paper, concept or theory in one sentence. If you ask for this regularly, it will become a routine part of their preparation for a meeting to think about this in advance.
- Perhaps you could require a single-sentence summary at the beginning of any piece of written work, or a single-sentence question at the beginning of any email. Emphasis on clarity of thought manifested like this will assist in developing the supervisory experience for both parties.
- It's not such an easy thing to do! Try to model this in your comments about (a) your own work and (b) the literature you are reading, with a liberal use of 'So, this is about X.'

As mentioned above, we believe that communication can only be said to have been achieved when the recipient has understood the message transmitted (by whatever means) by the communicator. Therefore, understanding who the audience is, what their needs and interests are and what they already know is essential for effective communication.

Do not judge your neighbour until you walk
two moons in his moccasins.
Cheyenne proverb

The chief example of where this empathy is required in the doctoral process is in the examination. The postgraduate's primary audience is the examiners, who require evidence that the candidate has achieved the standard required for the doctorate. Examiners are likely to focus on the areas in which they themselves are expert, so a candidate who is demonstrating the required empathy will communicate their own message in a way that is aligned with the examiners' niche expertise.

In contrast, when writing a journal article, the audience is the academic community in the relevant field, and their requirements are more closely related to the research itself: a clear presentation of what has been done, what the results were and how the author interprets those results.

Supervisory Ideas about Communicating Research

When seeking to communicate – by whatever means – to a different audience, encourage your student to answer the following questions:

- What is the message I want to convey in this talk/paper/review?
- Who am I communicating with, primarily?
- What does the audience already know about this? What is the audience interested in?
- What do I need to tell them about my research in order to achieve communication of my message?
- What, therefore, should I leave out?

You could set out these or other relevant questions on a pro-forma, which your student completes then brings to supervision meetings. The question for discussion may not necessarily be any of these, but a more general one, along the lines of 'How has your thinking about the audience had an impact on what you want to include?'

It is worthwhile for the supervisor to notice what activities a student is involved in generally, and to use these as an opportunity to enhance audience-focused communication. For example, increasing numbers of academic researchers are engaging with social media as a way of communicating their research. The supervisor could take advantage of this by considering how this media platform could be used productively to help develop clarity of expression while bearing in mind the audience's understanding of a particular subject.

Supervisory Task Ideas about Concise Expression

The following are summaries of successfully completed doctoral Theses, each adhering to the Twitter limit of 140 characters:

> 'Variation in expression of aspect in past tense English is not entirely driven by linguistic factors and is subject to longitudinal change.'
>
> 'Human melanoma cells show reduced attachment and motility when treated with anti-oestrogenic compounds in vitro.'
>
> 'International law can't deal with failed states (e.g. Somalia and Yugoslavia). Their treatment is politics abusing the vocabulary of law.'

Could you do this for your own Thesis? Would it help your students to express their ideas in this way? How might a summary for a specialist be 'tweaked' in order to demonstrate empathy with a wider audience?

Clarity of Expression

When we ask researchers to describe what makes good academic writing, the predominant answer is 'clarity'. The academic community disapproves of ambiguity, prizing instead the precision that comes from using exactly the right word or phrase to describe a given concept or entity. Empathy with the audience is necessary here in order to ascertain whether the correct phrase needs to be explained or defined, and if the right judgement is made, the message will be clear.

This is an occasion where native speakers of other languages can sometimes help to clarify matters. I was recently discussing the issue of clarity in academic English with a group of postgraduate researchers with a range of first languages. I used an example of the way English is often used figuratively, which obscures the exact meaning: 'the kettle is boiling'. The native English speakers in the room were so familiar with this phrase that there were frowns and bemusement as they failed to see my point. However, a non-native speaker piped up quickly, 'But that makes no sense! Why would you say that? In Portuguese, we would just say "the water is boiling", because that is what is happening.'

Supervisory Ideas about Encouraging Clarity

Consider a simple action you have done today – for example, teeth-brushing. Express this as simply and straightforwardly as possible:

> 'I brushed my teeth.'

Then consider what aspect of this is most important? Is it the subject (I), the verb (brushed) or the object (teeth)?

What extra detail could enrich the most important element?

> 'I, a competent adult, brushed my teeth.'
>
> 'I brushed my teeth thoroughly.'
>
> 'I brushed my teeth with an electronic toothbrush for exactly two minutes.'
>
> 'I brushed my upper and lower incisors, but ignored my molars.'

Remember that all of these may be right, so this isn't about correct use of English, but about the exact message one wants to convey. Have a conversation – what exactly does your student want to convey in the description of an action in their speech or writing?

On several occasions above we have discussed the idea of encouraging peer support: groups of postgraduate students supporting each other. This is not to get students to do the work of supervisors, although the increase in the effectiveness with which a supervisor's time will be used is no doubt an advantageous by-product. The primary purpose of such activity is to encourage creative thinking and peer-to-peer communication.

Of course, when an international student has made a choice of university based on the prospect of receiving expert guidance from a particular academic, it's possible they may be disappointed at being asked to talk about their work with 'inexpert' peers. Simply expressing the educational advantage of learning together may ensure that the student doesn't feel that they are simply being fobbed off.

There are several ways the supervisor can counter any disappointment and encourage this kind of communication within their own department.

Supervisory Ideas about Communicating Expertise

- Find out where each student's expertise lies – particularly those who are professionals in their own country. Notice what skills students pick up particularly well. Make it a practice to point students in each other's direction for suggestions with phrases such as: 'You should talk to X about that, he's been doing that for a while in his job' or 'Get Y to show you how to do this.'
- Check in with your students about suggestions like this, to reinforce that this kind of support is important. 'How did it go when you asked Y to show you …?' or 'Was it useful talking to X about …? Did they have another perspective?' Hearing that you are interested in the outcome will reduce the likelihood of the student feeling they have been dismissed when encouraged to talk to one of their peers.
- It's also a good idea to give informal acknowledgement or thanks to the student who has provided assistance. This encourages a culture where expertise is valued, regardless of the source, and builds up confidence.
- Get the students together socially every now and again. It doesn't matter whether this is for a meal in a restaurant, a visit to a tourist attraction nearby or simply coffee in the department. Not only will it help them to get to know you a little, it will help them form social relationships

with one another, from which useful professional relationships are likely to grow. This is a genuine first step in developing a student's ability to network, which will pay dividends during coffee breaks, mealtimes and long evenings during conferences!

- In a group setting, when presenting ideas to each other/talking to each other, assign one student at a time to critique the communication with questions such as:
  - Is the message clear? Is the method of communication helpful?
  - Are correct assumptions being made about what is or isn't common knowledge?
  - Is sufficient detail provided to be clear about what has been done and found?
  - Is too much detail provided, thus obscuring the main message?
  - Are visual aids being used appropriately?
  - Are appropriate examples used productively?
  - What suggestions do you have for alternative methods?

What else about the communication of a message is appropriate to ask in your field?

Of course, the term 'peers' is not restricted to those within a student's own department. When at conferences, my supervisor used to introduce me to her peers' students. These relationships became important both professionally and socially, as we talked about our work, shared expertise and ideas, and found solace in the fact that, though from different nations and university systems, we were all having the same struggles.

Communicating with the wider scholarly community generally refers to participating in conferences and publishing in peer-reviewed journals. There is often a degree of diffidence about doing this that is not unique to international students, but is exacerbated when English is not the student's first language. The supervisor's attitude can make all the difference:

> *'A PhD in the UK makes you less independent, I think, because you are not automatically part of teaching or giving talks, seminars, conferences, writing articles etc. You are not expected to take part in these activities if you don't want to pursue them.'*
>
> *Research student – Arts and Humanities*

The impact of the supervisor's opinion on matters like those expressed by this postgraduate should not be underestimated. The difference between 'not expected to take part' and 'expected not to take part' is a subtle one, and there are times when a well-meaning supervisor who wants to avoid putting pressure on an international student may be perceived as discouraging the student from taking part in external activities.

In terms of the research, it's possible to present at conferences at an earlier stage than it is to write a paper for peer-reviewed publication. This is true both of oral and poster presentations, and both can be used to encourage a student to share their work with the wider scholarly community.

Supervisory Enquiries about Formal Presentations

- When did you first present your research outside your own department? What stage were you at in terms of your career?
- How did you do it – a poster, a talk, on your own, or with others? How did you find the experience?
- How did your supervisor encourage you to do this, or support you in doing this?
- What lessons did you learn that you would like to pass on?

When we talk to postgraduates about presenting their work to the wider scholarly community, we often find that they are nervous about doing so. This is exacerbated when their confidence in the use of English is not great, but generally the nervousness arises from having people look at their work rather than their expression of it.

In most cases it helps considerably to remind students that the presentation is not about them – rather, it is about the research and what the audience needs to understand about the message of the research. This is a lesson that could be learned by many academics at all stages of their academic careers. However, the lack of role models does not negate the usefulness of the concept.

Supervisory Ideas about Formal Presentations

When you are encouraging your students to prepare a talk or to create a poster, first ask them what the message is that they want to portray:

- What is the point of the talk/poster?

Then, together, consider the audience. It's very likely that you, as an experienced academic in the field, will have far greater knowledge of the likely audience at the conference in question:

- Are they likely to have specific, technical knowledge of the subject area, or will they need an introduction to the area as well as the precise topic?
- What is important to them? What will interest them? Do share your experience here as well as asking your student to reflect on what they know.

Bearing the information about the audience in mind, ask your student what is absolutely necessary to include in the talk/on the poster:

- What would be useful? What would be 'nice to have'?

This could be done in a conversation, face-to-face, or it could be achieved by posing the questions in advance for the student to consider and bring the answers to a meeting. If an international student whose confidence is not great either in English language or in their research is put on the spot with questions like these, it's unlikely they will respond positively. Sometimes simply having a bit of time to think can be productive.

Research presentations in all forms represent a major part of the academic experience, so there is frequently some focus on this within the generic training a university will provide. It's certainly worth the supervisor finding out a little about what's available in university training programmes for doctoral candidates. If the supervisor points their students in the direction of the skills development resources available and then follows up by asking about the learning that has been derived from these, not only will the students see the sessions as enrichment rather than addressing of some kind of deficit, but the value of the experience will be increased. We are all aware that training courses will offer useful information and ideas, but these will be trumped by the opinions of a respected or dominant supervisor on all occasions:

> *'The PhD here is different, as it is not usually by publication. Therefore, do not necessarily expect to finish your PhD with many publications, as the opportunities may not be there.'*
>
> *Research student – Biological Sciences*

Unless engaging in a PhD by Publication, the process of publishing work in peer-reviewed journals is not an integral part of the doctoral qualification. However, our experience is firstly that there is an increasing desire on the part of students to engage in publishing work, and secondly that with increasing pressure on academic staff to publish regularly, there is a distinct advantage to supervisors writing jointly authored papers on their students' research.

The submission of a research student's work for publication will be a viable possibility at different points in the doctoral process, depending on discipline and the nature of the individual research project. However, considering publication from the outset has advantages, especially since targeting publication outlets early on can be helpful in both writing and in the research itself.

Having said that publication is not necessarily an integral part of the doctoral process, it's worth spending a few moments considering why the academic community increasingly feels that publishing is a good thing for doctoral candidates to do. Many international students lack confidence in communicating their work and struggle with the practicalities of the process, so why would it be a useful thing to expend considerable effort and time on this?

We believe there are a number of reasons why both the process and product of publication are useful for international students:

- It informs the research agenda.
- It may be a requirement of stakeholders.
- It is the objective means of ascertaining quality (see Chapter 9).
- The Research Excellence Framework exerts (indirect) pressure.

- It is motivating, as many international students want to publish.
- Publication can represent a confidence boost and a milestone for marking progress.

Student and Supervisor Discussions about Publishing

When your student's project is formed – at least in the first instance – consider asking them to identify different sections of the project, each of which could be published. Determining which journals to target is a useful process for students to engage in – especially if they are unfamiliar with the range of journals available.

Consider asking them to review some relevant journals, asking the following questions for each of them:

- What is the audience of this journal interested in?
- How relevant are the articles to your research project?
- Are there particular methodologies that are commonly adopted?
- What is the impact factor?
- What is the rejection rate?
- What other questions would you ask yourself before targeting a journal?

Armed with the answers to these questions, then follow up with:

- Where do you want to publish your first paper?
- When might it be reasonable to do this?

With the increase in emphasis on 'impact' across the entire spread of academic disciplines, there has been an increase in pressure to communicate the message of academic research throughout the community at large. Some academics have been engaged in what have become known as 'outreach activities' for quite some time, but for others such activity is new.

Pearls are of no value in the desert.
Indian proverb

Our experience is that researchers often have the attitude that communicating sophisticated research to a lay audience is tantamount to dumbing down the results of their labours. However, this does not need to be the case. In fact, communicating expertise to those who don't share academic experience is a sophisticated skill in itself. It's the skill of discerning the purpose and value of the research, rather than the technical detail – a skill worth acquiring for its own sake.

For international students there are additional challenges to engaging in outreach activities. Many of the activities will involve addressing cultural differences. Imagine walking into a classroom of schoolchildren. This prospect alone is frightening enough for many, but imagine the added confusion when the classroom doesn't look like the ones you remember, when the children don't behave in the way you remember, when the relationship the pupils have with their teacher is perplexing. And now imagine needing to express the purpose of your research to these schoolchildren, and the value of the results for them.

Supervisory Enquiries about Outreach Activity

- What outreach activities are you engaged in?
- What challenges does this pose for you?
- How could you encourage your student to support you in your own engagement in the wider community, then to take on their own responsibilities in this area?
- What opportunities are available across the university that your student could take advantage of? If not in your own department or faculty, often there are opportunities through the careers service, graduate school or specific outreach or community relations offices in the central university administration.

Sufficient understanding of their own research and the expertise to communicate it effectively to a range of audiences are likely to develop later in a student's doctoral candidature. However, an awareness that this is a goal can't come too early, and students can usefully be encouraged to discuss their research with friends, family and neighbours, as well as with their peers and the academic community at large, from the initial stages.

Of course, it's true that the 'impact agenda' has the UK economy as its primary driver, so the argument that impact is not necessarily a concern of international doctoral students is valid. However, our contention is that the ability to communicate to a varied audience has intrinsic value for the student, in relation to both their current study and their future career, wherever that may be.

Regardless of whether the doctoral candidate is communicating with their peers, the wider scholarly community or society at large, it's essential that we focus on the communication of sophisticated ideas rather than worrying too much about the use of academic English. If a researcher can, as a doctoral candidate, develop the skill of expressing these sophisticated ideas clearly and simply to a variety of audiences, then, as we shall see in the next chapter, it's a small step to being able to promote research within society.

Chapter 12
Onwards and Outwards

The final Dublin Descriptor states that a successful doctoral candidate can 'be expected to be able to promote, within academic and professional contexts, technological, social or cultural advancement in a knowledge based society'. This descriptor is about taking the knowledge and experience acquired during doctoral study and using it for the good of general society. It's about applying expertise in such a way that society advances, whether in terms of furthering academic research in progressing technology, deepening understanding, or in transferring knowledge beyond academia. It's about making knowledge count.

One who does not look ahead remains behind.
Brazilian proverb

For the knowledge to count, the doctoral candidate must develop an understanding of the impact of their work and appreciate the value of that impact. And building on that knowledge and appreciation, they must have the ability to communicate the importance of their research in the appropriate contexts. Thus, they are able to promote the notion that knowledge is good, something to be shared and disseminated, rather than held close to one's chest.

When we talk to researchers, both doctoral candidates and their supervisors, about the doctoral experience, the skills encapsulated in this Dublin Descriptor don't arise naturally, and frequently don't arise at all. Therefore, we have comparatively little material from students or supervisors on this topic. In many ways it's understandable that doctoral researchers tend to focus on the immediate task at hand (the research project that will form the basis of the Thesis) rather than the impact this will have more widely. This is despite the 'impact agenda' stirring the UK academy, which, although perhaps not originally intended by this descriptor, must now be taken account of by all academics seeking funds for their research.

Does this mean we should skate over the topic because it's not of immediate interest to many? We don't think so. At the risk of sounding overly idealistic, we believe that those of us who have the privilege to study at doctoral level and beyond have a responsibility to contribute to the society within which we will operate.

This Dublin Descriptor doesn't specify how exactly the contribution is to be made. It could be that the research carried out is applicable enough to be of direct benefit to society in itself, such as the development of a new drug or piece of technology; it could be that our research will be of indirect benefit, by promoting or fostering other research that's of direct benefit. Or it could be that the skills and aptitudes developed during doctoral study are of value in a different way.

There are three main aspects of this descriptor that are relevant to our focus in this chapter:

1. the impact of research;

2. the question of which society should be advanced by an international student;

3. what it means to be able to promote advancement.

A social scientist we spoke to reported that she had recently attended a series of workshops about grant writing. Each workshop had been useful and well received by the participants, until the one entitled 'Impact'. Her main comment about this was how high the feelings of the participants had run at the very mention of the word, and how the skilled facilitator had needed to exercise peace-making skills.

There is some resistance within parts of the academic community towards participating in the increasing requirement to provide an account of the impact a piece of research might have. It seems that this is often a result of feeling that the account must provide some kind of economic justification for something whose value isn't easy to express in monetary terms. There is resistance to this requirement for economic justification, though resistance to a financial reality is generally futile.

The term 'knowledge-based society' is often used in economic and political contexts to mean a civilization that isn't reliant on buying and selling manufactured goods for its survival, but leans instead on the knowledge of its citizens to drive innovation and entrepreneurship. Training and education are prized, as are the wider contributions to society and culture.

> *'I think it's almost impossible for anyone (be they a PhD candidate or established academic) working in such an overtly policy-oriented discipline as mine to ignore the possible impacts of their work on the "real world".'*
>
> *Research supervisor – Social Sciences*

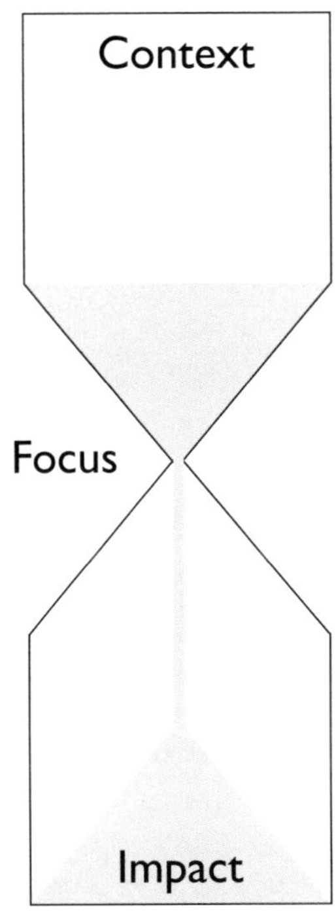

Figure 12.1 Thesis structure

For some disciplines, such as the one in the quote above, the link between academic work and the impact on the world outside academia is clear. For others, including for each of the three of us when we reflect on our doctoral research, the link to wider society, or even to the rest of the academic field, is less obvious.

However, this is not to say that the link is not there. In Chapter 7 we introduced the hourglass image we use frequently when describing the Thesis. To return to this analogy (see Figure 12.1): the Thesis is broad at the beginning, with a description of the context into which the research is set provided by the introductory chapters and literature review or theoretical foundations; it then narrows to the specific piece of work the doctoral candidate is undertaking, then it broadens out again with the final discussion and conclusion which detail what the research means for the field and the questions raised and not yet answered – the impact.

However, it's our experience that many doctoral students focus entirely on the middle of the hourglass – at least in part due to their supervisor's guidance. Frequently this results in sections such as the literature review being seen as a necessary evil, a distraction from the real business at hand. The same is often true of the concluding chapters. But in order to be able to address this Dublin Descriptor, to understand the value of one's investment in time and study, some appreciation of what comes at the top and bottom of the hourglass must be attained.

Supervisory Idea about Knowledge Transfer

Early in your student's doctoral candidature, get them to read a newspaper – on paper or online – each day for a week. They should identify an academically based story that interests them, one that includes the phrase 'Researchers at X University …', then search for the original academic publication the article is based on. The student could then come to you with the answers to the following questions:

- What are the differences between the academic publication and the newspaper piece? What is the central message of each of them?
- In the newspaper article, where has the core intellectual content of the journal article been well represented, and where has it been misrepresented?
- Why has this story become newsworthy? Do you think the researchers contacted the press, or vice versa?
- Who might benefit from the research?
- How might they benefit?

In this way, in addition to the cultural and linguistic advantages of the exercise, the international doctoral candidate will start to identify the ways research feeds into wider society. They will also start to appreciate the different ways the central message of the research must be communicated in order for the transfer of knowledge to happen.

Articulating impact is not simply about providing economic justification for the worth of one's research. Research Councils UK, a partnership between the UK's seven research councils, has outlined the different ways which research can be said to advance society in its Pathways to Impact Model.[1] These include the academic impacts of worldwide academic advancement, the development of new methodologies and cross-disciplinary approaches, contributing to the strength and longevity of academic disciplines, training highly skilled researchers, and the improvement of teaching and learning more generally, as well as a wide range of economic and societal impacts. To return to the hourglass analogy, the impact can be seen to extend beyond the end of the Thesis, towards societal change.

The Dublin Descriptor discussed in this chapter demonstrates the need to engage with impact in its broadest sense. Researchers can consider following a number of different pathways in order to extend the impact of their work.

Scholarly Publications

Scholarly publications and other dissemination of research within the academic community can be said to advance academic knowledge, thus having an impact in an academic context. It may also be argued that by increasing one's skills, an impact is discernable in this context in the improving of teaching and learning within higher education, and in the development of high levels of technical and other skill in researchers.

1 See 'What Do Research Councils Mean by "Impact"?': www.rcuk.ac.uk/ke/impacts/mean byimpact (accessed 19 June 2014).

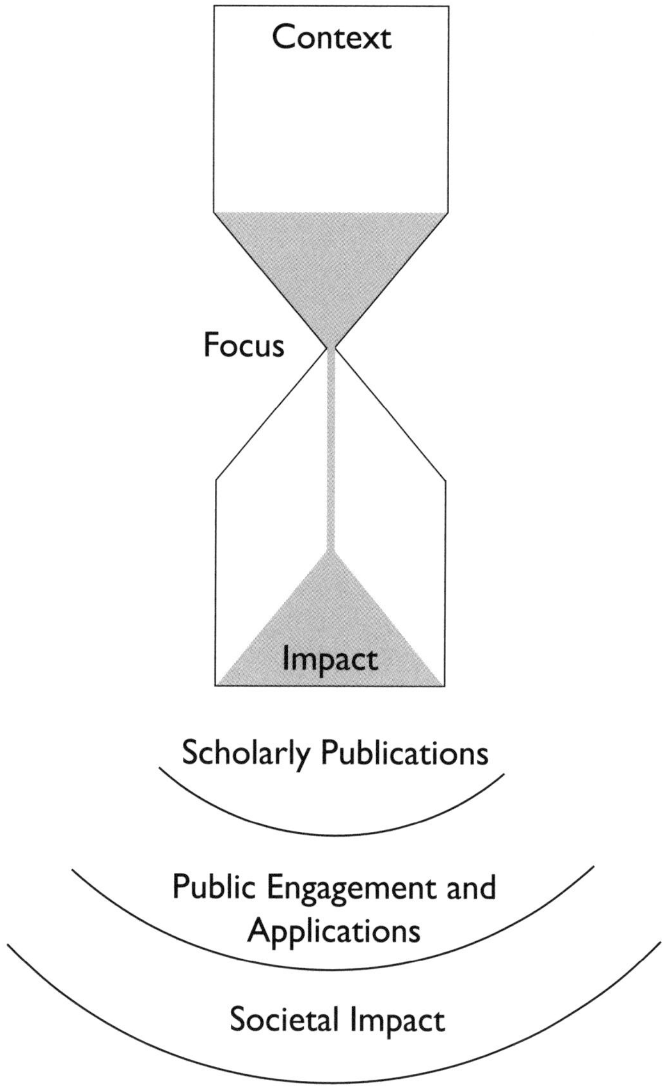

Figure 12.2 Thesis structure including the impact on society

However, if this knowledge remains in the academic context, all that is ultimately achieved is the perpetuation of a discipline. In order to meet the demands of society that is footing the bill for research, at least one of the public engagement, knowledge exchange, economic or societal pathways to impact must be followed.

Public Engagement and Applications

Public engagement is often described as 'outreach' (see Chapter 11), and describes the notion of inspiring those outside academia to be involved in some way with research and related issues. Knowledge exchange goes a step further, creating a bridge between research in higher education institutions and the public, private and third sectors, thus enhancing the research capacity, knowledge and skills in those sectors. This may involve developing and sharing innovative methodologies, equipment, techniques and cross-disciplinary approaches. This sharing of information and wisdom is at the foundation of the advancement of a knowledge-based society. Economic impact is achieved through the commercialization of research, and the exploitation of that research leads to the creation of economic prosperity and regeneration.

Societal Impact

Societal impact is achieved when public policy is influenced by evidence-based research and when research results enhance the effectiveness and sustainability of public, private and third-sector organizations. In addition, if practices and cultures within these organizations are changed, or where there is an improvement in social welfare, cohesion or national security, research can be said to have had a societal impact.

There are occasions when academic research is shown to have contributed to an improvement in public health and well-being, or to the enhancement of quality of life and cultural enrichment. Such occasions are rare, largely due to the difficulty of providing evidence for this kind of impact.

Supervisory Enquiries about Research Impact

In what ways does your own work have an impact?

- Who might benefit from your work?
- How might they benefit?
- Is it important to you that your work has a non-academic benefit?
- How important is it that the benefit should be both measurable and measured?

In Chapters 1 and 2 we discussed the UK doctorate in a global context. Many international doctoral candidates have chosen to study in the UK simply because by doing this they can have a greater impact in their home nation. The reality of twenty-first-century life is that education and training gained in one country has currency in others, and it is often apparent to us that there is an advantage of travel as part of the whole doctoral experience. In a context where this is the case, it's inevitable that there are certain political and economic realities that must be acknowledged within the European Union, and increasingly, it seems, beyond it.

One of the realities faced by UK academics is that each application for funding must now be accompanied by a statement of how the potential impact of the proposed piece of research can be maximized.

Supervisory Ideas about Research Impact

- When you have a research proposal under way, in order to raise your student's impact-awareness, give them the task of considering the impact statement. After ensuring that they have a grasp of the essence of the proposed project, ask them to come back with ideas about the potential areas of impact and what the content of the impact statement could be.
- Ask the student to draft a similar impact statement for their own research.

It's frequently a source of relief and pleasure to academics that research can be said to have impact due to its significance in terms of academic practice. If an academic's research informs their teaching at either graduate or undergraduate level, or if it's interesting and attractive to students, thus contributing to the health of the academic discipline, the research is considered to be impactful.

Supervisory Enquiries about the Research–teaching Interface

- How much does your research inform your teaching, both in content and method?
- What could you do to increase undergraduate interest in your research speciality?

Supervisory Idea about the Research–teaching Interface

- If you're trying something new in relation to bringing your research into your teaching, ask your student to sit in on a lecture or seminar of yours. Ask in advance for comments and suggestions on specific areas, such as student engagement or communication of complex ideas, and then discuss the experience afterwards.

This could be a wonderful exercise for your undergraduates as they are drawn closer to the cutting-edge of your research, useful for you as you receive supportive and constructive feedback on your endeavours, and invaluable for your research student as they see the promotion of knowledge in action.

Of course, if contributing to an academic discipline is a way of promoting the advancement of a knowledge-based society, we can't ignore the impact of peer-reviewed publications on this.

Some years ago a colleague and I were delivering a supervisory training course, and as part of the activities involved we asked the supervisors to form groups and to depict the research student journey as a Bayeux Tapestry-style picture. Following much debate and several cartographic drafts, one sub-group agreed that following the 'Pre-Induction', 'Induction' and 'Becoming Competent' stages of the journey there was usually a stage or phase that they agreed to call 'Usefulness'. When asked to explain this stage to the rest of the cohort, the group reported back that this was the phase where the 'harvesting of all the effort that had been put into the induction and training phases' took place. By this they meant joint publications, research outputs and tangible 'crops' from all their supervisory efforts. There was widespread agreement from the rest of the supervisors present about the need for 'doctoral harvesting'.

While this story is not meant to indicate that all supervisors think in these terms, it's a clear indication that some supervisors do. And neither is this philosophy confined to the sciences, where larger research project teams are more common. Harvesting also occurs in the arts, humanities and social sciences, which are, it seems, being financially urged towards the bigger and longer models of research practice.

And whether or not the notion of harvesting sits easily with the supervisor's core values , there can be no denying that a relationship that has tangible and practical benefits for both parties will be advantageous over one where the advantage is only one-way. As Rugg and Petre (2004) observe: 'Supervisors are research-active academics and research-active academics are hideously overworked. PhD students take up time, which is the supervisor's scarcest resource, and are in that sense a liability. A sensible student will reduce their liability rating; a good student will find ways of being a positive asset.'

Publishing clearly offers advantages for both doctoral researchers and supervisors, so it's something that can bring unity of purpose to even a flimsily constructed relationship. As a doctoral researcher progresses, it may be possible for them to begin publishing in collaboration with their supervisor. As discussed in Chapter 9, the publication process is valuable in its own right in helping the international doctoral student to gain confidence and credibility as an academic, or as highlighted by the contribution below, as a skilled professional with a contribution to make. Publications are evidence of impact; co-authored publications are advantageous to both doctoral candidates and time-pressured supervisors alike:

> *'A third of all my publications to date have been co-authored with my own students. Those same students, if they have pursued an academic path, have subsequently gone on to publish their own work in major journals. If they have gone outside the research sector for employment, they have often excelled in their positions.'*
>
> *Research supervisor – Arts and Humanities*

Of course, as an academic, at a superficial level it's obvious why publication is important. It's important to publish because research academics simply must do so in order for fulfil their institutional obligations to the Research Excellence Framework. However, the same is not (yet) true of their doctoral researchers.

Doctoral students are not subject to the pressures of the REF, neither is their solely authored work eligible for the research quality count in the same way. Indeed, according to this superficial view of publishing, it could be argued that *providing they can obtain a post-doctoral research contract,* it's almost as advantageous for doctoral students not to publish until they are eligible to be entered into the REF exercise in their own right.

As an aside, we often talk to doctoral researchers (both UK and international) about the REF. Those who have even heard of it are consistently in the minority, which is an interesting comment on their appreciation of the workings of the UK higher education sector and the value placed on contributing to the health of the academic discipline. This lack of awareness is also possibly a reflection of the degree to which supervisors inform their students about the reality of the context in which they are both working:

> *'It's brilliant to have so many international students, but when they go back home they take everything they've learned with them.'*
>
> *Research supervisor – Business School*

International doctoral students are unquestionably contributing to UK society and its economy with the substantial fees they pay the universities at which they are studying. So there's a moral and ethical question to be posed about whether it's acceptable to require them to be advancing the technological, social and cultural development of UK society in addition to this.

We have argued throughout this book that it's necessary to supervise individuals in the context of a relationship that is specifically designed for the precise doctoral candidate and supervisor involved. Doctoral candidates' motivation has been discussed at length in Chapter 3, and will not be revisited here apart from to highlight the fact that while seen as a distraction by some, the possibility of making a difference to society with either specific knowledge or advanced transferable skills may be exactly what motivates a student to begin their research, or to carry it through to completion. It may well be useful for the supervisor to acknowledge their individual student's motivation, and indeed to use this attraction to the 'So what?' of the research rather than simply the 'What?' in order to help motivate the student if passion for the topic fades.

In short, what this Dublin Descriptor requires is not an economic output from a doctoral research project to UK society specifically, but rather that the student be able to contribute to whichever society is relevant, in whatever way is relevant for them. The doctoral candidature must be a period of training for this.

A good tree bears good fruit.
German proverb

There are advantages for both supervisors and doctoral students in this regard when different countries or cultures of origin provide different perspectives from which to look at research topics and what they might mean. When encouraged to articulate their points of view, both parties can enrich their understanding of the breadth of impact their research may have.

Supervisory Ideas about Societal Benefit

Previous activities have suggested a discussion of who is funding the international student's research and what the funders require. But to look at the wider advancement of society, it may be relevant to look with your student at the source of these funders' funds.

Ask your student to consider the ultimate source of their funding and to come to a supervision meeting with answers to the following questions:

- What does the source of funding say about the ultimate impact of the research?
- What is the student's responsibility in the light of this?
- Which part of which society will benefit from the doctoral research?
- What about similar considerations for other stakeholders contributing to the student being able to do their research in the UK – employers giving study leave, families and so on?

The writing of the Thesis is a concrete contribution to knowledge, a tangible piece of evidence that will sit in a library, often undisturbed until someone comes across the abstract in some electronic format and requests a copy of it to check a detail of the research. This is important in terms of qualifying for the doctorate itself, but in terms of promoting the advancement of a knowledge-based society, the effects are limited. What's significant here is not the writing up of the Thesis itself, but an appreciation of the actual 'contribution through original research that extends the frontiers of knowledge' as discussed in Chapter 9, and of why this contribution matters.

In order to be able to fully communicate the essential message of one's research and to use this to promote the advancement of society, it's necessary to be passionate about it. I recently heard a senior academic speak to early-career researchers about his professional journey. He spoke with integrity, detailing the times when he had been fortunate, the people he had been privileged to work with, what opportunities he had grasped. He was engaging and interesting to listen to. But it was when he spoke about his current research and how he had come to appreciate the value of cross-disciplinary work that he lit up like a beacon. Soon members of the audience were all but queuing up to share their research with him and discuss what the possibilities might be for them. It became abundantly clear how he was having an impact. Some of this impact was due to the details of his specialist research, for which he is internationally renowned. But mostly what was communicated was his professional passion for research.

Supervisory Enquiries about Professional Passion

- What do you love about your academic career?
- What does your work mean to your field?
- What does it mean to your academic discipline?
- What does it mean to the research sector more generally?
- What does it mean to wider society?
- How do you share your passion?
- How do you promote the advancement of a knowledge-based society in your own work?

> *[Why did you decide to do a PhD?] 'I wanted to become an academic. My PhD has taught me that I was incorrect.'*
>
> *Research student – Psychology, Brazil*

It's sometimes the case that a researcher's specialist knowledge will provide any kind of advantage only if the researcher remains in the academic environment. However, not only is the university research sector extremely competitive, meaning that many bright and committed doctoral researchers don't go on to an academic career, but many doctoral students, regardless of domicile, *do not have the aspiration* to follow an academic career even if the opportunity were presented.

Supervisory Enquiries about Career Destination

- How attached are you to the idea of your student staying in academia?
- What impact does this have on the way you supervise?
- Does their career destination *really* matter to you as a supervisor?
- Do they know at the beginning, in the middle or at the end of their candidature what they aspire to do? Does this change? Have you discussed this with your student?

Incidentally, this Dublin Descriptor, doesn't include the necessity of the student continuing with their field of study. It simply states that they should be able to contribute. It's entirely consistent with this descriptor for the student's aspirations to lie outside academia. We are not suggesting, by any means, that it's part of the supervisor's role to be a careers adviser. However, as part of a productive relationship, these matters can usefully be discussed while maintaining a focus on the task in hand –the completion of the doctorate.

The supervisor's interest lies in the student's well-being and in their gaining something useful from the experience of the doctorate in order to contribute to the technological, social or cultural advancement of a knowledge-based society. As Julie Reeves (2007) observes: 'the PhD experience should result in a portfolio of skills for life, not simply a hard-bound manuscript that sits in a library'.

This observation is of increasing value in a context where many of those holding a doctorate don't remain in academia, as testified by the (albeit Europe-focused) research conducted by Vitae and published under the title *What Do Researchers Do?* finding that only 17 per cent of those canvassed who completed a doctorate in 2010 remained in higher education research occupations.[2]

However, in addition to collecting that portfolio of skills, the student is changed by the experience of attaining a doctorate. That experience is part of what makes them who they are, and (particularly where it has been a positive experience) will mean that they can make a valuable contribution in whatever field they choose to adopt in the future.

2 *What Do Researchers Do? Early Career Progression of Doctoral Graduates*: www.vitae.ac.uk/CMS/files/upload/What-do-researchers-do-Early-career-progression-2013.pdf (accessed 18 June 2014).

Supervisory Ideas about Career Destination

- Ask your student to produce a map of their life's journey post-doctorate – any kind of graphical representation of the possible routes their life could take, showing significant events and turning points. Get them to bring it to a meeting and talk you through it.
- What is interesting for you about this?

There are many things about this exercise that could prove useful. You may discover that you have an accomplished artist! You may find that you understand your student better when they have an opportunity to really let you know where they see themselves ending up. It's also a way they can use to express themselves without relying too heavily on the written word; this can be liberating if the use of English is an added pressure.

If you know your student is looking for a career outside academia:

- Encourage your student to research alternative careers, and show an interest in what they find out.
- Support them in networking appropriately by allowing time away from research where necessary.
- Discuss whether an ongoing professional as well as personal relationship could be of mutual benefit if your student moves on from academia. What are the possibilities here?

While this may seem like a distraction from the research, there's some evidence that certain personality types are likely to delay completion of a task while they're unsure what they will do next. As timely completion of a Thesis is one of the supervisor's aims, it may be an effective investment of time for a doctoral candidate to explore their future options.

What you see in yourself is what you see in the world.
Afghan proverb

In common with many achievements, the completion of a doctorate is more than simply an academic qualification. Once a person achieves a doctoral qualification, they are forever entitled to use 'Dr' as their title, regardless of their subsequent occupation. Whether that researcher chooses to remain in the UK, in academic research or in research at all is incidental. The simple fact is that this person has had the privilege of participating in doctoral research, and consequently they have a responsibility to share that advantage with others in whatever way is right for them to do so:

> *'I strive to provoke curiosity, to foster questioning, initiative and self-direction, to transmit the thrill of discovery and to convey the satisfaction that comes from taking on a problem and figuring it out.'*
> *Research supervisor – Arts and Humanities*

The final question for us, then, concerns the supervisor's role in this development. Is there a mutual advantage in the supervisor providing support in this metamorphosis? Much of the value of a supervisor's role lies in modelling the analysis of their own impact on society and sharing that self-analysis with their student for the student's benefit.

Student and Supervisor Discussions about Value

What value does each of the following add to society:

- this research project?
- this thesis?
- this student?
- this relationship?

What does 'society' mean for you both?

The discussions outlined above are particularly useful when coupled with a model provided by a supervisor. Together they can enable the international student to appreciate the need to take responsibility for sharing not only the information they gather during their research, but also their identity.

In this way the supervisor, regardless of style or approach, can become not simply a guide, but also a catalyst.

Chapter 13
Fit for Purpose? Preparing the Candidate for their Viva

This book, and in particular the previous six chapters, has engaged with the questions of what the doctorate is and how the supervisor can help and guide their student through to the point of scholarly independence. There is, of course, a final test for the student to pass: the doctoral viva. This process is designed to check whether the candidate is fit for purpose and worthy of the title 'Doctor'. This final chapter examines how supervisors can help their students to ensure they are ready for this test.

Experiences of the Viva

There were four people in the room. I sat at a large table with my back to the door; my external examiner was to my left, and my internal examiner was to my right. My supervisor, present at my invitation, was behind me, slightly to my right and out of my line of vision. She had no active role to play; she didn't speak throughout the entire two-hour period, and honestly, after the first few moments I forgot she was there.

So, since the supervisor usually plays no real part in the examination of the thesis and many are not present at the viva itself, why have a section on the viva in a book about supervision?

The physical presence of a supervisor in the viva may not be the norm, but the supervisor's influence will always be a factor in the candidate's experience. How the supervisor prepares their student for the viva can be crucial. Discussions of the viva process and actual practice of the likely types of examination interactions will benefit the student's preparation both in terms of their confidence and their intellectual performance.

In the UK system (both as it applies in the UK and in 'franchise universities' in other parts of the world) the PhD viva is far from a formality. In contrast with vivas in many other countries, in the UK the viva voce examination is just that: an oral examination of the candidate's worthiness of the doctoral qualification.

A UK viva has none of the ceremony and festivity associated with the public defence as conducted in North America and much of Europe, where family and friends gather to hear a candidate discuss their work. In such public vivas the result is all but a foregone conclusion as the thesis has already been read, commented upon and revised. If this is what a candidate for a UK viva expects, the reality will prove something of a shock. A meeting behind closed doors where two (or three if there are two external examiners) senior academics have the responsibility of judging whether or not the candidate meets the criteria for the award of PhD can seem a daunting prospect – even if the candidate fully understands what may happen:

> *'I want to know how I will be measured and judged. It is unknown, and I feel anxious.'*
>
> *Research student – Biosciences*

Due to the private nature of the UK viva – together with the fact that candidates have often left the department and even the country, return for their viva, then leave again with little opportunity to share their experience with others – an air of mystery surrounds the viva, and in the vacuum of clear information, myths and horror stories abound. Therefore, the role of the supervisor in preparing the student for the viva is partly a matter of providing accurate and representative information about what is involved, then ensuring the candidate is equipped intellectually and emotionally to meet the requirements.

On many occasions through this book we have discussed the need for the PhD candidate to be independent and for the supervisor's role to be to facilitate that independence. Many of our supervisory enquiries and suggested methods centre on the supervisor passing on responsibility to the candidate. In its widest possible sense, this student-centred approach is the best preparation for the viva that can be imagined.

The tips throughout the book can help to increase the student's confidence and equip them to function independently in the academic field. However, it often helps the candidate if there are explicit conversations about the viva, as this will make it clear that there is a specific reason for requiring the student to be independent. The primary purpose of the viva is to establish that the candidate is responsible for the creation of the thesis. So talking about the thesis, asking questions about details and probing the underlying assumptions will assist in increasing the student's ability to cope when the challenges come from the examiners.

There are some great resources already available which are designed to help with the viva process (for instance, Tinkler and Jackson 2004; Trafford and Leshem 2002). Our intention is not to attempt to replace these, but to focus specifically on how supervisors can help to prepare their candidates for the final challenge of the doctoral process.

> *He who is well prepared has half won the battle.*
>
> *Portuguese proverb*

This book has taken the Dublin Descriptors as one of its structuring ideas and has emphasized throughout that there are specific success criteria that must be met in order for a PhD to be awarded. We suggest that providing explicit 'mock viva' questions concerning each of the Dublin descriptors as a matter of course throughout the candidature will be great preparation for the viva. The student will become accustomed to answering such questions in a 'safe' environment, and able to discuss their work at a sophisticated level with confidence. Many universities have a rigorous 'upgrade' or 'transfer' process which may help the student to understand the process of postgraduate oral examinations (though many of the concerns students have about the viva are also applicable to any prior formal oral defences).

Potential Viva Questions Addressing Each Dublin Descriptor

What follows is a selection of itemized questions designed to access and test the different aspects of the doctoral candidate's competency and understanding. They can be used throughout the process of candidature, or as part as a formal 'mock viva', or even as part of a 'mini-viva', where an individual chapter of the Thesis is objectively 'examined' by the supervisor. Many of these questions are based on actual ones asked by examiners we've spoken to, supplemented by the writings of Trafford and Leshem (2002) and Tinkler and Jackson (2004). What follows is not intended to address the specific technical elements of the research, but to help the candidate to contextualize it and frame it within the holistic nature of the doctoral qualification.

1. DOES THE CANDIDATE DISPLAY FIRM INTELLECTUAL FOUNDATIONS?

... can demonstrate a systematic understanding of a field of study and mastery of the skills and methods of research associated with that field.

- What do you believe makes for good academic research? What led you to select this model of academic practice?
- What are the key theories that underpin your study?
- Who are the key thinkers in the field, and how does your work compare with theirs?
- How did you arrive at your conceptual framework?
- How did you decide on the variables to include in your conceptual framework?
- How did you use your conceptual framework to design your research and analyze your findings?
- How does your work build on the work of others?
- How does your Thesis fill a gap in the literature?

2. DOES THE CANDIDATE SHOW SOUND SCHOLARLY CONSTRUCTION?

... can demonstrate the ability to conceive, design, implement and adapt a substantial process of research with scholarly integrity.

- What other forms of research did you consider? Why did you select this particular design for your research?
- What methodologies did you reject, and why?
- If you could start the work again, what would you change? Why didn't you make those changes sooner?
- How would you explain you research approach?
- How would you defend your methodology?

- What other interpretations of your data may there be?
- How did you relate the various stages of your research to each other?
- How did you analyse your data, and how did you arrive at meanings from that analysis?

3. IS THE CANDIDATE MAKING A VALID INTELLECTUAL CONTRIBUTION?

... has made a contribution through original research that extends the frontier of knowledge by developing a substantial body of work, some of which merits national or international refereed publication.

- How can you be certain that this work is original?
- What was your literature search strategy?
- How do your findings contribute to the discipline? What is their significance, and what further questions do they invite or leave open?
- How would you justify your choice of methodology/sampling/data?
- What value does this work add outside academia?

4. IS THE CANDIDATE SOPHISTICATED IN THEIR THINKING?

... is capable of critical analysis, evaluation and synthesis of new and complex ideas.

- How would you critique your thesis?
- What are the weaknesses in the work?
- How was your hypothesis formed?
- In what ways were you not fully objective in your approach?
- How would you use this Thesis in a different context?

- How would incorporate a complementary aspect of research into your work...?
- How could you have achieved a better result?
- If you wanted to continue this work, how would you do so?
- What has the doctoral process taught you about being an academic?

5. CAN THE CANDIDATE SPREAD THEIR MESSAGE?

... can communicate with their peers, the larger scholarly community and with society in general about their areas of expertise.

- In a sentence, what is your thesis?
- With which researchers would you like to collaborate, and why?
- How are you intending to disseminate this work in an effective manner?
- How would you go about explaining your work to a non-specialist?
- How would you justify further economic investment in this area of study?
- What aspects of your work would you want to include in future undergraduate/master's degree programmes?

6. IS THE CANDIDATE CONTEXTUALLY WELL PLACED FOR THEIR FUTURE PROFESSIONAL CONTRIBUTIONS?

... can be expected and able to promote, within academic and professional contexts, technological, social or cultural advancement in a knowledge-based society.

- What has doctoral research taught you that will be useful for you?
- How is gaining your doctorate going to help your career?
- What are you going to publish from your thesis?

- How would you go about supervising a doctoral candidate?
- What advice would you give to a potential doctoral applicant?
- How might your work have a wider impact?
- Does this work represent value for money?

The purpose of these questions is to ensure that the candidate can demonstrate confidently that they broadly meet all of the scholarly requirements of the six Dublin Descriptors. If they're able to do this – provided they fully understand the technical elements of their work and the work is actually their own – they are by definition well prepared for their viva. Of course, we can provide no guarantees in terms of an examination process that is governed by individual examiners with their own idiosyncrasies and biases. However, a candidate who is well prepared as set out above, and whose written work is carefully constructed to meet the regulations and academic requirements, is unlikely to encounter too many problems.

Final Thoughts

A good, well-lived today makes every yesterday a dream of a good future and every morning a vision of hope.
Sanskrit proverb

The doctorate is a journey, akin to a trek through uncharted territory. The supervisor has undertaken many journeys before, and though they too are in alien territory, they know how to read the stars, use a compass, find the right sort of berries and intuitively know which dark caves to avoid. The student is learning this craft of exploration. The start of the journey is potentially a huge shock for any student, and the international researcher may face cultural, institutional, intellectual and methodological shocks. At embarkation they will have to place a huge amount of trust in their supervisor.

'Don't panic! Your supervisor knows what he is doing.'
Research student, Saudi Arabia

The purpose of their journey is twofold: to discover new worlds and to attain independence so that in future they can travel alone. The first could be gained by the student simply following in the considered footsteps of the supervisor and taking advice on which direction to take. The second, as we hope we've demonstrated, requires something more – certainly intellectual fieldcraft in the forms of skills and knowledge – but more than this, it requires *confidence*:

- It requires that the student is confident and trusts the supervisor and is certain that they are providing good advice and sound direction.
- It requires that the supervisor is confident and trusts the student to have sufficient stamina, drive and ability to learn the craft of academic exploration.
- It requires that the student is confident that they won't be abandoned if they make a mistake or seem to take too much responsibility too soon.

- It requires that both parties have confidence in each other as the journey develops and the expertise starts to shift so that the student is the one with superlative knowledge of the territory in question.

This confidence doesn't come about by accident. It requires both travellers to think about the journey, the purpose of discovery and the relationship they have. And we hope that we've argued successfully that the doctoral journey and experience can only be truly enhanced if the alliance between the travellers is one that is consciously designed. With co-travellers who start the journey from different cultural places and with different languages and previous experiences, this design process can be difficult, so it's sometimes avoided or forgotten. Here, the responsibility for leadership lies with the supervisor – not in leading the journey, but leading the design.

This may seem like a huge additional weight for a supervisor who is already incredibly busy, but much of the burden is front-loaded. Once the alliance is well designed, the doctoral process is likely to be smoother and more trouble-free, allowing supervision to be more of a joint academic endeavour than a burden. Thus, if by the end of the journey both parties trust the other implicitly and are able to take the lead, this can open up whole worlds of joint international discovery in the future. This is the real pay-off to the travellers for all their work.

We hope that this book has offered inspiration and practical advice, or has simply encouraged the reader to pause and consider their own actions. However, the value of anything we've written will come the next time the supervisor prepares for a supervision, or the next time student and supervisor sit down together in a supervisory meeting. Will anything change? Will there be a focus on the 'Why?' and the 'How?' as well as the 'What?' and the 'Where?'

Here we throw the challenge to the reader. But be aware of the proverb that appears in some form in many countries and cultures:

I dreamed a thousand paths.
I woke and walked my old one.

References and Literature Cited

Anthony, J.S. (2002) 'Re-examining Doctoral Student Socialization and Professional Development: Moving Beyond the Congruence and Assimilation Orientation'. In Smart, J.C. and Tierney, W.G. (eds) *Higher Education: Handbook of Theory and Research*, vol. 17. New York: Agathon Press, pp. 349–79.

Apfelthaler, G. et al. (2007) 'Cross-cultural Differences in Learning and Education: Stereotypes, Myths and Realities'. In Palfreyman, D. and McBride, D.L. (2007) *Learning and Teaching Across Cultures in Higher Education*. Basingstoke: Palgrave Macmillan.

Atkinson, D. (1999). *Scientific Discourse in Sociohistorical Context: The Philosophical Transactions of the Royal Society of London 1675–1975.* Mahwah, NJ: Lawrence Erlbaum Associates.

Austin, A.E. (2011) 'Preparing Doctoral Students for Promising Careers in a Changing Context: Implications for Supervision, Institutional Planning and Cross-institutional Opportunities'. In Kumar, V. and Lee, A. (eds) *Doctoral Education in International Context: Connecting Local, Regional and Global Perspectives*. Serdang: Universiti Putra Malaysia Press, pp. 1–18.

Barker, J. (1997) 'The Purpose of Study, Attitudes to Study and Staff–student Relationships'. In McNamara, D. and Harris, R. (eds) (1997) *Overseas Students in Higher Education*. London: Routledge.

Beattie, C., Hutchinson, S. and Marshall, S. (2001) 'What Makes for Effective PhD Training and Supervision in the Arts and Humanities?', *Higher Education Academy English Subject Centre Online Newsletter*, 2: www.english.heacademy.ac.uk/explore/publications/newsletters/newsissue2/beattie.htm (accessed 6 June 2014).

Binsardi, A. and Ekwulugo, F. (2003) 'International Marketing of British Education: Research on the Students' Perception and the UK Market Penetration', *Marketing Intelligence and Planning*, 21(5), pp. 318–27.

Bolker, J. (1998) *Writing your Dissertation in Fifteen Minutes a Day: A Guide to Starting, Revising and Finishing Your Doctoral Thesis*. New York: Holt.

Brewer, R. (2007) *Your PhD Thesis: How to Plan, Draft, Revise and Edit Your Thesis*. Abergele: Studymates Books.

Briggs-Myers, I. and Myers, P. (1980) *Gifts Differing*. Mountain View, CA: Davies-Black Publishing.

Brockbank, A. and McGill, I. (1998) *Facilitating Reflective Learning in Higher Education*. Buckingham: Open University Press.

Burnapp, D. (2009) *Getting Ahead as an International Student*. Buckingham: Open University Press and McGraw-Hill.

Calvert Scott, J. (2004) 'Researching Abroad: Actual Experiences and Lessons Learned', *Delta Pi Epsilon Journal* (Spring/Summer), 46(2), pp. 65–75.

Canagarajah, A.S. (2002) *The Geopolitics of Academic Writing*. Pittsburgh, PA: Pittsburgh Press.

Caruna, V. and Spurling, N. (2007) *The Internationalisation of UK Higher Education*. London: Higher Education Academy.

Chan, S. (1999) 'The Chinese Learner: A Question of Style', *Education and Training*, 41(6/7), pp. 294–304.

Clegg, S. (1997) 'A Case Study of Accredited Training for Research Awards Supervisors through Reflective Practice', *Higher Education*, 34, pp. 483–98.

Collini, S. (2012) *What are Universities For?* London: Penguin Books.

Cortazzi, M. and Jin, L. (1997) 'Learning Across Cultures'. In McNamara, D. and Harris, R. (eds) *Overseas Students in Higher Education*, London: Routledge, pp. 76–90.

Cotterall, S. (2011) 'Six Outsiders and a Pseudo-insider: International Doctoral Students in Australia'. In Kumar, V. and Lee, A. (eds) *Doctoral Education in International Context: Connecting Local, Regional and Global Perspectives*. Serdang: Universiti Putra Malaysia Press, pp. 50–63.

Cryer, P. (2010) *The Research Student's Guide to Success*. Buckingham: Open University Press.

Davey, G. (2008) *The International Student's Survival Guide*. London: Sage.

Delamont, S., Atkinson, P. and Parry, O. (2004) *Supervising the Doctorate: A Guide to Success*, 2nd edn. Buckingham: Society for Research into Higher Education and Open University Press.

Denicolo, P. and Pope, M. (1999) 'Supervision and the Overseas Student'. In Ryan, Y. and Zuber-Skerritt, O. (eds) *Supervising Students from Non-English Speaking Backgrounds*. Buckingham: Society for Research into Higher Education and Open University Press, pp. 63–74.

Dunleavy, P. (2003) *Authoring a PhD: How to Plan, Draft, Write and Finish a Doctoral Thesis or Dissertation*. Basingstoke: Palgrave Macmillan.

Earley, C.P and Ang, S. (2003) *Cultural Intelligence: Individual Interactions Across Cultures*. Stanford, CA: Stanford Business Books.

Eley, A. and Jennings, R. (2005) *Effective Postgraduate Supervision: Improving the Student/supervisor Relationship*. Buckingham: Open University Press.

Eley, A. and Murray, R. (2009) *How to Be an Effective Supervisor*. Buckingham: Open University Press and McGraw-Hill.

Evans, T. and Liou, I.Y. (2011) 'Institutional Pedagogical Waypoints: Reflections on Doctoral Journeys between Taiwan and Australia', *Innovations in Education and Teaching International*, 48(4), pp. 401–11.

Fallon, G. and Berman Brown, R. (1999) 'What about the Workers? Academic Staff Opinions about Working with non-UK Postgraduate Students in Higher Education', *Journal of Further and Higher Education*, 23(1), pp. 41–52: http://dx.doi.org/10.1080/0309877990230104 (accessed 19 June 2014).

Foskett, N. and Foskett, R. (2006) *Postgraduate Study in the UK: The International Student's Guide*. London: Sage.

Furnham, A. (1997) '*The Experience of Being an Overseas Student*'. In McNamara, D. and Harris, R. (eds) *Overseas Students in Higher Education: Issues in Teaching and Learning*. London: Routledge.

Gatfield, T. (2005) 'An Investigation into PhD Supervisory Management Styles', *Journal of HE Policy and Management*, 27(3), pp. 311–25.

Geake, J. and Maingard, C. (1999) 'NESB Postgraduate Students at a New University: "Plus ça change, plus c'est la même chose"'. In Ryan, Y. and Zuber-Skerritt, O. (eds.) *Supervising Postgraduates from Non-English Speaking Backgrounds*. Buckingham: Society for Research into Higher Education and Open University Press, pp. 48–60.

Graves, N. and Varma, V. (1997) *Working for a Doctorate: A Guide for the Humanities and Social Sciences*. London: Routledge.

Greenfield, N. (2000) *How I Got My Postgraduate Degree Part Time*. Lancaster: Guardian Newspapers/Lancaster University Independent Studies.

Gundara, J. (1997) 'Intercultural Issues and Doctoral Studies'. In Graves, N. and Varma, V. (eds) *Working for a Doctorate: A Guide for the Humanities and Social Sciences*. London: Routledge.

Gurr, G. (2001) 'Negotiating the "Rackety Bridge": A Dynamic Model for Aligning Supervisory Style with Research Student Development', *Higher Education Research and Development*, 20(1), pp. 81–92.

Halai, N. (2011) 'Becoming and Being a Doctoral Supervisor in Pakistan: A Lived Experience'. In Kumar, V. and Lee, A. (eds) *Doctoral Education in International Context: Connecting Local, Regional and Global Perspectives*. Serdang: Universiti Putra Malaysia Press, pp. 37–49.

Hall, G. and Longman, J. (eds) (2008) *The Postgraduate's Companion*. London: Sage.

Halse, C. and Mowbray, S. (2011) 'The Impact of the Doctorate', *Studies in Higher Education*, 36(5), pp. 557–70.

Harman, G. (2003) 'International PhD Students in Australian Universities: Financial Support, Course Experience and Career Plans', *International Journal of Educational Development*, 23, pp. 339–51.

Hersey, P. and Blanchard, K.H. (1977) *Management of Organizational Behaviour: Utilizing Human Resources*, 3rd edn. Englewood Cliffs, NJ: Prentice Hall.

Hinchcliffe, R., Bromley, A. and Hutchinson, S. (eds) (2007) *Skills Training in Research Degree Programmes: Politics and Practice*. Buckingham: McGraw-Hill and Open University Press.

Hockey, J. (1995) *Strategies and Tactics in the Supervision of Research Students*. Cheltenham: Cheltenham & Gloucester College of Higher Education.

Hofstede, G. (1991) *Cultures and Organisations: Intercultural Cooperation and its Importance for Survival: Software of the Mind*. London: HarperCollins.

Hofstede, G. and Hofstede, G.J. (2005) *Cultures and Organisations: Software of the Mind*. Maidenhead: McGraw-Hill.

Humfrey, C. (1999) *Managing International Students*. Buckingham: Open University Press.

Hutchinson, S. and Lawrence, L. (2011) *Playing With Purpose: How Experiential Learning Can Be More than a Game*. Farnham: Gower.

James, R. and Baldwin, G. (1999) *Eleven Practices of Effective Postgraduate Supervision*. Melbourne: Centre for the Study of Higher Education, University of Melbourne.

Johnson, L., Alison, L. and Green, B. (2000) 'The PhD and the Autonomous Self: Gender Rationality and Postgraduate Pedagogy', *Studies in Higher Education*, 25, pp. 135–47.

Joyner, R. (2003) 'The Selection of External Examiners for Research Degrees', *Quality in Higher Education*, 11(2), pp. 123–7.

Kam, B.H. (1997) 'Style and Quality in Research Supervision: The Supervisor Dependency Factor', *Higher Education*, 34, pp. 81–103.

Kamler, B. and Thompson, P (2006) *Helping Doctoral Students Write: Pedagogies for Supervision*. London: Routledge.

Kim, H.Y. (2011) 'International Graduate Students' Difficulties: Graduate Classes as a Community of Practices', *Teaching in Higher Education*, 16(3), pp. 281–92.

Kim, T. (2009) 'Shifting Patterns of Transnational Academic Mobility: A Comparative and Historical Approach', *Comparative Education*, 45(3), pp. 387–403.

Kogan, M. and Kogan, D. (1983) *The Attack on Higher Education*. London: Kogan Page.

Kolb, D.A. (1984) *Experiential Learning: Experience as the Source of Learning and Development*. Englewood Cliffs, NJ: Prentice Hall.

Kouzes, J. and Posner, B. (2003) *Encouraging the Heart: A Leader's Guide to Rewarding and Recognizing Others*. San Francisco, CA: Jossey-Bass.

Ku, H.Y., Lahman, M., Yeh, H.T. and Cheng, Y.C. (2008) 'Into the Academy: Preparing and Mentoring International Doctoral Students', *Education Technology Research and Development*, 56, pp. 365–77.

Kumar, V. and Lee, A. (eds) (2011) *Doctoral Education in International Context: Connecting Local, Regional and Global Perspectives*. Serdang: Universiti Putra Malaysia Press.

Lee, A. (2008) 'How are Doctoral Students Supervised? Concepts of Doctoral Research Supervision', *Studies in Higher Education*, 33(3), pp. 267–81.

Leonard, D., Metcalfe, J., Becker, R. and Evans, J. (2006) *Review of Literature on the Impact of Working Context and Support on the Postgraduate Research Student Learning Experience*: www.heacademy.ac.uk/assets/York/documents/ourwork/postgraduate/web0581a_review_of_literature_on_the_impact_of_working_context_and_support_on_postgraduate_research_students_learning_experience.pdf (accessed 6 June 2014).

Lewis, V. and Habeshaw, S. (1997) *53 Interesting Ways to Supervise Student Projects, Dissertations and Theses*. Bristol: Technical and Educational Services.

Lin, Z. (2001) 'Discovering English as Foreign Language Learners' Perceptions of Prior Knowledge and its Roles in Reading Comprehension', *Journal of Research in Reading*, 25(2), pp. 172–90.

Livermore, D. (2011) *The Cultural Intelligence Difference*. New York: Amacom.

Lord, P.A. and Dawson, C. (2002) *The Induction Needs of International Students at Postgraduate Level*: https://www.llas.ac.uk/materialsbank/mb080/LO_3/lord_business_sc.pdf (accessed 6 June 2014).

Lee, N.Y.L. and Johnson-Laird, P.N. (2006) *Are There Cross-cultural Differences in Reasoning?*: http://mentalmodels.princeton.edu/papers/2006xcultural.pdf (accessed 18 June 2013).

Manathunga, C. (2007) 'Intercultural Postgraduate Supervision: Ethnographic Journeys of Identity and Power'. In Palfreyman, D. and McBride, D.L. (2007) *Learning and Teaching Across Cultures in Higher Education*. Basingstoke: Palgrave Macmillan.

Manathunga, C. (2012) 'Supervisors Watching Supervisors; The Deconstructive Possibilities and Tensions of Team Supervision', *Australian Universities Review*, 54(1), pp. 29–37.

Marshall, S. (1999) 'Supervising Projects and Dissertations'. In Fry, H., Ketteridge, S. and Marshall, S. (eds) *A Handbook for Teaching and Learning: Enhancing Academic Practice*. London: Kogan Page, pp. 105–20.

Maslow, A. (1987) *Motivation and Personality*, 3rd edn. Upper Saddle River, NJ: Pearson.

Matsuda, P., Ortmeier-Hooper, C. and You, X. (2006) *The Politics of Second Language Writing*. West Lafayette, IN: Parlor Press.

Mazzarol, T., Kemp, S. and Savery, L. (1997) *International Students Who Choose Not to Study in Australia*. Canberra: Australian Education International, Department of Education Training and Youth Affairs.

McCulloch, A. and Thomas, L. (2012) 'Widening Participation to Doctoral Education and Research Degrees: A Research Agenda for an Emerging Policy Area', *Higher Education Research and Development*, 32(2), pp. 214–27.

McNamara, D. and Harris, R. (eds) (1997) *Overseas Students in Higher Education*. London: Routledge.

Morrison, T. and Conaway, W. (2006) *Kiss, Bow or Shake Hands*, 2nd edn. New York: Adams Media Corporation.

Murray, R. (2011) *How to Write a Thesis*, 3rd edn. Maidenhead: McGraw-Hill.

Nisbett, R.E. (2003). *The Geography of Thought*. New York: Free Press.

Okorocha, E. (2007) *Supervising International Research Students*, Issues in Postgraduate Education: Management, Teaching and Supervision, Series 2, no. 4. London: Society for Research in Higher Education.

Okorocha, E. (2010) *International Students' Experiences in UK Higher Education*. Bury St Edmunds: Abramis Academic Publishing.

Oxford, R.L. and Anderson, N.J. (1995) 'A Cross Cultural View of Learning Styles', *Language Teaching*, 28, pp. 201–15.

Palfreyman, D. and McBride, D.L. (2007) *Learning and Teaching Across Cultures in Higher Education*. Basingstoke: Palgrave Macmillan.

Paltridge, B. (2002) 'Thesis and Dissertation Writing: An Examination of Published Advice and Actual Practice', *English for Specific Purposes*, 21(2), pp. 125–43.

Paltridge, B. and Starfield, S. (2007) *Thesis and Dissertation Writing in a Second Language: A Handbook for Supervisors*. London: Routledge.

Park, C. (2007) *Redefining the Doctorate*. Discussion paper, Higher Education Academy: https://www.vitae.ac.uk/policy/hea-redefining-the-doctorate-february-2007-vitae.pdf (accessed 6 June 2014).

Park, C. (2008) 'The End of the Secret Garden: Reframing Postgraduate Supervision', *Research Supervision: An Online Journal*: www.lancs.ac.uk/celt/celtweb/current_journal (accessed 22 September 2010).

Peelo, M. (2011) *Understanding Supervision and the PhD*. London: Continuum.

Phillips, E. and Pugh, D. (2010) *How to Get a PhD: A Handbook for Students and Their Supervisors*, 5th edn. Maidenhead: McGraw-Hill.

Powell, S. (ed.) (2003) *Special Teaching in Higher Education: Special Strategies for Access and Inclusion*, London: Kogan Page.

Powell, S. and Green, H. (2007) *The Doctorate World Wide*. Buckingham: Society for Research into Higher Education and Open University Press.

Premkamolnetr, N. (1999) 'Doing Research Overseas without Tears: Adventures of an Innocent Abroad'. Paper delivered at 65th IFLA Council and General Conference Bangkok, Thailand, 20–28 August 1999. International Federation of Library Associations and Institutions Conference Archive: www.ifla.org/IV/ifla65/papers/060-141e.htm (accessed 6 June 2014).

Pyvis, D. and Chapman, A. (2005) 'Culture Shock and the International Student "Offshore"', *Journal of Research in International Education*, 4, p. 23.

Ramsden, P. (2003) *Learning to Teach in Higher Education*. London: Routledge Falmer.

Rees, W.D. and Porter, C. (1998) 'Management Training for International Students', *Industrial and Commercial Training*, 30(6), pp. 209–13.

Reeves, J. (2007) 'Getting Beyond Supervision'. In Hinchcliffe, R., Bromley, A. and Hutchinson, S. (eds) *Skills Training in Research Degree Programmes: Politics and Practice*. Maidenhead: McGraw-Hill.

Rizvi, F.A. (2009) 'International Students and Doctoral Studies in Transnational Spaces'. In Walker, M. and Thompson, P. (eds) (2010) *The Routledge Doctoral Supervisor's Companion*. London: Routledge.

Robinson-Pant, A. (2009) 'Internationalisation of Higher Education: Challenges for the Doctoral Supervisor'. In Walker, M. and Thompson, P. (eds) *The Routledge Doctoral Supervisor's Companion*. London: Routledge.

Rugg, G. and Petre, M. (2004) *The Unwritten Rules of PhD Research*. Buckingham: Open University Press.

Ryan, J. and Hellmundt, S. (2003) 'Excellence Through Diversity: Internationalisation of Curriculum and Pedagogy'. Paper submitted to the 17th IDP Australian International Education Conference, October 2003.

Ryan, Y. and Zuber-Skerritt, O. (eds) (1999) *Supervising Postgraduates from Non-English Speaking Backgrounds*. Buckingham: Society for Research into Higher Education and Open University Press.

Samara, A. (2006) 'Group Supervision in Graduate Education: A Process of Supervision Skill Development and Text Improvement', *Higher Education Research and Development*, 25(2), pp. 115–29.

Scheyvnes, R., Wild, K and Overton, J. (2003) 'International Students Pursuing Postgraduate Study in Geography: Impediments to Their Learning Experiences', *Journal of Geography in Higher Education*, 23(3), pp. 309–23.

Seagram, B.C., Gould, J. and Pyke, S.W. (1998) 'An Investigation of Gender and Other Variables on Time to Completion of Doctoral Degrees', *Research in Higher Education*, 39(3), pp. 319–35.

Senge, P. (1994) *The Fifth Discipline Fieldbook*. London: Nicholas Brearley.

Steiner, G. (2003) *Lessons of the Masters*. Cambridge, MA: Harvard University Press.

Sullivan, S. and Glanz, J. (2000) *Supervision that Improves Teaching: Strategies and Techniques*. Newbury Park, CA: Corwin Press.

Taylor, S. and Beasley, N. (2005) *A Handbook for Doctoral Supervisors*. London: Routledge.

Tinkler, P. and Jackson C. (2004) *The Doctoral Examination Process: A Handbook for Students, Examiners and Supervisors*. Buckingham: SRHE and Open University Press.

Trafford, V.N. and Leshem, S. (2002) 'Anatomy of a Doctoral Viva', *Journal of Graduate Education*, 3, pp. 33–41.

Trahar, S. (2011) *The Doctorate: International Stories of the UK Experience*, Higher Education Academy ESCalate Education Subject Centre: http://escalate.ac.uk/8137 (accessed 6 June 2014).

Trompenaars, F. and Hampden Turner, C. (2004) *Managing People Across Cultures*. London: Capstone Publishing/Wiley.

Vilkinas, T. (2002) 'The PhD Process: The Supervisor as Manager', *Education and Training*, 44(3), pp. 129–37.

Walker, M. and Thompson, P. (eds) (2009) *The Routledge Doctoral Supervisor's Companion*. London: Routledge.

Watson, D. (2004) *Gobbledygook: How Clichés, Sludge and Management-speak are Strangling Our Public Language*. London: Atlantic.

Weidman, J.C. and Stein, E.L. (2003) 'Socialization of Doctoral Students to Academic Norms', *Research in Higher Education*, 44(6), pp. 641–56.

Weidman, J.C., Twale, D.J. and Stein, E.L. (2001) *Socialization of Graduate and Professional Students in Higher Education: A Perilous Passage?* ASHE-ERIC Higher Education Report 28. San Francisco, CA: Jossey-Bass.

Wellington, J., Bathmaker, A., Hunt, C. McCulloch, G. and Sikes, P. (2005) *Succeeding with Your Doctorate*. London: Sage Study Skills.

Wilkinson, D. (2005) *The Essential Guide to Postgraduate Study*. London: Sage.

Winchester-Seeto, T. et al. (2013) 'Doctoral Supervision in a Cross-cultural Context: Issues Affecting Supervisors and Candidates', *Higher Education Research and Development*, 33(3), pp. 610–26: http://dx.doi.org/10.1080/07294360.2013.841648 (accessed 19 June 2014).

Wisker, G. (2001) *The Postgraduate Research Handbook*. Basingstoke: Palgrave.

Wisker, G. (2004) *The Good Supervisor: Supervising Postgraduate and Undergraduate Research for Doctoral Theses and Dissertations*. Basingstoke: Palgrave Study Guides.

Wu, S. (2002) 'Filling the Pot or Lighting the Fire? Cultural Variations in Conceptions of Pedagogy', *Teaching in Higher Education*, 7(4), pp. 387–5.

Zhao, F. (2003a) *Enhancing the Effectiveness of Research and Research Supervision through Reflective Practice*, UltiBASE, July: http://peoplelearn.homestead.com/PGDipHET/ACADLeader/Reflective.Supervision.pdf (accessed 19 June 2014).

Zhao, F. (2003b) 'Transforming Quality in Research Supervision: A Knowledge Management Approach, *Quality in Higher Education*, 9(2), pp. 187–99.

Zuber-Skerritt, O. and Ryan, Y. (eds) (1994) *Quality in Postgraduate Education*. London: Kogan Page.

Index

If you have found this book useful you may be interested in other titles from Gower

Researching Amongst Elites
Challenges and Opportunities in Studying Up
Edited by Luis L.M. Aguiar and Christopher J. Schneider
Hardback: 78-1-4094-2955-5
e-book PDF: 978-1-4094-2956-2
e-book ePUB: 978-1-4094-8423-3

Design Education
Learning, Teaching and Researching Through Design
Philippa Lyon
Hardback: 978-0-566-09245-9
e-book PDF: 978-0-566-09246-6
e-book ePUB: 978-1-4094-5978-1

Action Learning in Practice
Edited by Mike Pedler
Hardback: 978-1-4094-1841-2
e-book PDF: 978-1-4094-1842-9
e-book ePUB: 978-1-4094-8689-3